9/22

EMS

MW01089919

BLACK POWER SERIES

General Editors: Ibram X. Kendi and Ashley D. Farmer

Fight the Power: African Americans and the Long History of Police Brutality in New York City
Clarence Taylor

Pasifika Black: Oceania, Anti-Colonialism, and the African World
Quito Swan

The Tuskegee Student Uprising: A History
Brian Jones

The Tuskegee Student Uprising

A History

Brian Jones

NEW YORK UNIVERSITY PRESS

New York

NEW YORK UNIVERSITY PRESS
New York
www.nyupress.org

References to Internet websites (URLs) were accurate at the time of writing. Neither the author nor New York University Press is responsible for URLs that may have expired or changed since the manuscript was prepared.

Please contact the Library of Congress for Cataloging-in-Publication data.
ISBN: 9781479809424 (hardback)
ISBN: 9781479809431 (library ebook)
ISBN: 9781479809486 (consumer ebook)

New York University Press books are printed on acid-free paper, and their binding materials are chosen for strength and durability. We strive to use environmentally responsible suppliers and materials to the greatest extent possible in publishing our books.

Manufactured in the United States of America

10 9 8 7 6 5 4 3 2 1

Also available as an ebook

For scholar-activists, past, present, and future

CONTENTS

ILLUSTRATIONS

Introduction

"Uppity for a Long Time"

On April 6, 1968, Tuskegee Institute's past, present, and future collided as twelve members of its board of trustees, thirteen Tuskegee staff members, and approximately twenty Tuskegee students assembled in a room of Dorothy Hall. The building traditionally housed prominent visitors to the campus and had become the location of the trustees' annual campus meeting. On the table before the dignitaries lay an eighteen-page typed document titled "General Philosophy: A Black University Concept." The first page declared, "The Black University Concept as applied to the Tuskegee Institute Situation includes, among other things, a redirection of the goals for the Institute as a whole and the instillment of a Black Community concept within the Black students for generations to come." Tuskegee student activists presented these goals as a mandate from the student body. That argument was supported by the presence of nearly three hundred students gathered outside the building, who were effectively holding the trustees hostage.

At the same moment, not far away, an equal number of Alabama National Guardsmen assembled, preparing to invade Tuskegee Institute. Governor Lurleen Wallace gave them orders, just days after the assassination of Dr. Martin Luther King Jr. in Memphis, Tennessee, to free the prestigious trustees. The troops gathered outside the campus gates in the early hours of April 7, with bayonets attached to their rifles. Tuskegee's dean of students approached, hoping to convince the guardsmen to turn around and avoid a bloodbath. One soldier heard his concerns, but told him that they would enter the campus anyway. "Well, you know," the guardsman explained, "you all at Tuskegee have been too uppity for a long time."[1]

In this standoff between students, administrators, and soldiers, Tuskegee Institute joined the geography of global revolt in that incendiary year, 1968. The 1968 uprising connected Tuskegee to the worldwide movements for social change, yet it played out in ways that were related to the unique history of the Institute. In the eyes of the state, this historically black college had been "uppity for a long time" and needed to be put back into its proper place. Yet, in the eyes of its students, the school hadn't been uppity enough. The 1968 student revolt at Tuskegee Institute was the highest expression of a long-standing tension on campus between the individual and collective ambitions of students and the cautious educational-political paradigms of its leaders, beginning with the founder, the nation's most famous black educator, Booker T. Washington. Although today Tuskegee University (as it has been known since 1984) is most commonly associated in public consciousness with a pathbreaking World War II pilot training program, with a fateful syphilis experiment, and, above all, with Washington himself, the 1960s Tuskegee student movement is worth our attention because it illuminates the southern roots of the broader Black Power movement, and because it provides a new vantage point from which to understand the history and meaning of Tuskegee Institute itself.

The students who took radical action at Tuskegee in 1968 were aware of the revolutionary struggles breaking out around the world, but knew less about student strikes that had rocked their own campus in the first decades of its founding in the late nineteenth century. Separated by nearly a century, these different eras of student protest were actually expressions of the same contradiction: between black people's aspirations for education as a lever of liberation and elite white people's desire to organize black people's education in such a way as to preserve a deeply entrenched racial hierarchy. This is not surprising given the timing of Tuskegee Institute's founding. After the defeat of Radical Reconstruction, when the prospects for black people to access formal education were bleak, Booker T. Washington, then only twenty-five years old, garnered support from wealthy and powerful white people in the South and in the North to create a Normal School for Colored Teachers in the town of Tuskegee, Alabama; the school opened its doors in 1881. The curriculum emphasized the morality and dignity of manual labor and de-emphasized civil and democratic aspirations. Through the decades, however, the school Washington founded grew in wealth and stature, and the modest teacher training institute became a university.[2] Ironically, in the 1950s and 1960s, Tuskegee Institute began to develop a reputation as a center of somewhat less than cautious political thought and action. By 1968, some of the most powerful white people in the state of Alabama openly loathed the school and feared that it was teaching "communism"; some less powerful white people apparently got the impression that the school community had become too "uppity." Tuskegee student activists, from their perspective, were aiming for a "redirection of the goals" of the school in order to transform Tuskegee Institute from a "White" university to a "Black" one.[3]

This book, *The Tuskegee Student Uprising: A History*, seeks to understand how and why the conflict between students, administrators, and, ultimately, the state of Alabama developed into such an extreme physical confrontation in April 1968. Based on archival documents and interviews with former Tuskegee students, professors, and administrators, *The Tuskegee Student Uprising* analyzes the meaning of this movement in relation to both the broader political landscape of the 1960s and the history of the institution itself, particularly the political and educational legacy of the school's founder. Despite his careful public presentation in countless public speeches and his influential memoir, *Up from Slavery*, Washington also faced the charge of "uppity"-ness. While some 1960s student activists imagined Washington as a forefather of their struggle, others saw their rapidly escalating movement and the ideas it produced as departures from his political-educational paradigm.

Like many other social movements, the Tuskegee student uprising was spurred by a tragedy. Following the murder of one of their classmates by a white man off campus in the first days of 1966, Tuskegee student activists began fighting for change under the banner of "Black

Power."[4] The old compromises with the white power structure were no longer tenable. Tuskegee students insisted on the full exercise of democratic rights in their city and county. In the pages of the student newspaper, the *Campus Digest*, Tuskegee activists interpreted their political work in terms of a new attitude toward blackness and debated the meaning of the word.

Their changing political views had pedagogical implications as well. Tuskegee students demanded the power to participate in shaping and reshaping their education. They wanted greater emphasis in the curriculum on African and Afro-American history and culture, and less emphasis on the dominant European and Euro-American history and culture. For some Tuskegee students, reconceiving their school's purpose meant deprioritizing aspirations for individual advancement in white society in favor of larger collective visions for social change; for most students, I argue, making Tuskegee a "Black University" meant fusing the two. The content of their dissent, distilled in the "Mandate" document they presented to the board of trustees, reveals the contradictory position of Tuskegee students in American society in the 1960s. As black students within the Jim Crow system, they were second-class citizens. They challenged manifestations of this status inside and outside the classroom and aligned themselves accordingly with anticolonial revolts in Asia and Africa. As upwardly mobile students in a school with strong connections to centers of American wealth and power, however, they were offered significant opportunities for individual advancement. When their ambitions were frustrated, when they wanted to climb farther or faster than their school or their world allowed, they rose up in protest. Like their postcolonial counterparts, Tuskegee student activists debated and discussed a wide range of answers to the question, How much has to change for us to be free?

By focusing on student activists, *The Tuskegee Student Uprising* reveals a familiar and historically significant place—Tuskegee Institute—in a new light. From the student perspective, we learn that the campus was a site of greater political and educational contestation and a wider range of political and educational thought than is commonly understood. *The Tuskegee Student Uprising* demonstrates that Booker T. Washington's political and educational paradigms were not hegemonic; they were debated, contested, and challenged, not just on the national stage but also on the very campus that he founded, from the late nineteenth century and throughout the twentieth century. And like student uprisings at other historically black colleges and universities (HBCUs), the 1960s Tuskegee student movement was animated by intense loyalty to the institution; Tuskegee student activists didn't want to tear down Tuskegee, they wanted to "redirect" it.

Located almost exactly in the middle of the region known as the "Black Belt" (named after the color of the soil and the folks who worked on it), by the middle of the twentieth century Tuskegee Institute represented an island of black affluence in a sea of poverty and white supremacy. The deep-rooted patterns and intensity of white supremacy in the region meant that Tuskegee students and administrators, despite their disagreements, relied more often than not on a sense of solidarity and commitment to each other. No matter how cautious or conservative their demeanor, there were always going to be white people who viewed the prosperous and well-educated members of the Tuskegee community as "uppity." Stepping off campus, students venturing into the surrounding Black Belt counties learned that that perception could mean death, as it did for one Tuskegee student in 1966. The dean's last-minute appeal to the soldiers at the campus gates in 1968 was neither the first nor the last time Tuskegee administrators intervened on behalf of students in the face of such threats.

This geographic position also meant that, as it developed, the Tuskegee student movement was well placed to make major contributions to the broader civil rights and Black Power movements. *The Tuskegee Student Uprising* builds on historical scholarship that emphasizes the continuity between these movement phases, and recovers the role of Tuskegee students in both. I argue that "Black Power" stood for an expansive conception of democracy in Macon County, Alabama, in the

1960s. Whereas some previous scholarship has celebrated civil rights battles and denigrated the growing militancy of the student movement, I show that the latter was an essential and important continuation of the former. Tuskegee students had a significant yet seldom remembered impact off campus, which politicized and radicalized them. Working to transform their world, student activists returned to their classrooms and found them intolerable. In the late 1960s, as the "Black University" reform concept spread across the nation's historically black colleges and universities, some of its first articulations came from Tuskegee students. By making the bold choice in 1968 to confront the school's trustees directly with their vision and demands, Tuskegee students gave us the clearest articulation of a long pattern of black student dissent at an institution whose history is foundational for Afro-American history, education, and politics. When the Black Power movement emerged on Tuskegee Institute's campus in the 1960s, what did that mean for the legacy of Booker T. Washington?

* * *

More than a hundred years after his death in 1915, Washington remains a figure of controversy. My interest in Tuskegee Institute's 1960s student movement grew out of my reading of the literature on the school's origins. Perhaps more than any other single volume, James D. Anderson's masterful *Education of Blacks in the South, 1860–1935*, is directly responsible for this study.[5] Anderson presents overwhelming evidence that the "Hampton-Tuskegee" model of schooling "represented the ideological antithesis of the educational and social movement begun by ex-slaves."[6] Whereas the freed people had self-organized schools from their own meager resources and used them to promote political literacy and preparation for political and economic action,[7] the northern philanthropists who created the Hampton Institute (and later backed the Tuskegee Institute) intended to train black people to accept subordinate roles in southern economic and social life. From the founding of both institutions into the late 1920s, neither Hampton nor Tuskegee was an actual trade school; they were not "academic schools worthy of the name," Anderson writes, "but schools that attempted to train a corps of teachers with a particular social philosophy relevant to the political and economic reconstruction of the South."[8] A long line of scholars and activists, starting with W. E. B. Du Bois, have criticized Washington for his complicity with this agenda.[9] But there is more to the story.

While Washington's critics are legion,[10] a new trend in scholarship shifts away from critique and attempts to exonerate him. The two-volume biography by Louis Harlan still represents the most well-rounded assessment of Washington's career to date,[11] but the new vindicationist literature sees it as skewed toward a critical perspective. Pushing in a different direction, recent scholarship emphasizes the fact that Washington carried on *sub rosa* advocacy for civil rights, and that his apparently disgraceful public statements opposing black civil rights were squarely within the Afro-American tradition of "wearing the mask" in the presence of white folks, and argues that, at the end of the day, he navigated the only possible path for building an educational institution given the pervasive anti-black terrorist violence of the post-Reconstruction South.[12] Both his critics and defenders are able to present considerable evidence to support their claims, and so Washington seems to remain an enigma.

Among the lacunae in a century's worth of scholarship on the Tuskegeean, as Pero Dagbovie observes in the most comprehensive historiographical essay to date on Washington scholarship, is the study of the experiences of Tuskegee students.[13] But the voices of Tuskegee students have been hiding in plain sight. Although Anderson's work focused on the interests and motives of northern philanthropists, he also pointed to the resistance of students and parents within the "industrial" model. His description of the Hampton student strike in 1927 led me to search for records of similar actions at Tuskegee Institute. Once I asked the question, I began seeing evidence of the long Tuskegee student movement sprinkled like bread crumbs throughout the literature on Washington.

Of course, Tuskegee Institute is not the only school to face such protests, and Tuskegee student activists never acted in political or educational isolation. A bountiful crop of new scholarship explores the ways black students worked, throughout the twentieth century, to transform a wide range of institutions of higher education nationwide, including private colleges, public colleges, and predominantly white institutions as well as historically black colleges and universities.[14] Following Jacquelyn Dowd Hall's reframing of the "long civil rights movement," Ibram Rogers (now Ibram X. Kendi) describes what he calls the "long Black student movement," stretching back to the origins of higher education for black people at the end of the nineteenth century, but rising in strength in the 1920s, 1930s, and 1940s.[15] Although the specific reasons for black student movements shifted over the decades, the overall pattern was that they resisted the imposition of the rules of Jim Crow segregation on their campuses, and fought to make their education live up to their aspirations.[16] When the southern civil rights movement began gathering strength in the late 1950s and early 1960s, HBCUs provided the youth leadership that transformed the nation.[17] In doing so, however, black students were also compelled to transform their campuses. There are familiar patterns in the Tuskegee student movement, including the activists' creative co-optation of campus resources for other purposes, courage in the face of pushback from administrators, and the ever-present danger of murderous state violence.[18]

Although popular consciousness often only recalls violent repression of white student activists in this period—particularly the murder of four white students by National Guardsmen at Kent State University in 1970—state violence was more frequently visited on black college campuses. Less familiar to popular memory is the police assault on Texas Southern University in Houston in 1967, the murder of three students at South Carolina State University in Orangeburg in 1968, a ground and air offensive against students at North Carolina A&T in Greensboro in 1968, the murder of two students at Jackson State College in Jackson in 1970, and the murder of two students at Southern University in Baton Rouge in 1972.[19] Accordingly, when the Alabama National Guard entered Tuskegee's campus in April 1968, it was not unreasonable for students and faculty to assume that the resulting confrontation might be fatal. State repression is a crucial part of the story of the Tuskegee student revolt.

Beyond looking at student actions, twenty-first-century scholars have also taken a fresh look at other figures on campuses who were previously dismissed as conservative (especially black faculty and administrators) and produced research on the hidden ways that people in such roles worked within HBCUs to challenge racism, white supremacy, and the Jim Crow system. Jelani Favors's use of the concept of *communitas* to describe the ethos of HBCUs in the twentieth century resonates with the midcentury Tuskegee experience, where student activists, even at their most radical, retained, with faculty and administrators, a shared sense of loyalty to the institution.[20] While this book shows the ways that Tuskegee administrators clashed with student activists, it is also true that they nurtured them. As Eddie Cole's work shows, some of these administrators courageously sought to use their positions to challenge the old order.[21] Administrators and students were negotiating new roles in a rapidly shifting social and economic context. Joy Williamson-Lott's recent research on the changing nature of mid-twentieth-century higher education in the US South (including but not exclusively at HBCUs) shows a broad pattern of activism on the part of students and faculty and structural transformations leading to expanding intellectual horizons and academic freedoms.[22] One of the structural changes was increased federal funding, which both undermined the Jim Crow system and made institutional leaders more reluctant to be seen as operating centers of opposition to the Vietnam War. Tuskegee certainly fits both of these patterns. Like much of the recent research in these fields, Favors's and Williamson-Lott's studies are national in scope and provide essential context for understanding Tuskegee Institute. However,

Tuskegee's own story is worth a closer look because of its distinctive historical position.

The Tuskegee student movement story is unique in several respects. Tuskegee Institute was a Deep South campus but was well funded, and its immediately surrounding black community was uniquely prosperous. Other historically black college campuses might fit that description, but none that did were situated in the Black Belt region. Other historically black colleges and universities may have a reputation for conservatism, but Tuskegee Institute is uniquely prominent in the history of black education; it was the foundation stone for a particular and, for a time, successful philanthropic-led strategy of cultivating a specific type of education for black people in the US South. Tuskegee Institute's founder, Booker T. Washington, is the nation's most famous black educator. Far from a settled matter, his legacy remains a matter of controversy, scholarly and otherwise. For all of these reasons, the story of the Tuskegee student uprising is shaped by Tuskegee Institute's unique history and importance.

Although this is the first study of the student movement at Tuskegee Institute, the topic has been examined in two other books, each taking a different approach to the question of the movement's relationship to Booker T. Washington's legacy. *Reaping the Whirlwind: The Civil Rights Movement in Tuskegee* by Robert J. Norrell, first published in 1998 and republished with an updated conclusion in 2013, tells the story of the struggle for voting rights in Macon County in the 1940s and 1950s, led by Tuskegee's faculty.[23] The star of *Reaping the Whirlwind* is Tuskegee professor Charles Gomillion, who patiently and systematically collected evidence of disfranchisement, leading to a landmark 1960 US Supreme Court case, *Gomillion v. Lightfoot*. Norrell connects the faculty-led voting rights battle with Booker T. Washington's philosophy. Washington was correct, Norrell argues, to think "that political rights would indeed follow from economic power," and thus the "Washington philosophy was vindicated, at least in its place of birth."[24]

By midcentury, Tuskegee was in fact a center of black prosperity, as Norrell demonstrates. It was home to perhaps the largest concentration of black professionals in the United States at that time. The disposable income of Tuskegee's black middle class—a resource that was essential to the *Gomillion v. Lightfoot* US Supreme Court victory—actually developed in ways that had little to do with Washington's prescriptions, however. Washington emphasized landownership and small business ownership, but Tuskegee's twentieth-century black middle class grew on the basis of academic salaries underwritten by northern philanthropy and medical professional salaries at the nearby veterans hospital paid by the federal government. So, indeed, political rights did follow from economic strength, but not exactly in the way Washington imagined, and not without the kind of open political struggle that Washington avoided.

Norrell rightly celebrates the voting rights victory, although he is more skeptical of the student movement that grew in its wake. Whereas professors like Gomillion were patient and careful, Norrell (accurately) describes the student activists as impatient and impetuous. The younger generation "tended to believe that change had come easily," in his assessment. "Gomillion knew it had not."[25] *Reaping the Whirlwind* focuses on Tuskegee's faculty and the voting rights struggle, while *The Tuskegee Student Uprising* shifts our attention to Tuskegee's students and their movement for Black Power and for a Black University. Whereas the faculty movement has entered the pantheon of celebrated civil rights battles against southern segregationists, the less often-remembered Tuskegee student movement aimed its fire on campus as well as off, raising thorny questions that, at the very least, complicate Washington's legacy.

In the aftermath of the murder of Tuskegee student Sammy Younge Jr. in 1966, Student Nonviolent Coordinating Committee (SNCC) leader James Forman wrote *Sammy Younge, Jr.: The First Black College Student to Die in the Black Liberation Movement*.[26] Forman had helped to recruit Younge into the movement and was personally devastated by his murder. While *Reaping the Whirlwind* was written from the faculty's perspective, published decades after the events took place, celebrating a faculty-led victory, Forman's text is student-centered, has the feel of immediacy (published just two years after Younge's death), and is brimming with radical anger at Tuskegee's faculty and administration. Much of the book consists of transcriptions of interviews Forman conducted with Younge's family and friends and with other activists (including Gwen Patton, George and Wendell Paris, and others), interspersed with Forman's analysis of the events. Thus, it serves as a primary source of contemporaneous eyewitness testimony in late 1960s Tuskegee, and as a source of Forman's theorizing about the southern student movement. The book's final chapter is titled "Postscript: Rebellion '68" and is composed primarily of an extended interview with Michael Wright, the lead student organizer of the occupation of the trustees' meeting in Dorothy Hall in April 1968. That twenty-page postscript is the most extensive analysis of the 1968 Tuskegee student revolt published to date.

In *The Tuskegee Student Uprising*, I treat Forman's text as a primary source document, and understand it as a product of its moment: the immediate aftermath of Younge's murder and the high point of the global student movement. In 1968 Forman and many of the students he quotes viewed Tuskegee's administration as outright enemies. In Forman's text, he and they direct significant ire at Tuskegee's dean of students, Bertrand Phillips. But Dean Phillips's relationship to the movement is complex. For most of the 1960s, Phillips was probably the most popular administrative figure on Tuskegee's campus. Phillips spent countless hours in those years advocating for students and defending their right to protest in various ways. He created the Tuskegee Institute Community Education Program (TICEP), which sent students into the surrounding Black Belt counties to work as literacy tutors, a program that radicalized many participants. Part of the reason the Tuskegee student movement was so dynamic, I argue, has to do with the ways faculty and administrators opened the door to its growth in its early phase. And of course, it was Bert Phillips who stood in front of the Alabama National Guardsmen at the campus gates in 1968, trying to prevent a massacre. *The Tuskegee Student Uprising* both builds on and departs from Norrell's and Forman's books, and could not have been written without them.

This book is also deeply indebted to the work of the late historian Manning Marable. Marable's scholarly writing about Washington and Tuskegee are all the more perceptive because of his intimate connections to the subjects. Marable's parents grew up in Macon County, and he taught briefly at Tuskegee Institute in the 1970s. Two book chapters and two articles in particular have provided crucial guidance for thinking about Black Power in Tuskegee and the legacy of Booker T. Washington. In the two articles (both published in 1977, while he was still teaching at Tuskegee Institute), Marable cataloged the struggles over the meaning of Tuskegee Institute and the efforts of black elites in Macon County to follow in Washington's footsteps after his death in 1915. In "Tuskegee Institute in the 1920's," Marable illustrated the contradictions of an institution clinging to nineteenth-century cultural and intellectual ideals in an era of growing militancy and cultural renaissance among black people.[27] In a second article, "Tuskegee and the Politics of Illusion in the New South," Marable argues that these contradictions came to a head in the 1970s because black people captured political office, but not genuine economic power. "Without an independent political party," he wrote, "and devoid of a critical political perspective, the black petit bourgeoisie of Tuskegee finds itself in a position of municipal power which increasingly means very little."[28] Marable concludes by drawing a parallel between the economic decline of Tuskegee under "Black Power" and the bitter postcolonial legacy of African independence. As discussed in chapters 3 and 4, this analogy played a particularly significant role in the Tuskegee student movement.

Marable's class-conscious approach is particularly useful here because of the class nature of the story's main characters. *The Tuskegee
Student Uprising* is a narrative of the actions of a particular group—the
black middle class. I use the term "middle class" to mean people who
are neither the wage laborers who work as directed nor the owners of
capital who set labor in motion, but are between the two. The middle
class is composed of people who stand between capital and labor and
share elements from both groups: small business owners, professionals, and managers who direct the labor of others, for example. In this
sense, "middle class" is neither a subjective designation, a statement of
absolute living standard, nor a moral approbation, but a way to label
a very real and particular relationship to production and to society.[29]
As Kevin Gaines puts it, the black middle class has a "contradictory
position as both an aspiring social class and a racially subordinate
caste denied all political rights and protections, struggling to define
themselves within a society founded on white dominance."[30] It is not
just the presence but also concentration of black middle-class people
in Tuskegee, I argue, that explains the unique nature of the civil rights
activism as it emerged there, led, in the first instance, by professors.
When student activists came to the fore in the 1960s, they were propelled by the confidence, resources, and actions of their elders and, at
the same time, had to overcome the limitations of their outlooks and
methods.

Tuskegee's middle-class community was also uniquely situated in
the middle of the Black Belt, and Tuskegee student activists cut their
teeth in the context of a dangerous battle for democracy there. Without
a doubt the boldest organization working in the Black Belt was the Student Nonviolent Coordinating Committee (SNCC). Through their experiences in the Deep South, SNCC activists radicalized quickly over the
course of the decade.[31] At least three Tuskegee students (Sammy Younge,
Gwen Patton, and George Ware) played a leading role in SNCC's history.
SNCC leaders Stokely Carmichael and James Forman both spent considerable amounts of time in and around Tuskegee in those years, and their

respective memoirs were consulted for this book.[32] While these male figures captured many of the headlines, women were often playing less publicly acknowledged leadership roles in SNCC, as new work on these histories attest.[33] Dr. Gwendolyn Patton's long activist career, beginning at Tuskegee, is rightfully a prominent feature in recent publications, a signal that her life and work are being taken seriously by a new generation of scholars, and her posthumously published memoir is an important new contribution.[34]

Patton is one of the figures whose story highlights the connection between southern student activism and the Black Power movement. Patton is also one of many Tuskegee students who stepped off campus to get involved in political struggles in the wider Black Belt. Some students, for example, who began working in the adjacent rural counties as literacy tutors ended up campaigning for the Lowndes County Freedom Organization (LCFO), the independent political party created by SNCC (and whose symbol was a black panther) to challenge the Democratic Party in the 1966 elections.[35] At the very end of 1965, two activists involved in the LCFO, Sammy Younge Jr. and Stokely Carmichael, discussed bringing that model of independent political organizing to Macon County. That did not exactly come to pass, but ironically it was Younge's murder just a week later that set Tuskegee students on a path to a different electoral project: campaigning to successfully propel to office the first black sheriff elected in the South since Reconstruction, an event that reverberated nationwide. Contemporary readers will be forgiven for not recalling that in the late 1960s, many observers looked at Tuskegee as a center of Black Power. We know that this was so in part because when two leading figures in the movement—SNCC activists Stokely Carmichael (later known as Kwame Ture) and former Tuskegee professor Charles Hamilton—sat down to coauthor a definitive book on the subject, they devoted an entire chapter to this prospect.[36] "Tuskegee, Alabama, could be the model of Black Power," Carmichael and Hamilton wrote in 1967. "It could be the place where black people have amassed political power and used that power effectively."[37]

The story of the Black Power era is both local and global. The explosive social movements in North America in these years were intimately connected to others in Asia, Latin America, and particularly Africa. The powerful currents of anticolonial African thought and action influenced Tuskegee students through a variety of means, not the least of which were African students at Tuskegee Institute, who introduced their classmates to the works of Frantz Fanon, Jomo Kenyatta, Kwame Nkrumah, and others. The concept of colonialism, for many Tuskegee student activists, was a compelling model for how to think about the situation facing black people in the United States. This tendency potentially represented a remarkable reversal of Tuskegee's relationship to the world, given its historic collaborations with European colonialism and the centrality of its relationship with the US military to its identity at midcentury.[38] Student activists drew strength from the process of making closer personal and political connections with leading figures in the African anticolonial movements. They also drew heat from the association; although almost no Tuskegee student activists identified with the socialist movement to the extent that anticolonial leaders abroad did, segregationists were quick to report as "communist" any and all student activism on and off Tuskegee's campus.[39]

Such conflicts highlight the inherently political nature of education. Student movements, especially when they take on and try to change the process of schooling itself, involve a process wherein students develop and fight for their own educational agendas. So, while school leaders have their philosophies, orientations, and plans, once they actually gather students together, the process of learning runs the risk of getting "out of control." For this reason, schooling can be a dangerous enterprise to those who favor the status quo. My approach to the study of student activism at Tuskegee is informed by scholarship in the field of education that emphasizes the unique nature of schools as sites of political contestation and the potential for schools to create opportunities for personal and collective transformation.[40] Looking at student activists' intellectual processes is a different perspective from which to consider institutional history. Through that lens, we see that the meaning of Tuskegee Institute and the legacy of Booker T. Washington cannot be reduced to statements by Washington or by the school's official leadership. Students, too, attempted to shape the institution, to varying degrees of success, throughout its history. As previously noted, during Washington's era as director, the volume of petitions, letters of dissent, student protests, and extensive disciplinary countermeasures is a record that demonstrates clearly that the founder's views did not necessarily represent a consensus. This book attempts to sort through the contending ideas that developed on Tuskegee's campus.

This process of educational contestation was most sharply expressed in the 1960s and 1970s in the United States. In those decades, different tendencies of thought and action crystallized, and activists tried to realize their respective visions. I have found useful typologies of these various political/educational schools of thought in works by Daniel Perlstein, Manning Marable, and Russell Rickford.[41] Their studies show that there is not a singular "black" political or educational philosophy, but rather an array of sometimes complementary and sometimes contradictory responses to the conditions of anti-black racism in the United States. Perhaps the clearest commonality is that black educational movements have been, on the whole, progressive, politically and educationally committed to enlarging prospects for freedom, democracy, and equality.[42] In general, when black-led movements for progressive social change have been thwarted, so, too, have their educational movements been thrown backwards.[43] Black Studies in higher education, simultaneously an enduring and tenuous institutional legacy of the Black Power era, bears the scars of this process of social ebb and flow.[44] I have tried to take these lessons to heart in the process of exploring the meaning of the "Black University" concept as it unfolded at Tuskegee in the late 1960s.

The Tuskegee student movement defies easy political categorization. Elements of black nationalism and cultural nationalism mixed frequently with fairly straightforward liberal reformism. Off campus, "Black Power" essentially meant expanding democracy in the Black Belt,

I argue. On campus, it was effectively a fusion of different trends and impulses. Taken together, however, the reforms proposed by students amounted to a revision of Tuskegee's prevailing political-educational paradigm. In that midcentury paradigm, Tuskegee Institute's administrators sought to prepare students to take roles in the technocratic management of the machine-age and, increasingly, computer-age society, and to assume positions as leaders who could ensure a smooth and thoughtful transition from Jim Crow segregation to the integration of black people into the American body politic.[45] The new "Black" consciousness encouraged a far more assertive stance, less concerned with managing the reactions of white people, and more oriented toward targeting the reins of power. Black students insisted that their universities should share this new perspective.

Not every demand to upgrade academic offerings required such a revision of the underlying paradigm, however. Many calls for improving the quality of teaching, of textbooks, and of physical plant and infrastructure were well within the universities' accepted self-conceptions. Therein lay the tension in the Tuskegee student demands. On the one hand, these students demanded a university fully equipped to help them compete in white society, and on the other hand, they demanded a new university, more oriented to a collective effort to transform that society. Rather than ask their classmates to reject individual aspirations altogether, Tuskegee student activists organized collective actions around those aspirations. The explosive power of the student movement at Tuskegee in 1968 is explained in part by the ability of organizers to fuse these disparate impulses under the same banner: Black Power.

* * *

In this book, I am passing on a story that was told to me by people who lived it. I listened to twenty-one different people's perspectives on it: fifteen former Tuskegee students (Lena Agnew, Lucenia Dunn, George Geddis, Warren Hamilton, Chester Higgins Jr., Ronald Hill, Caroline Hilton, Robert Jones, Cozetta Lamore, George Paris, Wendell Paris,

Gwendolyn Patton, Arthur Pfister, Melvin Todd, and Michael Wright); two former Tuskegee administrators (Bertrand Phillips and Richard Wasserstrom); two former Tuskegee professors (Maggie Magee and Sue Pendell); and two people who grew up in the town of Tuskegee (Kathleen Cleaver and Guy Trammel). These interviews were conducted over three years, from 2015 to 2017. Their respective campus careers at Tuskegee fall roughly into two temporal phases of activism: among the pre-1967 group are Gwen Patton, George and Wendell Paris, and Melvin Todd; whereas the 1967–1968 story features students such as Michael Wright, George Geddis, and Caroline Hilton more prominently.

Two clear patterns emerged in the interviews: first, the intense loyalty the participants feel toward Tuskegee University and the profound sense of the loss of its stature from the 1960s to today; and second, the importance of understanding the class nature of the town of Tuskegee. Again and again, in their own ways, interviewees returned to either or both themes. Although the administration had tried to expel him many times, Michael Wright told me that Tuskegee's campus was "hallowed ground." The former students describe Tuskegee as a kind of middle-class utopia, very much wrapped up in the ideals of upward mobility and of acquiring the material trappings of middle-class American life. For example, Gwen Patton stressed, repeatedly, the importance of understanding "the class within the caste," the middle-class black community in which she was rooted. Most of the activists were from a similar echelon, themselves the children of college-educated professionals. There were also some poorer students, the first to go to college, and some arrived without any money in their pockets whatsoever.

Another crucial source of information came from Chester Higgins Jr. (who later became a world-famous photographer). As a student at Tuskegee Institute in 1968, he collected every leaflet, letter, memo, manifesto, and other document produced by students, faculty, and administrators in the heat of that year's struggle. Higgins received assistance from a professor and the approval of the administration for the final product, which consists of typed versions of all of these documents, running to

166 pages. Tuskegee Institute published it as *Student Unrest, Tuskegee Institute: A Chronology*. *Student Unrest* is invaluable as a documentary history of all parties involved in the 1968 conflict and as an authoritative timeline of its unfolding. It is, perhaps, a testament to the historical significance of the events in question that two people involved (Higgins and Forman) had the impulse to archive them as they happened.

I was also fortunate to have SNCC veteran and former Tuskegee student government president Gwen Patton guide me through her own papers, stored at Trenholm State Technical College in Montgomery. I reviewed hundreds of documents from the collection, which include letters, speeches, and writings tracing her activist trajectory from Tuskegee in the mid-1960s (she helped to found the Tuskegee Institute Advancement League, the student activist wing of the civil rights movement at Tuskegee) to a veritable tour of the most radical wing of the Black Power movement through the late 1960s and early 1970s, including the Lowndes County Black Panther Party, the Black Panther Party initiated by Huey Newton and Bobby Seale years later, the Revolutionary Union Movement in Detroit, and more. Patton claims to have organized the first Black Power conference in the United States at Tuskegee Institute in February 1967. She never actually made it to the conference, though, as she was badly injured in a mysterious car accident en route. For the rest of her life, one of her legs was shorter than the other. She lectured for a time at Brooklyn College, but eventually returned to Alabama and remained a sought-after public speaker on civil rights, Black Power, and the role of women in activism. Patton's archive contains several lengthy speeches and articles from the 1970s assessing the prospects for broad social change, even socialism, and ideas about how schooling, women's rights, and the fight against racism fit into those perspectives. Patton is probably the best-known activist to emerge from Tuskegee in the 1960s. When she died in the spring of 2016, I attended her funeral, spent time with her family and friends in Montgomery, and became further convinced that she deserves to be the object of her own study.[46]

Although this book does not tell my story, it is personal to me. My father, Robert Jones, attended Tuskegee Institute from 1957 to 1961. To hear him tell it, Tuskegee's professors bent over backwards to make sure he was successful, and that required a lot of bending. He was "under-prepared" for college-level work, by his own admission, and it was due to the care, attention, and persistence of his professors that he thrived. After graduation, my father went to Vietnam as a commissioned officer. When he returned from the war, he moved back to the Detroit area, where I was born. As a light-complexioned black man with a college degree from a prestigious university, he quickly found his way to the management fast-track in a series of corporations. Detroit's auto companies hoped to use him to help them deal with the black insurgency rocking the city. He remembers serving as a middleman, negotiating the relationship between the rising black radicals (such as leaders of the Revolutionary Union Movement, some of whom he knew) and the white titans of the auto industry. As we watched the film *Black Power Mixtape* together, my father commented, "Those people [black radical activists] kicked open doors that I walked through." Although he had gotten to know the radicals in Detroit, he had missed the explosion at Tuskegee Institute. By the time he was leaving the campus in 1961, the student movement was just beginning to emerge. My father attended precisely one protest march, in the spring of 1960, in solidarity with the student sit-in movement sweeping through the South. So, when he and I traveled to his alma mater together in the summer of 2014 to explore the archival evidence of the late 1960s uprising, he was poleaxed. The images and headlines from the student newspaper, the *Campus Digest*, revealed an escalating crisis on campus, increasingly dramatic protests, student organizing, and stridently radical political language. This was not the Tuskegee Institute he had known. But holding the evidence in his hands, my father acknowledged the importance of understanding what had happened. "This is part of Tuskegee's history, too," he said.

* * *

I have organized the chapters of this book like a telephoto lens, with the scope of time narrowing in each successive chapter, in the hope that this approach will allow the reader to understand the way the story of the 1960s Tuskegee student uprising resonates both in the context of the contemporaneous global movements and in the long view of Tuskegee Institute itself. The first chapter's scope is eighty years, then the next is just six years, then two years, then one. In order to explore the connection between the 1960s student movement and the legacy of Washington, who died in 1915, I needed to write a history of Tuskegee Institute.

The first chapter tells roughly eighty years of that history, starting with the school's origins in the late nineteenth century, and paying special attention to the pattern of intra-campus debate and dissent, beginning with a Tuskegee student strike in 1896. To understand the nature of such conflicts over many decades, I also describe the changing political economy of black education in general and of Tuskegee Institute in particular. Northern philanthropy gave the school its start, but by the middle of the twentieth century, a new sponsor became even more important to the school's success and growing national influence: the federal government. Tuskegee's transformation, by midcentury, into a prosperous middle-class black community is essential to understanding both the story of the faculty-led voting rights struggle and the more ambitious student-led movement that followed.

In the second chapter, I "zoom in" my lens to focus on the actions of students in just a six-year period: 1960 to 1965. I show how, in those years, Tuskegee students joined the southern civil rights movement, and how their organizing efforts had a much wider influence than is generally remembered. Tuskegee Institute was truly an organizational and intellectual center of the southern student movement, and Tuskegee students were instrumental in the fight for democracy in the surrounding Black Belt counties.

Focusing the telephoto lens even more tightly in the third chapter to look at just two years, 1966 and 1967, I explain the radicalization of the student movement and how Tuskegee came to be an influential model of Black Power nationwide. After Tuskegee student Sammy Younge Jr. was murdered in 1966 in an off-campus dispute over a segregated restroom, his classmates turned their attention back to their school and decided that it, too, must change. Tuskegee students were among the first to publish systemic critiques of HBCUs and to imagine what a "Black University" might look like.

In the fourth chapter, the focus tightens to just one explosive year: 1968. I narrate the events of that year, including when Tuskegee students held the trustees hostage for two days until the Alabama National Guard arrived, threatening to invade the campus. The further development of the student movement was stalled when the president closed Tuskegee Institute completely for two weeks, but activists still registered an impressive list of victories. I unpack the "Black University" concept and show that the demands students fought for represented a marriage of their desire for individual upward mobility with their aspirations for collective social change. In the final chapter I offer concluding thoughts about the history of Tuskegee's student movement, the legacy of Booker T. Washington, and implications for the present and future of black education.

* * *

I have often reflected on a tension I perceived in interviews I conducted for this book: between loyalty and reverence for Tuskegee Institute on one hand, and criticism of it on the other. At a time when many HBCUs are struggling financially, supporters naturally emphasize the historic strengths of these institutions and their continuing importance. Tuskegee Institute graduates have no shortage of reasons to be proud. Their school remains celebrated and highly regarded, and continues to produce distinguished graduates in many fields.[47] Yet, this book focuses our attention on the historic pattern of student criticism. What is the value in that? I think it is important to state that the internal critics I write about in this book always aspired to reform (or "redirect") the institution, to improve it; and they did. More than forty years ago sociologist Daniel C. Thompson pointed out the irony in the fact that HBCUs trained most of the leading black activists yet were the institutions "most harassed by the racial revolution."[48] Thompson may not have known that the same pattern existed prior to the 1960s. "Oddly enough," noted one white visitor to Tuskegee's campus in 1930, "Tuskegee and its methods receive more criticisms from the Negroes themselves than from the Southern whites."[49] Those who bristle at the idea of a critical history may, as they read the stories contained here, find themselves in accordance with these student protesters. In the end, such internal critics succeeded in their aim: "redirecting" Tuskegee Institute to make it a better place.

Following their example, I offer this research not as a dig at Tuskegee Institute, but as a new way to understand its complicated history. In this view, Tuskegee students played an important role in changing their school over time, pushing it toward new horizons to match their growing social and political ambitions. Instead of emphasizing the singular genius of the founder, by studying the history of student dissidents we see this historic campus community as a contested space, one whose success owed much to the advocacy of parents, teachers, and students. As a former student activist, a former teacher, and now an administrator, I know how complicated our institutions can be. In many ways Tuskegee Institute is just like all schools, a mixture of compromises and constraints, combined with space to think and dream beyond those constraints. This history also reminds us of the role that elite white people played in both making such spaces possible and attempting to define the boundaries of acceptable black dreaming. All of our institutions continue to grapple with the necessity and difficulty of reform.

In telling this story, I have endeavored to embrace the contradictions of Tuskegee Institute and not to flatten them. I make space for critique of Washington, but I also understand the power of his legacy as the founder of a black-led educational institution. I highlight student critics, but try to appreciate what we can learn from the fact that their school was a place that consistently nurtured such critical voices. The campus was confining and restrictive while also a "haven for activist people," as one former student described it.[50] Tuskegee Institute has a proud military history that is also a controversial history. It was a military outpost that was nearly invaded by the military—twice. Tuskegee students in one era traveled abroad to collaborate with European colonialism in Africa, and in another era sought to learn from and imitate the process of African liberation from European control. In one decade students were hired by mine owners to convince black workers not to join unions, and in the next decade Tuskegee students ventured off campus to organize black workers into unions. The truth of Tuskegee Institute is that it has been a home to a wide range of political and educational ideals, many of which do not neatly fall within the philosophies laid down by Booker T. Washington.

There is a broader significance to this history, I believe. Today, paradigms of black education are once again hotly debated and black college students coast to coast are organizing to demand institutional change.[51] There is no singular "black" perspective on these questions, but a range of responses by black people, including stances that conflict. Often, but not always, different classes of black people have different imaginations about what kinds of changes are possible or necessary. The radical history of student movements at historically black colleges and universities provides an opportunity to expand our contemporary political and educational imaginations. That history can also enrich our understanding of HBCUs. Too often our knowledge of institutions comes from the people in leadership, not the broader community that makes up an institution. Understanding the perspective of student activists gives us a richer picture of the educational and political life of Tuskegee Institute. When, in April 1968, various echelons of Tuskegee's hierarchy were forced to confront each other in Dorothy Hall, the reckoning was not just physical, but intellectual. The legacy of Booker T. Washington has been examined for almost a century from every angle except this one: the arrival of the Black Power movement on the campus that he founded. For the first time, the students at the school he founded will have their say in the scholarly record. I sincerely hope that *The Tuskegee Student Uprising* does justice to their story.

1

The Contradictions of Tuskegee Institute, 1881–1960

In 1896, while traveling outside Alabama, Booker T. Washington received a letter from his clerk at Tuskegee Institute. "The students all struck here today because they were given nothing to eat," the missive stated. "I think every thing [*sic*] has been settled peaceably; it was a sure enough strike."[1] This student strike was probably the first, but definitely not the last. We don't know much about student protesters in the early years of Tuskegee Institute; unlike the protests of their twentieth-century counterparts, the early Tuskegee students' actions were not well documented. Still, their presence in the historical record reveals the campus as a contested space, not just in national discourse but also within the school's community. Some of these protests—over food and other material conditions—questioned the stringent management of student life. In 1902, perhaps under pressure from students, Washington actually proposed a slight relaxation of the Victorian rules governing student comportment, suggesting that "dancing might be permitted," but the dean of women warned him that doing so would "open Pandora's box."[2] But other protests, including a student strike in 1903, discussed below, developed in opposition to the school's curricular priorities, and represented a more fundamental challenge to Washington's educational-political enterprise. Washington remained the director of Tuskegee Institute until his death in 1915, and was an obsessive micromanager, argues historian Kevern Verney. The Booker T. Washington Papers are "peppered with complaints by Tuskegee staff and students about Washington's authoritarian management," Verney writes. "Moreover," he concludes, "it is probable that recorded grievances represented but a small proportion of the discontent, for individuals who allowed their doubts to become public risked hurtful letters of rebuke from Washington."[3]

Eighty years after Tuskegee Institute's founding, the recorded grievances of students exploded as one small part of a global movement, calling into question all of higher education and its purpose in a rapidly changing society. The 1960s Tuskegee student movement developed in relation to that worldwide conflagration. In the United States in particular, the student movement owed its dynamism to the revolt of black people, particularly black students. But when the fires of protest spread to Tuskegee, Alabama, in those years, they found kindling in an institution that stood apart from its peers; for much of the twentieth century, Tuskegee Institute was a symbolic capital of Black America, a school that was both behind the times and ahead of them, ripe for revolution and well-practiced at the art of reform. In the 1960s, Tuskegee students were well aware that their uprising reflected, one way or another, upon the legacy of Booker T. Washington. What they didn't know was that their protests had eighty years of precedents in the very halls and classrooms they occupied. Of course, Tuskegee Institute in the 1960s was very different from the teacher training school founded by Booker T. Washington in 1881. When Washington's compromises were no longer tenable, new ones had been negotiated. Tuskegee Institute was durable over many decades precisely because, under pressure, it changed with the times. Still, certain patterns of thought, organization, and pedagogy remained. The contradiction between the aspirations of students and elite intentions for social engineering—a defining tension in all US educational institutions in the twentieth century—was particularly acute at Tuskegee Institute. In each era, the clash between the hopes black people invested in Tuskegee Institute and the dollars that powerful white people invested there, too, found some expression in picket signs, in petitions, in literature, or in attrition. The meaning of Tuskegee Institute is contained not only in the designs of its leadership or its funders, but also in the context of black students and teachers struggling to realize their dreams. Tuskegee Institute was stamped by this contest from the moment of its birth, when black people's hopes were raised by revolution and dashed by counterrevolution.

Industrial Education and Counterrevolution

Tuskegee Institute was born in a counterrevolution. What was destined to become the nation's most famous school for black people came into existence just as the self-organized movement of newly freed black people after the Civil War to build and sustain their own schools was thwarted. It didn't have to be so. At the height of the nation's democratic experiment after the war, six hundred black people joined southern state legislatures, and sixteen were elected to the US Congress.[4] In Macon County, future site of Tuskegee Institute, a formerly enslaved person, James Alston, was elected to the state legislature, representing, among his constituents, the man who had once owned him.[5] The freed people set to work immediately building schools, bringing out into the open their heroic, long-standing pursuit of literacy in slavery.[6] Alabama's first public schools for black people were established in Huntsville in 1863 when the city was captured by federal troops.[7] By 1870, every single southern state constitution contained specific language about the formation of a state-supported public school system.[8] Many white students in the South went to school for the first time thanks to the efforts of their black neighbors. "Public education for all, at public expense," W. E. B. Du Bois wrote, "was, in the South, a Negro idea."[9]

The counterrevolutionary "redemption" of the South was a reign of terror. Schools for black people were systematically defunded and destroyed.[10] "The sight of blacks carrying books often had the same effect on whites as the sight of armed blacks," as one historian put it, "and many would have found no real distinction between the two threats."[11] In Alabama's Black Belt, terrorism largely succeeded in excluding black people from politics and confining them to a form of social and racial subordination (later known as "Jim Crow").[12] Nine out of every ten people lynched in the United States before the Civil War were white; now the reverse was true.[13] More than two thousand black people were lynched in the United States between 1882 and 1903. Macon County's two state representatives, both black, were convicted of felonies and sentenced to chain gangs.[14] There had been 181,000 black people registered to vote in the state in 1900, but only 3,000 were registered by 1902.[15] The freed people wanted to be independent farmers, but through debt accumulation and harsh legal repression and violence were stuck working as tenant farmers.[16] As late as 1925, 90 percent of black farmers in Macon County were still tenants, paying their rent in cash, cotton, or other crops. And since white landlords kept all of the records of debt and controlled all of the courts (in which any disputes might be settled), the typical tenant fell further in debt year after year.[17]

Tuskegee Institute was able to come into existence in this context in part because the counterrevolution in the South did not, as a rule, sweep away all schools for black people. The counterrevolutionaries (the so-called Redeemers) sought many mechanisms to defund black schools and redirect public funding to white schools. However, in their attempt to erect and preserve a segregated social system, it was necessary to allow a small layer of black professionals to be trained to serve their segregated communities. The maintenance of segregated schools required black teachers. Thus, for many years, higher education for black people mainly took the form of teacher training institutions, like Tuskegee Institute.[18]

From Hampton to Tuskegee

The model for the Tuskegee Institute was the Hampton Institute, where Booker T. Washington enrolled as a student in 1872, and it was there that the contradiction between the ambitions of the freed people and of northern and southern white elites was forged. In 1868 the Hampton Normal and Industrial Institute was founded by Samuel C. Armstrong, a white Civil War veteran who saw a potential "solution" to the "Negro Problem" in the South through the model of so-called industrial education provided to the colonized indigenous people in Hawaii, where he was raised as the child of missionaries.[19] The "industrial" moniker indicated a curriculum oriented toward manual labor, but "normal" schools were for training teachers, not mechanics.[20] Through long hours of work, necessary for the maintenance of themselves and the school, students learned to "value" manual labor, and the curriculum emphasized the inherent harmony of the interests of capital and labor.[21] Training teachers in this worldview, school leaders hoped to reconcile the aspirations of the freed people to the counterrevolutionary social order. "The ex-slaves struggled to develop a social and educational ideology singularly appropriate to their defense of emancipation and one that challenged the social power of the planter regime," historian James D. Anderson writes. "Armstrong developed a pedagogy and ideology designed to avoid such confrontations and to maintain within the South a social consensus that did not challenge traditional inequalities of wealth and power."[22] In the aftermath of the defeat of Reconstruction, the "great problem," said one Hampton trustee, was "to attach the Negro to the soil and prevent his exodus from the country to the city." Teacher training that emphasized manual labor was the solution to this problem. "Let us make the teachers," Armstrong said, "and we will make the people."[23]

When Armstrong tapped Washington, his star pupil, to build a new school in Tuskegee, Alabama, the student outshone the teacher. Fusing the curriculum with a political stance, Washington followed directly in his mentor's footsteps and also surpassed him. Black people needed moral education and manual skills, Washington taught, not the broad liberal arts education they sought. "No race can prosper," he said, "till it learns that there is as much dignity in tilling a field as in writing a poem. It is at the bottom of life we must begin, and not at the top."[24] Washington personally oversaw the construction and expansion of the school's facilities, most of which were built by the students themselves. Washington initially forbade the introduction of liberal arts courses popular at other Black colleges, such as Greek or Latin. Instead, students focused on technical skills. Male students studied carpentry, printing, and agricultural techniques, while female students learned how to do laundry, sewing, and "kitchen duties." "We are not a college," Washington told students in 1896, "and if there are any of you here who expect to get a college training, you will be disappointed."[25] Under Washington's leadership, Tuskegee acquired land and erected impressive buildings on a sprawling, immaculate, and handsome campus. By directing resources to "little Tuskegees" and away from schools with classical liberal arts offerings, philanthropists hoped to force all of higher education for black people in the South into one mold.[26] For many years, they succeeded. Hampton and Tuskegee stood apart from their peer institutions. By 1915, Hampton had a $2.7 million endowment, and Tuskegee's was $1.9 million. Together, these sums were greater than half of all of the private black college endowments in the country combined.[27]

Tuskegee Institute quickly became as much a symbol as it was a school. It "operated as a propaganda agency," Horace Mann Bond concluded.[28] To black supporters, it was a symbol of pride, an inspiring example of what an institution run by black people could achieve. To white philanthropic supporters, it promised to teach black people to forgo political and social agitation in favor of the kind of humility and deference that would foster good "race relations." To white southern detractors, any kind of schooling implied revolution: black people at Tuskegee were, by seeking education, attempting to rise above their assigned station in the social hierarchy. For the school's black critics, the problem was the opposite, that the school encouraged black people to accept their political and social subordination. Whatever the outward appearance, Tuskegee students formed their own judgments, and acted upon them.

The Black Student Voice

While most scholarship has focused on external critics of Washington and Tuskegee (most famously, W. E. B. Du Bois), the voices of Tuskegee students have been underexamined in the assessment of Washington's legacy. Like all students, those at Tuskegee have held a wide range of opinions on matters of curriculum and politics. Student critics and dissidents cannot be said to speak for the entire student body, nor do they express the sum of Tuskegee student experiences. However, given the perpetual danger facing their school from racist officials wielding budget axes and vigilantes wielding other weapons, the fact of raising their voices loudly enough to leave a mark in the historical record speaks to the strength of their convictions. Whatever the inciting incident, many of the protests on Tuskegee's campus in its early years were over the low level of instruction or the strict enforcement of moral codes (the latter was a common feature of college life across the color line as well). The same was true at its predecessor and sister school, the Hampton Institute, where "industrial" education didn't always mean what pupils hoped it would. Some students who were attracted to Hampton, for example, because of its printing press "commented bitterly" when they realized that the printing trade was not taught.[29] One "distinguished" black visitor to campus complained that Hampton was "teaching the Negroes to be hewers of wood and drawers of water, and . . . servants to the white race." It was the most beautiful campus he had ever seen, but because of the restricted nature of intellectual pursuits, he said it was also a "literary penitentiary."[30]

The Hampton Institute's emphasis on strict supervision of their morality angered students who felt insulted by the rules of behavior. At times this anger motivated Hampton students to organize themselves to strike. One such incident in 1889 actually involved the future president of Tuskegee, Robert Russa Moton, who ended up the reluctant leader of a student strike, initiated by students insulted by a matron who had prohibited male students from escorting female students to a dance.[31] The students weren't the only ones to express dissent. Increasingly, Hampton's political stance came under fire within the broader school community. In 1889 alumni wrote a petition of protest against the school's support of Jim Crow segregation on campus. Samuel Armstrong, Hampton's founder, admitted that criticism of the school was "common in the negro papers."[32] This undercurrent of protest and internal critique of "industrial" education was no odd occurrence, but a sustained and permanent feature of the Hampton Institute.

Likewise, the central issue animating most of the protests through-out Tuskegee's history was the gap between students' aspirations and the school's governing philosophy. Most protesters were black Americans, from Alabama and the surrounding southern states.[33] Whatever initially drew them to Tuskegee, once they arrived, they frequently chafed at the emphasis on manual labor. In his memoir, Washington recalls that "quite a number of letters came from parents protesting against their children engaging in labour while they were in the school."[34] Black students from abroad had the same reaction. Black Cuban and Puerto Rican students were recruited as part of a collaboration with the US federal government to strengthen its ties with those colonies, but Washington encountered great difficulties winning them over to the "industrial" model of school-ing. The new students protested against their work duties so often that Washington eventually had a guardhouse built so he could put disrup-tive students in "jail" if necessary. In one incident, Cuban students went on strike and refused to eat, and "guns were flourished" when a teacher attempted to put a student leader in the campus jail.[35]

Washington always insisted that Tuskegee was a secondary school, not a college; but by necessity he was compelled to hire black college-educated people to work as teachers, and so, in its earliest days, Tuske-gee harbored intellectuals and intellectualism despite itself. Washington hired the eccentric agricultural genius George Washington Carver in 1896.[36] Carver's discoveries became legendary and increased the associa-tion of Tuskegee with serious intellectual effort. Despite Washington's fear that the faculty would catch the "Niagara spirit" (referring to the civil rights organization headed by W. E. B. Du Bois) and infect Tuske-gee with it, he recruited Monroe Work, one of that movement's found-ers, in 1908.[37] Work founded Tuskegee's Department of Records and Research, where he compiled statistics on the conditions of black life in the United States. His career at Tuskegee exemplifies the tensions on campus between academic work and industrial education. Initially en-thusiastic about the opportunity to use Tuskegee's resources to expand his research, Work was disappointed to find when he arrived that he was expected to essentially serve as a propagandist for Washington's growing political machine. He sufficiently impressed the founder, however, who gradually gave him more leeway. Work used the opportunity to gather evidence that would shatter myths about black people and expose the realities of segregation. In 1913 he published the first of what became an annual "Tuskegee Lynching Report," making the school the nation's premiere source for information on the topic.[38]

Tuskegee's students, meanwhile, resorted to strikes and sit-ins to protest the emphasis on industrial education. In 1903 a group of students took the opportunity of another of the founder's sojourns to strike in favor of more academic instruction and less manual labor. Their protest was prompted by an administrative change in their schedules: a new division of time between academic and industrial work put more emphasis on the latter at the expense of the former. "About a week after Washington had left," writes Harlan, "and after student petitions and complaints had been rejected, student dissatisfaction became so general that it was easy for a few leaders to bring about 'an open rebellion.'" The male students marched from their breakfast hall to the chapel, "locked themselves in, and after some haranguing voted not to work or study until changes were made."[39] The board of directors wrote to Washington for advice; he responded simply: "No concessions."[40]

Eventually, however, there were concessions. After the strike ended, the school's governing council reduced the frequency of mandatory chapel attendance from every night to two nights a week. Tuskegee trustee and railroad magnate William H. Baldwin (no fan of strikes) investigated the student strike and concluded that there was merit in the students' complaint that "they were required to devote too much time to both industrial work and studies with too little time for preparation." From an "efficiency" perspective, Baldwin thought that Washington should reduce their burdens. However, rather than grant greater freedom from manual labor, Washington elected (against the protest of the academic faculty) to ease the students' burden of time spent in preparation for their academic courses.[41]

The school's disciplinary records tell us more about student resistance to industrial education. For 1907, to take one year as an example, 41 percent of the students (676 out of 1,621) were subject to disciplinary actions (ranging from warnings to suspensions).[42] If they couldn't follow the rules, coursework allowed little reward, either. The vast majority of students never advanced beyond the lowest-level classes, and most of those did not graduate. The few who did "survive" to graduate did in fact go on to college and joined the professions that defined the "Talented Tenth."[43] Others left to pursue higher education elsewhere. The poet and activist Claude McKay was a student at Tuskegee in 1912; he described it as a "semi-military, machine-like existence."[44] McKay withdrew and transferred to a liberal arts college in Kansas.

"There is not a scintilla of evidence that the officials here are overbearing," wrote one visitor to Tuskegee in 1916, "that the discipline is unduly severe or that the students are discontented or depressed."[45] Whatever the intentions of this visitor, his report, published in a New England educational journal, begins with an unmistakably defensive tone, as if responding to very specific criticisms not explicitly referenced. From the perspective of some Tuskegee students, school officials were, in fact, overbearing. Criticism of Washington's educational philosophy and methods emerged within the Tuskegee campus community, an endogenous expression of the fundamental contradiction between black people's desire for educational opportunities that matched their political and social ambitions after the Civil War, and the orientation of the founders of the Hampton-Tuskegee "industrial" model of schooling. Ironically, the industrialization of the South and the crisis of southern agriculture spelled the doom of "industrial" schooling. After Washington's death in 1915, it wasn't just students and parents who made new demands of black education; the southern economy did as well.

From Cotton to Steel

In his famous oration at the Atlanta Cotton States and International Exposition in 1895, Washington had called upon black people to "cast down their buckets"—to stay and work in the US South. When it comes to business "pure and simple," he continued, "it is in the South that the Negro is given a man's chance in the commercial world."[46] In the first few decades of the twentieth century, rather than cast their buckets down, black people picked them up, and headed for southern and northern cities. From 1900 to 1930 the percentage of black people living in rural areas dropped by 20 percent, and the number living in Alabama's cities doubled.[47] The migrants were drawn to opportunities in the North and to the growth of industries such as coal mining in southern cities. If cotton had dominated Alabama's economy in the nineteenth century, steel would take its place in the twentieth.

As Horace Mann Bond observed in his influential study of education in Alabama, it was impossible for such an enormous economic transformation to occur and leave the social status of black people untouched; with new status came new approaches to their education.[48] Industrial employers had different attitudes toward schooling. Unlike planters, who benefited from a social arrangement that required black people to be illiterate, innumerate, and socially ostracized, the industrialists saw an advantage in opening up skilled positions to black workers, since they could be paid lower wages and were believed to have less experience with unions. Tuskegee officials collaborated with coal operators, sending students to the mines to convince black workers not to join biracial unions in return for coal-sponsored scholarships for employees.[49] By 1923, more than half of Alabama's coal miners were black.[50] This transformation of the working life of black people rendered outdated both the terms of Washington's "Atlanta Compromise" and the governing philosophy of Tuskegee Institute. Between the changing status of black workers, migration, and the shifting needs of industry, resistance to black education beyond the moral training of the "industrial" model broke down after Booker T. Washington's death in 1915.[51]

While philanthropists had successfully made "industrial" education the model of black schooling in the first decades of the twentieth century, what black teachers accomplished is not entirely contained by that label. A generation of activists and thinkers who wrote boldly and took bolder action (such as Carter G. Woodson, Richard Wright, Rosa Parks, and Ida B. Wells) were nurtured in these schools, where, despite the emphasis on manners and morals, an implicit lesson was pride. "By and large eschewing revolutionary or left-wing doctrines, they espoused Christian values, middle-class virtues, and American ideals. In that sense, they were a conservative force," historian Adam Fairclough concludes. "Yet they resisted white efforts to place a ceiling upon black achievement and refused to indoctrinate black children into white supremacy."[52] And, within a wide variety of institutional constraints, black teachers have long carried on a tradition of what education scholar Jarvis Givins calls "fugitive pedagogy"—pushing their students toward greater personal and social aspirations despite politicians' and school leaders' attempts to limit them.[53]

World events in the twentieth century further transformed black people's political, social, and educational horizons. Black soldiers traveled to Europe to fight in a world war and came home armed, literally and figuratively. Black people increased their migration to urban centers in the South and in the North, and the South industrialized. All of these dynamics shifted power away from the planters and gave force to calls for educational change. The philanthropists were slow to respond to black students' rising expectations. They assumed that black people could be socialized into particular industrial occupations. Accordingly, they funded "industrial" education in order to promote social stability and productivity. Both social stability and productivity proved fragile in the 1920s, however, as the American economy contracted. Employers turned "black jobs" into "white jobs" and thus rendered many black workers superfluous, frustrating philanthropists' plans. They eventually abandoned their commitment to "industrial" education and higher education and shifted their attention to elementary schools for black people. With Washington deceased and the economy changing rapidly, both Tuskegee and Hampton became liberal arts colleges. The "New Negro" of the 1920s would not accept anything less.[54]

The New Negro on Campus Fights Back

Black colleges in the 1920s faced extreme contradictions. Southern states raised teaching standards and expanded education, which placed greater pressure on colleges to raise academic standards as well.[55] However, philanthropists, the federal government, and some black educators tried to hold on to the industrial model in the form of vocational education and continued to challenge the rise of academic curricula.[56] At the same time, black students grew in numbers and expectations. While the population of college students in the United States doubled in the 1920s, the number of black college students nearly quintupled. Only 400 received bachelor's degrees in 1920, while 1,903 did so in 1929.[57] There were 2,132 black students nationwide in 1917 and 13,580 by 1927. These were no longer meek, grateful vocational students. Rather, they were often bitter, fearing that their aspirations had been traded for philanthropists' money.[58] Black students fought back. Their protests, with growing support from their parents and communities, and in the context of the changing political economy of the South, changed "institutes" into genuine colleges and universities.

In response to low academic standards, enforced vocationalism, and Jim Crow on campus, black students in the 1920s launched what one black newspaper called "an epidemic of student strikes." At Fisk in 1924 students demanded greater freedom, the right to form sororities and fraternities, and a student newspaper. In a flashpoint, students erupted, overturned chapel seats, and smashed windows, shouting, "Du Bois! Du Bois!" The students went on strike, shutting down the campus for ten weeks, ultimately winning their demands. At Howard, student protests ended mandatory chapel attendance in 1922. Two years later, Howard students threatened a strike and won joint power—alongside the administration—in student disciplinary cases. In 1925 Howard students struck against compulsory military participation in the Reserve Officer Training Corps (ROTC), and succeeded in having the program reclassified as an optional way to satisfy Howard's physical education requirement.[59] Students at Tuskegee would have to wait fifty years to win comparable changes.[60]

Many observers saw the revolt of black students in the 1920s as part of a global radicalization. "Youth the world over is undergoing a spiritual and an intellectual awakening," wrote the black poet Countee Cullen, "[and] is looking with new eyes at old customs and institutions, and is finding for them interpretations which its parents passed over." President McKenzie at Fisk said that the uprising of black students raised similar issues as the Russian Revolution, particularly the issue of control: "This problem in the college is quite similar to that occasionally presented, of recent years, by radicals everywhere. Shall the factory be turned over to the workers and be run by the workingmen's council? Shall the colleges be turned over to the students and be run by undergraduate committees?"[61] Visiting Tuskegee in July 1920, former US president William Howard Taft hopefully asserted that the legacy of Booker T. Washington would be the answer to this global movement. Washington's philosophy could, he said, "save us from anarchy and Bolshevism."[62]

The two black colleges with the largest endowments, Hampton and Tuskegee, were seen as immune from the strike wave. According to one observer, "Nobody considered the possibility that anything could happen at Hampton."[63] But something did in fact happen, and Hampton would not be the same afterwards. Students at Hampton went on strike in 1925 and then again in 1927 against the low level of instruction and against strict moral regulation. Tuskegee, meanwhile, mostly avoided such clashes in the 1920s for three reasons: dissidents often decided to leave campus on their own; the administration moved quickly to upgrade the academic programming; and the school faced external threats that united students, faculty, and administrators.

Following Booker T. Washington's death in 1915, Dr. Robert Russa Moton was selected as the next leader of Tuskegee. Moton successfully embraced and celebrated the educational philosophy of Booker T. Washington in words, while quietly abandoning many—but not all—aspects of it in practice. Moton inherited a college that was effectively a high school. After the state of Alabama initiated a policy of only hiring teachers with college degrees, Tuskegee graduates were unemployable in the state's primary schools. Moton decided that he had "to advance the curriculum of Tuskegee Institute to the college level in order to meet this requirement." In 1925 Moton initiated a major campaign to raise $5 million and ended up raising $10 million, proving that, while shifting course on the curriculum, he was able to continue Washington's success in courting wealthy donors.[64]

As in the past, the money came with strings. Student life was strictly regimented and surveilled in order to perpetually prove that Tuskegee was instilling the proper values in its students, including acceptance of Jim Crow segregation. Thus there were "continual rumors" of "student unrest" in the 1920s, and students found creative ways to "secretly" rebel. Tuskegee students were "divided," Marable wrote, "about the new racial consciousness of the twenties." Some embraced the Eurocentric cultural norms on campus, while others wondered, "Is it a humiliation to be identified with a race that has produced such men and women as Frederick Douglass, Booker T. Washington, Sojourner Truth, Phillis Wheatley and many others of such character?"[65] Some of the faculty considered the observance of Jim Crow rules on campus "obsequious." Tuskegee hired some of the best and brightest black scholars in the country, but they often bristled under the restrictions of the campus culture. The famous social scientist E. Franklin Frazier, for example, recalled that when he began teaching at Tuskegee, he was summoned to the dean's office and "admonished for carrying too many books on the campus." Apparently, the dean "feared that whites 'would get the impression that Tuskegee was training the Negro's intellect rather than his heart and hands.'"[66]

Although Moton moved to upgrade academic offerings, at the same time, Tuskegee experienced a rapidly revolving student body. Student attrition (following the pattern of the low graduation rates of the nineteenth century) helped reduce activism at Tuskegee. Moton himself admitted that "too large a percentage of our students, for one reason or another, discontinue their studies before completing their courses." Students who wouldn't conform simply removed themselves from the campus. As Claude McKay did a few years earlier, Nella Larsen, another such nonconformist, worked at Tuskegee in 1915 and left in 1916. In her novel *Quicksand*, the protagonist, a young teacher at a school clearly modeled on Tuskegee, becomes disillusioned with the "hypocrisy, cruelty, servility, and snobbishness," and decides to leave.[67] The departure of figures like Larsen and McKay in the first few decades of the twentieth century may explain why "the institute was free from the student and faculty protests that brought turmoil to other black colleges in the 1920s."[68] Still another factor may be the conduct of its president, Moton, when the school came under attack.

Transforming Tuskegee Again: Health, Wealth, and War

Tuskegee Institute went through a series of restructurings in the twenties, thirties, and forties: finding new sources of revenue, significantly upgrading its academic offerings, and deepening its relationship with the federal government. At times, students protested and even went on strike when their ambitions were out of sync with the administration. At other times, when the campus was under racist attack, students linked arms with administrators to defend their school. Maintaining its status as a "capital" of Black America, Tuskegee's leadership entered into new compromises and contradictions, setting the stage for the explosive battles of the 1960s.

Like most black leaders (including Du Bois), Moton saw the First World War as an opportunity.[69] Tuskegee Institute gave technical training to 1,229 men during the conflict,[70] and, on government-sponsored trips to France and Haiti, Moton lent his personal prestige in Black America to President Woodrow Wilson's effort to manage the rising expectations of black soldiers and to "dampen radical agitation among Negroes."[71] For his loyalty and service, Moton and Tuskegee were rewarded with a US veterans hospital. Interestingly, both black militants and white racists objected to the locating of a federal hospital for black veterans at Tuskegee. The NAACP worried that placing it at Tuskegee would further strengthen the school's standing as a "capital" of black America. An Alabama state senator, meanwhile, feared that a government hospital would put local black people beyond the control of state officials. "[A] bunch of negro officers," Senator R. H. Powell said, "with uniforms and big salaries and the protection of Uncle Sam—negroes who are not responsible to our local laws and not regardful of local prejudice—will quickly turn this little town into a place of riot."[72]

When Tuskegee's veterans hospital opened on May 20, 1923, the professional staff was entirely white. White nurses were assisted by black nurse-maids (earning one-third to one-fourth what white nurses made). In July, when the first black professional—an accountant—appeared, the hospital's director ordered the security guards to escort him out. Soon after, approximately a thousand local white people marched with the Ku Klux Klan directly through Tuskegee's campus in a single-file line that stretched two miles. Among the procession were at least twenty hospital employees. Moton struck a defiant pose. He was prepared to defend Tuskegee, ordering ROTC students to take up positions along the parade route, among campus buildings, and some reserves were posted in the nearby countryside "ready to speed in if trouble broke out."[73] The NAACP's Walter White sat with Moton in his home during the Klan procession, and remembered: "He pointed to a rifle and a shotgun, well oiled and grimly businesslike, that stood in a corner. . . . 'I've got only one time to die. If I must die now to save Tuskegee Institute, I'm ready. I've been running long enough."[74]

Standing up to the Klan was not the same as defying the federal government, but Moton achieved his goal in the end. By July 1924, only one year after a black accountant had been physically removed from the hospital and the Klan had marched through campus, the Tuskegee veterans hospital had an all-black staff and, with no fuss or protest from white people, a black director. By the 1940s, medical residency programs were initiated in the hospital, and by the 1970s, it had an all-black staff of 1,200, including 37 physicians and dentists and 136 nurses.[75] Moton's conduct is probably the major reason students and faculty at Tuskegee did not erupt in protest as they did at virtually every other black college in the 1920s. Transforming Tuskegee into a proper college, defending the campus from the Klan, and fighting for an all-black staff at the veterans hospital, Moton seemed to many to have broken from the "servile deference" of the Washington years. As one historian concluded, "It is doubtful that any considerable number of students and professors would have risen in rebellion against a militant principal who, at least in the mid-1920s, was seen as an embattled major leading a campaign for racial self-determination."[76] In 1929 Moton published *What the Negro Thinks*, in which he forthrightly asserted what Washington never did: that black people oppose segregation and discrimination and demand equality.[77] Rather than stifling the new militancy, Moton appeared to many to have joined it. Moton's boldness remained part of campus lore into the 1960s, contributing to the idea that student activists were operating in concert with the school's traditions, not opposing them.[78]

By departing from key elements of Washington's formula, however, Moton all the more effectively preserved Washington's institution. If many of Washington's specific proscriptions were no longer useful, his legend certainly still was. Moton inaugurated "Founder's Day," an annual commemoration of Booker T. Washington at Tuskegee, and on one such day in 1922 he presided over the unveiling of the infamous statue (still standing) at the campus's main entrance, depicting Booker T. Washington "lifting the veil" of ignorance from an enslaved person.[79]

The statue became a symbol of the still hotly contested legacy of Booker T. Washington and the school he built. The controversy deepened decades later in 1972 when the public became aware that the institution had willingly participated in a racist medical experiment. Ironically, Tuskegee and its leaders had always taken a particular interest in promoting good health. Just before he died, Booker T. Washington initiated what later became National Negro Health Week.[80] In a region where medical care was scarce, Tuskegee's campus had two hospitals: Andrews Hospital and the veterans hospital.[81] But in 1932 a program began that would, four decades later, make the word "Tuskegee" synonymous with racism in medicine. It came to be known as the "Tuskegee Syphilis Experiment," but is most accurately named the US Public Health Service Study at Tuskegee.[82]

The facts are known: white doctors from the US Public Health Service (USPHS) found four hundred black men in the Tuskegee area with late-stage syphilis; they gave them iron tonic and aspirin as a fake cure in exchange for permission to perform autopsies when they died and the promise of a decent burial, free of charge. Tuskegee Institute was a willing participant, and both of its hospitals lent resources to the effort. It was one of the school's philanthropic backers, the Rosenwald Fund (and one of the pioneering foundations supporting the construction of schools for black people in the South), that suggested to the USPHS that Tuskegee be the site of the study.[83]

The USPHS researchers were guided by racist assumptions and proceeded in a manner that was profoundly unethical. The syphilis study at Tuskegee did not involve injecting people with syphilis and was not aimed at "genocide," as some later believed. Rather, it was an attempt to use manipulative and deceitful methods to understand the late stages of syphilis. The subjects were not informed of their condition, were offered treatments that were fake, and were not given genuine treatments as new ones were developed. Sadly, it was not uncommon at the time for the USPHS to conduct research without subjects' consent. By 1936, researchers had demonstrated that late-stage syphilis caused neurological and cardiovascular damage, and still the study wasn't stopped.[84] By the 1940s, researchers knew that penicillin could be an effective treatment, but it was not administered to the Tuskegee participants. In fact, the Public Health Service went out of its way to prevent the patients from knowing they had syphilis and from seeking any treatments.[85]

When an Associated Press reporter broke the story in 1972, the impact was tremendous.[86] As the tale spread, so did outrage and misinformation, which unfortunately made subsequent public health initiatives all the more difficult to implement. For example, when health officials tried to promote needle exchange programs to prevent the spread of AIDS in African American communities in the 1980s, some black leaders responded with fear and suspicion, invoking the legacy of what happened at Tuskegee.[87] False information about the study at Tuskegee persists in the twenty-first century and is widespread.[88] In 1997 US president Bill Clinton officially apologized for the Tuskegee syphilis experiment. Surrounded by family members of the study's subjects as well as eight survivors, the president announced, among other things, a planning grant for the establishment of a bioethics center at Tuskegee University.[89] In 1999 the Tuskegee University National Center for Bioethics in Research and Health Care opened its doors.[90]

The War at Home and Abroad

When student protesters occupied Dorothy Hall in 1968, they had no idea that such a study was in progress, or that for the next several decades, their school would be associated with medical racism. They were also most likely unaware that, at that very moment, Tuskegee had become associated—in the eyes of Alabama's governor George Wallace—with communism. Wallace was wrong, of course. Tuskegee was not a communist training ground. The grain of historical truth, however, was this: everywhere black people in the South were fighting against Jim Crow in the 1930s and 1940s, radicals played an important part, and the Tuskegee Institute student community was not immune to those influences, either.

The New Deal, the federal government's intervention during the Great Depression, reorganized the shattered economy, ushered in new ways of life, and raised black people's expectations. Hundreds of thousands of former sharecroppers and farmers became factory workers and soldiers.[91] Black people slipped out of the grip of the planters and found new opportunities with new employers, including the federal government. From 1926 to 1933 the number of black federal employees jumped from fifty thousand to two hundred thousand.[92] Among the new opportunities they sought was higher education. Black people's college attendance soared. Only twelve thousand black people were college students in 1928, but by 1941 there were thirty-seven thousand, and that number more than doubled by 1950.[93] In the 1930s black students continued to protest, reflecting the fact that campus offerings still did not rise to the level of their aspirations. Ibram Kendi notes that "at least" eight big demonstrations "rocked HBCUs" in 1936 alone, over poor food, racism of professors, and the push for student councils.[94] As mentioned earlier, a white visitor to the campus in 1930 observed that "Tuskegee and its methods receive more criticisms from the Negroes themselves than from the Southern whites."[95]

One such critical testimony comes from the novelist and former Tuskegee student Ralph Ellison. Ellison was drawn to the campus in 1933 to study music under the famed black composer William Levi Dawson. Unable to pay tuition, Ellison was allowed to work in the school's bakery, but didn't earn enough for his musical instrument, the required uniforms, and boarding fees, and he found himself quickly sinking into debt. He found solace in reading, and got a job at the library, but the "historic ethos of Tuskegee was a constant worship of practicality," which left him feeling isolated from his peers. He also bristled at the strict regulation of student life and behavior. The student handbook was explicit: "Here, you will find every phase of your life systematically regulated and supervised for the purpose of aiding you in getting the most from your courses." Even the students' gait was a matter of scrutiny: "Pick up your feet when you walk. . . . Never drag yourself along. Some people think that heavy feet indicate a light head." The handbook reminded students that "Tuskegee is a vast workshop. . . . Work is the chief element awaiting you at every turn."[96]

In 1952 Ellison published his first novel, *Invisible Man*, in which the protagonist attends a Tuskegee-style college in the South. The portrait of the school—echoing *Quicksand*—is not flattering. Dr. Bledsoe, a thinly veiled representation of Moton, was described as a man with not one but two Cadillacs, who knew just how to put on a mask for the white people who funded the school, and reveled in the power he wielded. "I's big and black and I say 'Yes, suh' as loudly as any burrhead when it's convenient, but I'm still the king down here," Bledsoe tells the novel's protagonist. "This is a power set-up, son," Bledsoe continues, "and I'm at the controls. You think about that. When you buck against me, you're bucking against power, rich white folk's power, the nation's power—which means government power!"[97] Horace Mann Bond corresponded with Ellison in 1967, chiding him about this portrayal. "I thought you laid it on a little thick," he wrote.[98] But perhaps the most enduring aspect of this fictionalized Tuskegee-inspired narrative is the protagonist's reaction to the statue of the founder, portrayed as "lifting the veil of ignorance" from an enslaved person. "I am standing puzzled," he says, looking at the statue, "unable to decide whether the veil is really being lifted, or lowered more firmly in place; whether I am witnessing a revelation or a more efficient blinding."[99]

This tension between revelation and blinding was in evidence across HBCUs in the 1930s and 1940s, a shelter from the storm of Jim Crow, and a unique space where competing ideals were given open expression.[100] Ellison, drawn toward the communist movement as a teenager, felt out of step with the culture of the campus as a whole. But he did find a few professors and other students who shared his love of literature.[101] There were both strict rules and the possibility of protesting them. "Students complained about Victorian codes of conduct," writes Fairclough, perceptively, "but the very frequency of student protests suggests that black colleges were not nearly as autocratic as some critics charged."[102] On campus, black students became exposed to ideas of collective protest and social change, while the administration remained, generally speaking, committed to personal advancement strategies and opposed collective bargaining and unions. Thus, despite a history of being supportive of black farmers, Tuskegee's administrators actively opposed the communist-led Sharecroppers Union. Monroe Work conceded that the school's "general policy . . . is to discourage the organization of Negro farmers." At one point, when sharecroppers had an armed conflict with authorities in a nearby county, Moton hoped to "quell black unrest in the area" and so "dispatched representatives to Tallapoosa in a calculated move to turn blacks away from Communism."[103]

But another communist-led initiative, the Southern Negro Youth Congress (SNYC), spread across HBCUs in the late 1930s, including among students at Tuskegee Institute. Following the Communist Party's new strategic orientation to the center-left of American politics (known as the Popular Front), the SNYC was founded in 1937, initiated by CP members, yet remained formally independent of the party, and attracted a wide range of support. At its height, the SNYC claimed eleven thousand black members in ten southern states.[104] The SNYC was able to take root in HBCUs because, however conservative in leadership, the nation's black colleges were, in fact, incubators of a generation of activists. As students pushed for greater academic offerings and more intellectual freedom in the 1930s and 1940s, they opened up a space for discussions about left-wing ideas, including communism and socialism. Students at Morehouse College could take a course on Karl Marx. And even in the Deep South's state schools, notes Fairclough, "students could hear the likes of Paul Robeson, Langston Hughes, and W. E. B. Du Bois"—three of the nation's most prominent black communists.[105]

Whereas Moton had tried to undermine the Sharecroppers Union, Frederick Patterson, Tuskegee's third president (who began his tenure in 1935), could embrace the aims of the SNYC. The new organization represented the new mood of protest among young black people in the South, and its center-left politics also fit with the ideas of black leaders. Patterson was the chair of the SNYC's adult advisory board (along with other leading black educators, including Du Bois and Alain Locke).[106] Patterson's niece, Thelma Dale, was elected its vice-chairperson.[107] At the SNYC's fifth congress, held at Tuskegee Institute in 1942, the most famous African American communist, singer Paul Robeson, gave his first Deep South performance.[108]

The Great Depression and the buildup to the Second World War shattered the old arrangements upon which Tuskegee had stood for the first fifty years of its existence. Between collapsing profit margins in the 1930s and "mounting taxation on private capital" in the 1940s, philanthropic donations to Tuskegee and other HBCUs plummeted.[109] "Between 1930 and 1943," notes Marybeth Gasman, "the overall income of black colleges decreased by 15 percent and income from private gifts decreased 50 percent."[110] When Patterson took over the reins in 1935, Tuskegee was operating with a $50,000 annual deficit. By his own admission, Patterson was not the fundraiser that Moton or Washington had been. "I really had to strike out on my own to develop resources," he wrote.[111]

The sharp decline in funding may explain the wave of food strikes that swept black colleges in the 1940s. Students struck over the poor quality of food at Spelman in 1942, Clark College in 1944, South Carolina's Benedict College in 1944 and 1947, North Carolina's Livingston College in 1946, Alabama A&M in 1947, and Alabama State in 1948. The "major campus protest" during Tuskegee's 1940–1941 school year was a food strike. As Kendi noted, "Nearly half of the 1,400 students went on strike. Dozens were arrested, suspended, expelled, or battered by policemen in remonstration of 'despicable' food sometimes seasoned with flies, ants, roaches, and tacks."[112]

Patterson's response to the protests was uniquely sympathetic. When the Tuskegee student strikers began interfering with delivery trucks entering the campus, state troopers showed up. "I had to prevail on the state troopers not to arrest the students who were blocking the entrance but to give us a chance to work things out," Patterson recalled, "which they did. We had wonderful cooperation from the troopers, but they had the biggest guns I'd ever seen in my life. I said, 'Don't touch these students.' They responded, 'We wouldn't do that, Dr. Patterson.' I said, 'I think we can get this situation under control.'"[113] Patterson did so with a clever deflection of the students' energies. "When students at Tuskegee Institute went on strike in 1940 demanding better food," writes Fairclough, "Patterson let them run the cafeteria. The students learned a valuable lesson in economics, gladly relinquishing control after a few days. But the strike also taught something to Patterson, who thereafter made a point of including students on college committees."[114] Twenty-eight years later, state troopers would threaten to invade Tuskegee's campus once again, this time in response to a student occupation of the trustees' meeting; Frederick Patterson would be one of their hostages.

Such maneuvers could placate students for a while, but they couldn't solve the underlying financial problem. With tuition at only $50 a year, raising fees would not be enough. Tuskegee still had a large endowment (roughly $7 million), but costs were rising faster than income. Instead, Patterson initiated a "Five Year Plan" for poorer students to save money by extending the amount of work they performed for the school. Students who couldn't afford tuition would work more and study less, and graduate in five years instead of four.[115] Patterson also agreed to allow the state of Alabama the ability to appoint more trustees to the board (from two up to six, out of twenty-four in total) in order to receive more funding from the state. And, since all of the black colleges were in the same bind, Patterson suggested they pool their collective fundraising resources. What started as the United College Drive Conference later became known as the United Negro College Fund.[116]

The economic crisis mandated educational shifts, Patterson believed. To go forward, he decided to reach back to the ideas of Booker T. Washington. It was "imperative that we give renewed effort in the direction stressed by Booker T. Washington and put brains and skill into the common occupations of life," Patterson told a black newspaper in 1941.[117] When he took over, many graduates went on to become teachers or "ag men"—agricultural agents of the state and county. Patterson created four new programs at Tuskegee in fields that were "up and coming": commercial food service, veterinary medicine, aviation, and engineering.[118] Composer William Dawson saw the writing on the wall, and left Tuskegee; his famed music program was shuttered soon afterwards. Ellison also departed.[119] Apropos of the curtailment (and given the anachronism in the school's original name, "normal" for teacher training), Patterson likewise shortened the school's name to "Tuskegee Institute."[120]

Patterson was also responsible for the formation of the now-famous Tuskegee airmen, which deepened Tuskegee Institute's relationship with the federal government, increased funding, and laid the basis for a new round of political conflicts in the 1950s and 1960s. Seeing aviation as an expanding industry, in 1939 Patterson sought and was awarded a government contract for civilian pilot training.[121] Once civilian pilot training had begun and an airfield built, it was a short step to considering Tuskegee as a site to train black pilots for the Army Air Force. But this, too, was a controversial move, which the NAACP and some black newspapers criticized as further entrenching segregation in the military.[122] The Cleveland Gazette called it a "jim-crow school of aviation at Tuskegee." Kansas City's Plain Dealer headline read, "$80,000 for Tuskegee Jim Crow Air Unit."[123]

Patterson, like Tuskegee's leaders before him, sought to collaborate with the American military for political and financial reasons. With help from the Rosenwald Fund, Tuskegee was awarded the government contract for the Army Air Forces pilot training program. Aviation requires a lot of non-flight staff, who also came to Tuskegee, bringing more well-paid professionals into the local economy.[124] Enrollment in Tuskegee increased as students pursued aviation and related aero-engineering studies.[125] As another symbol of continuity in the collaboration, Booker T. Washington III (grandson of the founder) was appointed to oversee the development of the military aviation training school at Tuskegee.[126] Altogether, from 1941 to 1946, some one thousand airmen were trained at Tuskegee Institute.[127]

The Tuskegee airmen sought to prove their worth as pilots and simultaneously challenge discrimination in the armed forces. After their training at Tuskegee, they were deployed to various bases around the United States and in the European theater. Nearly everywhere they went, they faced harassment and discrimination. By merely attempting to use all-white facilities, Tuskegee airmen forced the US military to confront the long-standing practice of segregation at military bases, risking their military careers in the process. The airmen's actions began with the Tuskegee base, which was also segregated. Twelve black officers took direct action to challenge segregation on the base, on August 3, 1944. There was some tension as they were seated and served, but the restaurant was thereafter desegregated (although white officers stopped eating there).[128] The airmen's activism represented another forerunner of the 1960s Tuskegee student movement. Since its founding, students had often led the way at Tuskegee, but in the 1950s a dam burst, and the school's political stance was irrevocably transformed by the actions of its faculty. Tuskegee's teachers in turn opened the door to the biggest student movement the campus had ever seen.

The Struggle for Voting Rights and Booker T. Washington

The publication of Robert J. Norrell's 1998 book *Reaping the Whirlwind: The Civil Rights Movement in Tuskegee* brought wider appreciation to the role that Tuskegee University's faculty played in the struggle for voting rights nationwide.[129] The lawsuit that Tuskegee plaintiffs eventually brought all the way to victory in the US Supreme Court case *Gomillion v. Lightfoot* in fact set an essential precedent for securing basic voting rights for black people across the country. It is not widely remembered today, but at the time the battle over voting rights in Tuskegee was national news.[130] One staff researcher at Tuskegee Institute collected over three thousand pamphlets, magazine articles, and news articles about the conflict between 1957 and 1959.[131]

Tuskegee professor Charles Gomillion, the central organizer of the campaign to win voting rights and the lead plaintiff in the famous court case, saw his work as a definitive break from Washington's legacy. Gomillion is known to have said, "Booker T. Washington came to teach the Negroes how to make a living. I came to teach them how to live."[132] Norrell, however, emphasizes the continuity with Washington. "Gomillion and Washington agreed on one especially important point: change in Macon County was a slow process," he wrote. "While he was not nearly as patient as Washington, Gomillion was prepared for a long struggle."[133] The duality in Norrell's account is more to the point: Gomillion both broke with Washington by pressing directly and openly for political equality and adhered to Washington's formula by consciously attempting to contain that struggle within certain limits that he knew to be acceptable to white people (which was the reason for "going slow"). While "going slow," Gomillion was willing to go further than the old leadership. In the aftermath of Gomillion's victory, Tuskegee students wanted to go further still. They took up a more militant approach, pushed past the boundaries Gomillion had marked out, and began moving toward the ideas of Black Power.

Tuskegee student activists in the 1960s did not build their movement from nothing; rather, they inherited a set of political and educational ideas about social change from the teachers who stepped forward in the 1950s to challenge their disfranchisement. Professor Gomillion's model of activism was both an inspiration to the students and a yardstick against which they were judged. In the 1960s many veteran faculty activists were still present on campus, and were vocal and active during the student movement, although they didn't always find themselves on the same side as their pupils. Gomillion, like other black educators in that decade, grappled with new opportunities and challenges created, in part, by their own success.

At a 1954 Tuskegee symposium titled "The New South and Higher Education," leading educators and businessmen from across the nation gathered to contemplate the meaning of black education in the rapidly urbanizing South. The symposium concluded, on the second day, with the inauguration of Tuskegee's new president, Luther H. Foster. Foster (who fourteen years later would navigate the 1968 crisis) skillfully linked Tuskegee's past and present, evoking the need for both continuity and change. Tuskegee could play the role of preparing students for full political participation in the new South, he said. "While focused on a core of vocational content," Foster told the gathering, Tuskegee would also work to develop in each student "an appreciation for personal qualities associated with effective citizenship." Building on Washington's theory of "race relations," Foster expanded Tuskegee's charge to the improvement of "human relations" generally. "Tuskegee Institute must work to improve human relations," Foster said. "People of goodwill applaud the current trend to judge individuals on their merit, and to have their rights, duties, and opportunities assigned accordingly." In addition to these responsibilities, he concluded, Tuskegee had another: "There is the added institutional duty to speak out for truth and justice in the general society."[134]

In addition to its political inheritance, the Tuskegee student movement had an economic one as well. By the time Foster took over the helm of Tuskegee, the town around it had grown into a uniquely prosperous village of several thousand black people. The anchors of the community were the approximately 1,800 black people employed either at the veterans hospital or at Tuskegee Institute.[135] The percentage of black people in town with yearly income above $5,000 was higher than in any other county in the state of Alabama, Gomillion noted.[136] Between 1940 and 1950 the number of black people in white-collar positions grew in Tuskegee by 172 percent, nearly doubling the town's black middle class.[137] When my father, Robert Jones, first arrived in Tuskegee in 1957 as an eighteen-year-old from Inkster, Michigan, he recalled that the Institute "was one of the most beautiful sights I had ever seen." Everywhere he looked, black people were in charge. "I had never seen institutions of this size that were operated by people of color," he said.

"You had physicians, attorneys, professors. . . . These people lived well. I had never seen people of color live like that. I had never seen swimming pools in backyards."[138]

Tuskegee was in transition from an institute to a university. Robert Jones observed that in the late 1950s, Tuskegee began de-emphasizing "industrial education" in the form of training in skills such as carpentry and shoe repair, and began transforming into a university. "I saw evidence that that was a dying era, that the school was transitioning to a liberal arts school with more emphasis on engineering and those kinds of disciplines." Yet, some of the old ways of the Institute remained. Participation in the Reserve Officer Training Corps (ROTC) was still mandatory for male students, as was attendance at weekly chapel services. Students were required to attend chapel services twice on Sundays, in the morning and again in the evening, Jones remembered, "and there was also a service on Wednesday evenings. If you missed three church services they would send you home." In the 1960s, mandatory chapel would become a target of student organizers. In the 1950s, however, there was a more subterranean mode of resistance. As they entered chapel three times a week, students dropped a ticket with their name on it into a collection box. "Of course," Jones added, "there was a good side business of people dropping other people's tickets in the box."[139]

Several of the leading 1960s Tuskegee student activists enjoyed a comfortable upbringing as the children of the 1,800 professionals employed at the university or the veterans hospital. Lucenia Dunn, who later became the first female mayor of Tuskegee, remembers the sense of safety she had as a child. "The only rule that we had was: be home by dinner. We could ride our bicycles all over the place and do all kinds of things."[140] The resources of the campus were available to the town's youngsters. "If we wanted to go swimming, we went swimming up on the campus at the pool. If we wanted to play basketball in a gymnasium, then we went to the gymnasium on the campus," recalled Wendell Paris, who became one of the most influential student activists. "I'm saying it was just an idyllic place really if you look at it in terms of having black people in charge of everything but the local political apparatus," he said. "Sometimes we would go maybe a week or two without even seeing a white person."[141] To Guy Trammell, it was a place to grow up without a sense of inferiority. "The only people that I knew could do anything ever, were black people," he said. "All the stores were owned by blacks, all my teachers were black."[142] Tuskegee Institute, as Chester Higgins put it, "gave you a sense of worthiness."[143] Wendell's older brother George recalled with pride that Tuskegee "was a totally independent African-American community." "We had two hospitals," he noted. "We had the university. Everybody's dad, mom, had a decent job. It was a black middle-class community. We used to say that Tuskegee is surrounded by Alabama, not a part of Alabama, but surrounded by Alabama."[144]

Some young people experienced the class nature of the Tuskegee community as snobbery. Kathleen Neal (later known as Kathleen Cleaver, a leader of the Black Panther Party) grew up in Tuskegee, where her father was on the faculty. "If your kid hasn't gone to a white liberal prep school in Massachusetts a year or two," she recalled, "then you're just nowhere." She remembered that "middle class people" from the campus or the hospital didn't associate with poorer black people at all, "except when the poor people are their maids and housekeepers and children-keepers," she said. "The whole thing is a parody of white society."[145] Melvin Todd, another student activist, grew up in a working-class family in Birmingham, but when he arrived at Tuskegee, he noticed class differences among black people for the first time in his life. "When I went to Tuskegee, I thought I was middle class," Todd said. "It was only when I got there and took sociology that I learned that I was poor," he recalled with a laugh.[146] Gwendolyn Patton called this echelon of black people "the class within the caste." Students from such families had come to expect a certain level of service on campus. "We didn't wash our own clothes. We didn't clean up our own rooms," Patton remembered. There were staff members who would "come and pick up our laundry and return them," she said. "How bougie can you get?"[147]

On a Collision Course with Jim Crow

Like the Tuskegee faculty, some members of the black middle class were playing a role in the pathbreaking bus boycott in Montgomery, just thirty miles away. There, future Tuskegee student activist and leader Gwendolyn Patton, as an adolescent, got her first taste of organizing. Patton grew up in Detroit and Inkster but spent summers with her grandparents in Montgomery. Her grandmother owned a rental property that was used as a base for civil rights organizations. Through her grandparents, Patton became something of a junior aide to the Montgomery Improvement Association (MIA), the organization established to coordinate the boycott. Patton witnessed the planning and organization from the inside.[148] At ten years old, she was assigned to gather donations to support the cause, specifically collecting shoes to replace those that people were wearing out by walking.[149] She went to the MIA office "all the time," listened to organizing meetings, and would run errands for the adults.[150]

Besides the organizational experience, Patton learned about what the struggle against segregation did—and did not—mean to the people involved. Her grandmother taught her that the bus boycott wasn't about sitting next to white people. Patton recalled,

> One time, there were no white people on the bus and so I went back there and said, "Mommy, why are you sitting in the back of the bus?" And she says, "Gwendolyn, it was not about sitting next to white people. It was about sitting anywhere you please. And I'm pleased to sit right here." I had to get a whole other outlook on what is this Movement about. It ain't about sitting next to white folks.[151]

Meanwhile, back at Tuskegee, a confrontation with white supremacy was brewing. Black people in the town of Tuskegee had long outnumbered white people, roughly four to one by the late 1950s. By 1961, 84 percent of Macon County was black, the highest percentage in the United States.[152] The Tuskegee political science professor Charles

Hamilton counted nine black people for every white person in Macon County, yet no black person had every held public office since Reconstruction. "The smooth-working accommodation system conformed to the pattern many felt had been advocated by Booker T. Washington, the Negro founder of Tuskegee Institute," Hamilton wrote. "Whether this is an accurate representation of Washington's position is not important. The central point is that many—both Negroes and whites—believed it to be."[153] The long-standing compromise, Hamilton co-wrote with Stokely Carmichael (later Kwame Ture), was a division of labor in which "the blacks would run Tuskegee Institute and the V.A. Hospital while the whites would provide commercial services (banks and stores) and hold all political offices—thus overseeing law-enforcement, the assessing and collecting of taxes, the public school system and so forth."[154]

The reputation Tuskegee enjoyed for so long as a "model" of "good race relations" was exposed as a façade when, for the first time since Reconstruction, a black person filed to run for public office. Mrs. Jessie P. Guzman, the director of Records and Research at Tuskegee Institute, ran for a seat on Macon County's school board in 1954. Less than one thousand black people were registered to vote out of nearly seven thousand county residents, and the vote was split on racial lines.[155] Guzman lost, but the election, "a considerable shock," transformed Tuskegee's image among the white people in Macon County.[156]

The number of black registered voters was small, but ticking upwards, making a confrontation inevitable. From 29 black voters in 1940, the number had risen to 855 by 1954: a "clear trend," Hamilton wrote, that could result in "political catastrophe" for white officials if it persisted.[157] Whereas before, black people in Tuskegee historically accepted political subordination, now, in light of the shifting regional context, doing so no longer seemed acceptable or necessary. They began to feel that there was no need to "submit to the system of accommodation of an earlier time," Hamilton wrote. "They could have economic security and political participation simultaneously, and they were beginning to believe that anything less was a denial of their dignity and self respect."[158]

Gomillion and the Tuskegee Civic Association

Charles Gomillion was a patient and persistent activist whose work spanned nearly three decades.[159] In 1941 he participated in reorganizing the Tuskegee Men's Club into the Tuskegee Civic Association (TCA), a political club that admitted women as members.[160] Gomillion was the president of the Tuskegee Civic Association from 1941 to 1945, then from 1951 to 1968 and again in 1970.[161] His strategy for winning voting rights was both a break from Washingtonism and a reformulation of it. He broke with Washington by forthrightly and publicly asserting black voting rights. He preserved elements of Washington's "race relations" concept by emphasizing the idea that black people had self-improvement work to do in preparation for citizenship, and by carefully restraining black people's demands within limits he thought would be acceptable to forward-thinking white people. As the faculty took the lead, Tuskegee students watched and learned.

Under Gomillion's leadership, the TCA aggressively and systematically organized attempts at voter registration, and then carefully documented the ways the law was violated to deny them the vote.[162] Over seven long years the TCA compiled a detailed record of every single black person who attempted to register to vote in Macon County. The registrar perfected the art of obstruction: changing office hours, working as slowly as possible, frequent turnover of the job, and elaborate literacy tests.[163] TCA records showed that from 1951 to 1958 precisely 1,585 black people had applied, but only 510 voter certificates were granted.[164]

Like Washington, Gomillion was sensitive to dominant white opinions, and cultivated a message of moderation. The TCA did not want to "take over" city or county governance, Gomillion frequently asserted; rather, they wanted to "co-manage" alongside white people. "There is no good reason why white and Negro citizens in Macon cannot develop a community which would be a model of democratic living," Gomillion told the Alabama House of Representatives in Montgomery in 1958.[165]

The TCA avoided any activity that would besmirch its upstanding image, even if that meant organizing with one hand tied behind its back. The TCA's leading officers feared feeding stories to reporters because they "did not want to give the impression that the TCA was trying to solicit the aid of the press." Whereas the activists in Montgomery had solicited funds from northern supporters, the TCA refused to do so, lest its character as an indigenous southern organization be questioned or it be perceived as a "money-grabbing organization."[166]

White elites were not assuaged by such moderation. Those who ruled by excluding black people from politics were frightened by any deviation from the status quo, and decided to act. Those elites, led by state senator Sam Engelhardt, redrew the city boundaries to remove the possibility of black voters gaining a majority.[167] On July 13, 1957, as the number of black voters approached the one thousand mark, the Alabama state legislature unanimously passed a bill to change the shape of Tuskegee's city limits from a simple square to "a curious twenty-eight-sided figure resembling a stylized sea horse."[168] Nearly 3,500 black residents (out of a total of 5,000) and roughly 400 out of 410 black voters now found that they lived outside Tuskegee's city limits.[169]

The gerrymander utterly shocked Tuskegee's black middle class. "All the time, the intelligentsia in Tuskegee had had the impression that white people regarded them as different from the black folks who worked on farms and so forth," Ernest Stephens, a Tuskegee graduate student who grew up in the town, observed. "The white folks showed them that there was no difference."[170] Tuskegee's black professionals felt that their degrees, manners, and lifestyle separated them from the mass of black people in the Black Belt. "For decades, many Negroes believed that their problems stemmed from a handful of white politicians and that, when glaring injustices were exposed, all the 'decent thinking white people' in the South would protest," Hamilton wrote. "Most of the whites who were previously 'friends' were nowhere to be found. . . . There was an intense feeling of betrayal."[171] The gerrymander threw cold water on their sense of status and forced them into a coalition with their poorer rural cousins. Professor Stanley H. Smith, a Tuskegee sociologist, conceded that "it was the gerrymander that brought us together." Whereas previously, professional black people had enjoyed certain privileges, they were now "shocked into the realization that we were still Negroes," he wrote. "The country people found our comeuppance rather amusing and, I think, subtly satisfying. They didn't rub it in, but there was some chortling. 'Well now, join us' was their attitude at the first . . . meeting. 'Welcome home.'"[172]

The next month, as the gerrymander went into effect, so did the response from Tuskegee's black middle class: a boycott, widening the social and psychological schism in town. Business receipts in town were cut by nearly 70 percent immediately, and almost twenty businesses closed.[173] Instead of conceding, though, white people dug in and continued to resist change. By the end of the decade, some black people's patience with Gomillion's strategy was wearing thin. Eager for further escalation, TCA members at various moments proposed marching or public demonstrations, but each time the leadership demurred. Gomillion's personal hostility to the idea of marching was well known. "He was berated by some for this," Hamilton wrote. When confronted by a student on this point, Gomillion replied, "Any dumbbell can march, no dumbbell can do what I'm doing."[174]

Gomillion was not alone. Tuskegee professors, despite their relative economic independence, were reluctant to associate themselves with "rabble rousers" or even with the most prominent civil rights movement leaders. When Martin Luther King Jr. came to Tuskegee in the late 1950s, university officials did not allow him to speak on campus (apparently fearful of reprisals from the white community). King spoke at a nearby church instead. A Tuskegee student who attended the event noticed that there was not a single Tuskegee professor in attendance, except for Charles Hamilton. "At a time when many people (both black and white) saw King as an outsider whose methods of nonviolent protest would only stir up more trouble for black people," the student, Wilbur

C. Rich, recalled, "Hamilton stood on stage with King and even had his photograph taken with him."[175] In 1960, after frequent clashes with Gomillion and the TCA leadership, Hamilton's contract with Tuskegee was not renewed.[176]

In August 1958 Gomillion and eleven other members of the TCA sued the mayor of Tuskegee, Phillip Lightfoot. Their lawsuit, dubbed *Gomillion v. Lightfoot*, traveled all the way to the US Supreme Court and set an important national precedent in the voting rights struggle.[177] Thousands of dollars in legal fees over two years were paid primarily by Tuskegee's black middle class.[178] On November 15, 1960, the court, citing "the inevitable effect" of excluding black voters with the gerrymandered city boundaries, ruled unanimously for Gomillion.[179] The Supreme Court sent the case back to a federal district court, where Judge Frank M. Johnson ruled in February 1961 that the old boundaries be restored.[180] The next month Johnson issued a "sweeping decree" ordering the Macon County registrars, in very specific, detailed instructions aimed at removing any opportunity for obstruction, to begin registering black voters.[181] As a result, by 1962, for the first time ever in Macon County, black voters outnumbered white voters.[182] Their success came too late for the 1960 elections, so the first black officials since Reconstruction were not elected in the county until 1964.[183]

Gomillion and the Tuskegee faculty had won an important victory, but it was not theirs alone. The nearby Montgomery bus boycott shifted the landscape of politics in Gomillion's favor, adding to the pressure on the federal government and local authorities, and certainly gave Tuskegeans the confidence to launch a boycott of their own (even as they hesitated to associate themselves with an "outsider" like King). Because of the ferocity of the "massive resistance" to voting rights and desegregation, Gomillion's legal victory, like others in the era, was rendered meaningless without a movement to make it a reality on the ground. After Montgomery, the southern civil rights movement did not reemerge on a mass scale until black college students took action at the very top of the following decade. When their professors went into motion in the 1950s,

Tuskegee students watched and learned. But in the 1960s, the students took action on their own, both building upon and rejecting aspects of their elders' outlook. Like Gomillion, they would reckon with the legacy of Booker T. Washington in the process. Before the decade was out, the students would have the opportunity to teach their teachers a thing or two.

2

Scholar-Activists, 1960–1965

The indignities of segregation in Alabama were countless, ranging from the profound to the mundane, from being barred at the voting booth to the humiliation of segregated shopping. For (a mundane) example, a white person could try on shoes in one of Montgomery's downtown department stores, but a black person could not. Every rule, of course, had its exceptions, this one included. One day in the early 1960s, a handsome, blue-eyed scion of a well-to-do family widely considered Macon County "aristocracy" (and dating its time in the county back before a black teacher training institute came into the picture) entered just such a department store, accompanied by a dark-skinned young man he introduced to the clerk as his servant. "I came in here to buy my boy some shoes," the blue-eyed man told the clerk. Here was one such loophole: a black person could try on shoes in a downtown department store if directed to do so by his white employer, the real customer in that case. "Those shoes fit you, boy?" the aristocrat barked. "Yes sir," his companion replied meekly. "You like them?" "Yes sir." He turned to the clerk with cash in hand. "All right, I want to buy this boy these shoes."[1]

The two young men left the store in fits of laughter. To people who knew him in and around Tuskegee, Sammy Younge Jr. was a blue-eyed, fair-skinned son of a prominent black family, and his dark-skinned companion, Wendell Paris, was his best friend.[2] What appeared to be strict adherence was, for them, a delicious resistance to the rules of segregation. Their joke on the system was one they were uniquely capable of making. Most black people in Macon County did not have the complexion to pass for white. The dark-skinned Tuskegee professor Charles Gomillion had attempted to shop in one such store nearly forty years earlier, but walked out angrily when the clerk mistook him for a minister because he was wearing a suit; he vowed never to return.[3] And even if they could "pass," most black Macon County residents were not professors or the children of professionals. They possessed neither the cars, the clothes, the money, nor the education and language to carry off such a prank. Sammy Younge had spent his high school years in one of New England's finest boarding schools, Cornwall Academy. He and Wendell Paris were different from most black people in 1965, but they were not different from most black people they knew. Like many of the other young people who grew up in proximity to Tuskegee Institute, their parents had gone to college and had professional jobs, nice homes, cars, and a corresponding sense of confidence and entitlement.[4]

There was a civil rights movement in Tuskegee, as in many other southern towns. Unlike other southern municipalities, however, the town of Tuskegee had a concentration of middle-class black people that shaped the movement in unique ways. Tuskegee faculty and staff embraced elements of the militant ethos of the time, but in ways that did not violate their sense of propriety. In the rapidly moving events of those years, however, today's militants could quickly become tomorrow's compromisers. Faculty led the earlier phase of struggle, but by 1965, students—like Sammy Younge and Wendell Paris—were setting the pace of events. Whereas the faculty cherished their social position, the students explicitly challenged it. The trappings and outlooks of middle-class life that faculty members saw as a weapon in their struggle for political equality became a liability in the eyes of many members of the student movement.

Building on the success and example of their elders, Tuskegee students entered the political arena expecting to get results. The faculty-led voting rights struggle in Tuskegee was, after all, victorious, opening the door to the student movement. As soon as the students walked through that door, however, and stepped off campus—to march in Montgomery, to offer literacy lessons to their rural cousins in the surrounding Black Belt counties, to challenge segregated churches in the town of

Tuskegee—they came face to face with the violent, legal and extralegal enforcers of the status quo, were labeled "communists," and increasingly found themselves working at odds with Tuskegee Institute's adminis- tration. These results surprised the students, challenging their sense of reality and their understanding of what it would take to get real changes; it was, in other words, a moment of learning more profound than what they had found in any classroom. Students who braved these experiences off campus returned to campus transformed, and they began asking new questions about Tuskegee Institute. Many of the activists, groomed as a rising generation of middle-class leaders, suddenly embraced a new identity as scholar-activists.

The Tuskegee student movement, mostly dormant since the 1940s, reemerged in a rapidly changing global context. In 1960 alone, some sev- enteen African countries gained independence from European colonial powers.[5] These newly liberated countries, their leaders, and the many pupils they sent to study at Tuskegee would have a tremendous effect on the student body in the years to come. At the time, Alabama state sena- tor Engelhardt articulated a direct connection between voting rights and decolonization. Given the Tuskegee Civic Association's victorious legal battle against gerrymandering, the choice for local whites, he said, was either to leave the county or "submit to Negro rule and await a situation comparable to the Congo, with local Lumumbas coming forward in ever increasing numbers."[6]

Engelhardt's fears were misplaced, to say the least. Despite the legal victories, "massive resistance" by whites had successfully retarded de- segregation. By 1960, six years after the Supreme Court's *Brown v. Board of Education* decision, only seventeen southern school districts were de- segregated.[7] Nowhere had the success of the Montgomery bus boycott been replicated. "All of Africa will be free before we can get a lousy cup of coffee," author James Baldwin lamented.[8] While the movement over- all stalled, black college attendance swelled. Between 1953 and 1965 the number of black students in four-year colleges nearly doubled (63,000 to 119,000).[9] As their ranks grew, black students came to campus with raised expectations and confidence. "Their youth had been marked by sweeping changes in the economy, in demography, in national and international politics, and in American attitudes about race," one historian wrote. "All this had conspired to raise their aspirations, to fuel their hopes. But the promise of change far outran the reality."[10]

In February 1960, black college students initiated a new phase of the civil rights struggle, making it, for the first time, a genuine mass movement on a national scale. Bypassing the cautious, legalistic approach pioneered nationally by the NAACP and in the town of Tuskegee by the Tuskegee Civic Association, they shifted to mass direct action. Four students from a local college sat down at a segregated lunch counter in Greensboro, North Carolina, on February 1, 1960, unwittingly launching the largest mass movement for civil rights in the twentieth century. By 1961, sit-ins swept a hundred southern cities, involving some fifty thousand people. Roughly twenty thousand activists were arrested between 1961 and 1963.[11] By one estimate, nearly one out of every four black college students in the South participated in the sit-in movement during the years 1960–1961.[12]

Future Tuskegee students Michael Wright and Gwen Patton were both energized as teenagers by the sit-ins. In 1960 Wright joined his first picket line in New York City outside a Woolworth's department store in Harlem "in order to support the student sit-ins in Greensboro, North Carolina," he recalled. "I was thirteen years old."[13] Gwen Patton remembers that in 1960, "when I was sixteen, I wanted to go to Raleigh, North Carolina for the historic sit-ins, but I couldn't." However, the next year she came to Tuskegee and was able to join the movement there.[14]

At Tuskegee Institute, young people leapt into action. Future Tuskegee student George Paris was inspired. The sit-in movement, he remembered, "just opened our eyes. Opened up a whole new world for us. There *is* something we can do!" He and his friends began thinking of how to desegregate everything everywhere. "We can go to Montgomery and sit in at a lunch counter, you know, and we can go to Auburn, go to the swimming pool."[15] At Tuskegee Institute, roughly four hundred students marched off the campus, through downtown Tuskegee, carrying placards calling for voting rights and civic equality.[16] Robert Jones, by then in his junior year at Tuskegee Institute, decided to join the protest. The administration worried about the students' safety, Jones thought. "Dr. Foster was very much opposed to this," he recalled. "A few days later Dr. Foster had an assembly where the impression I got was that things were happening throughout the South and our business [was] academics and we should probably stay out of it for now."[17] No doubt Foster was aware that Alabama State College, under pressure from Governor John Patterson, expelled nine students for their participation in similar protests happening at the same time.[18]

Feeling optimistic about the growth of their movement, the sit-in activists decided to form a new national civil rights organization, the Student Nonviolent Coordinating Committee (SNCC) in April 1960. Their founding statement affirmed their view that love would conquer hate: "Nonviolence as it grows from Judaic-Christian tradition seeks a social order of justice permeated by love," they wrote. "Through nonviolence, courage displaces fear; love transforms hate. Acceptance dissipates prejudice; hope ends despair. Peace dominates war; faith reconciles doubt. Mutual regard cancels enmity. Justice for all overthrows injustice."[19] This confidence was not unfounded; nonviolent civil disobedience was, for the time being, a winning formula. By the end of 1961, the use of public accommodations in upper and border South states was transformed as almost two hundred cities began to desegregate.[20]

No Tuskegee students were present at SNCC's founding convention at Shaw University, but some immediately joined, and links with SNCC developed quickly over the next few years. Gwen Patton joined SNCC in 1962 and would continue working with the group for the next five years.[21] At Tuskegee, students formed a new civil rights organization, the Tuskegee Institute Advancement League (TIAL, an organization that would fade and then reorganize itself two years later); through its auspices SNCC chairman John Lewis was invited to speak to the campus community.[22] Foster gently opposed the first student marches, but his administration quickly shifted gears and began seeing itself as a steward of the student movement.

Reflecting this shift, one Tuskegee administrator developed a program to harness the students' desire to contribute to social change. In the summer of 1963, Bertrand Phillips, a recent graduate from Columbia University's Teachers College, was recruited by Foster to be the dean of students. When Phillips and his wife arrived in Macon County, they were struck by what they saw. "We drove around and saw a lot of poverty. . . . We also saw a lot of people who were trying to help themselves," he recalled. "It kind of inspired us." In his second semester on campus, Phillips suggested to an assembly of students that they follow the examples of Booker T. Washington and George Washington Carver, who "didn't hide themselves on the campus. They reached out into the community, they made this institute a living part of Macon County and some of the surrounding counties." Phillips issued a challenge: "To those students who really are interested and think that they can bring about some change, why don't you meet me in the morning and we'll talk about it in the gym. I'd like you to be there at five in the morning." Remarkably, at that early hour the next morning, Phillips found 150 students waiting for him in the gymnasium. They decided to call their mission a "domestic peace corps," with the idea that students would "use our talents to help people repair their homes if they were trying to repair their homes, to grow their crops if that's what they were doing, to tutor the children who wanted to get further ahead in their schooling, to just relate to the needs of the community," he said.[23]

Venturing out into the surrounding communities, Phillips's volunteers would find themselves again and again in the company of SNCC workers. SNCC had quickly distinguished itself as the boldest of the civil rights organizations. It sent students (often ex-students, actually) into the Deep South to challenge segregation and disfranchisement in the most dangerous contexts. Much of this work took place in the Black Belt. Given Tuskegee's location in the center of that region, it is not surprising that Tuskegee students were involved in all of SNCC's Black Belt campaigns. Like other SNCC workers, Tuskegee students were radical-ized by the resilience of rural black people and the murderous southern regimes they braved in order to assert their rights. SNCC recruited a small number of Tuskegee students for their voter registration, freedom school, and community center projects in the Black Belt in the fall of 1964.[24] Fourteen Tuskegee students worked in Mississippi on the mock election that propelled the SNCC-initiated Mississippi Freedom Demo-cratic Party into open conflict with the national Democratic leadership at the party's convention that year in Atlantic City.[25] By this time, some SNCC members, guided by James Forman, had moved on from the ideas of Christian nonviolence and began organizing study groups on Marxism, the Cuban Revolution, and African liberation struggles.[26] As young people in SNCC explored increasingly radical ideas, the state of Alabama observed their movement with growing alarm.

The Alabama Legislative Commission to Preserve the Peace

Leading the charge against the "communist menace" was the newly elected governor of Alabama, George Wallace. Wallace rarely missed an opportunity to link civil rights, the federal government, and com-munism. In 1963 he appeared before the US Senate Committee on Commerce to voice his opposition to a bill to desegregate interstate public accommodations. Wallace began by noting the recent push to desegregate all facilities on military bases. Whereas black civil rights leaders hoped to connect desegregation to military victory, Wallace made the opposite case. "Is the real purpose of this integration move-ment to disarm this country as the Communists have planned?" he asked. In the next several pages of his prepared remarks he attempted to portray civil rights leaders as communists and to shame the federal government for bowing to them. "As a loyal American and as a loyal Southern Governor, . . . I resent the fawning and pawing over such people as Martin Luther King and his pro-communist friends and asso-ciates," he wrote. Interestingly, while a staunch segregationist, Wallace aggressively promoted expansive funding for public education. Again and again he emphasized his support for the "up-lifting of the Negroes in Alabama" through education. Wallace noted that during his first year in office, "we have increased the appropriation to Negro educational institutions 22 per cent," he wrote. "We are building three new trade schools to train them for the jobs that we are making available to them by a fast growing industrial expansion in our state."[27]

And that rapidly expanding education system was a primary site of radicalization, a fact not lost on the governor's supporters. Tuskegee's practice of allowing radical (including communist) leaders to speak on campus provoked outrage among conservative white Alabamians, who in turn put pressure on Foster. In 1961 Tuskegee sponsored a sixteen-day speaking tour by a black journalist, William Worthy, who traveled to several colleges to talk about his recent trip to Cuba, criticizing the Kennedy administration's anti-communism and the "hatchet job" the US media were doing on Cuban leader Fidel Castro.[28] In 1963 Tuskegee's student government invited US Communist Party leader Gus Hall to speak, but then rescinded the invitation under pressure from the campus administration. The *Campus Digest* printed President Foster's defense of the reversal alongside a student rebuttal. Foster claimed that communism was a worthy topic of intellectual discussion, but that it was better to hear about it from an expert, "rather than one whose presentation would . . . be oriented strongly to his political views and to the fulfillment in some significant way of his political purposes." The student respondent, O'Neal Smalls, called the cancellation an "infringement upon the right of academic freedom" and "not in line with democratic principles." "I dissent from the belief that our students are intellectually incapable of debating these ideas when they are combined with such articulate personalities," he wrote.[29]

Anti-communism became institutionalized in Alabama in the early 1960s. Following Wallace's lead, the state legislature created the Alabama Legislative Commission to Preserve the Peace (ALCPP) in 1963 to investigate civil rights and campus activism in the state. The ALCPP's purpose was to "study, investigate, analyze and interrogate persons, groups and organizations who may be engaged in activities of an unlawful nature against the sovereignty of the State of Alabama." The new commission was charged with reporting to both houses of the legislature and to the governor.[30] For the rest of the decade, the ALCPP wrote breathless, hysterical reports that attempted to confirm the connection between black activists and a global communist conspiracy. The commission reported that SNCC "is extensively Communist dominated, and its leadership substantially follows the Communist Party line." The ALCPP found "that SNCC is an agent for the Communist conspiracy and measures up to every definition of a Communist Party Front." The CPUSA's goal, the commission's report alleges, is "using civil rights as a Springboard [*sic*] to achieve a Soviet America." The ALCPP noted that SNCC members, including John Lewis and James Forman, had traveled to Africa and had met with communist leaders in Algeria. "The danger signal cannot be ignored," the report warns. SNCC must be watched closely and "eventually it must be controlled by legal action," or else "the State and nation will court major disaster."[31]

There are two important truths here. One is that anti-communism, while at times hysterically exaggerated, gained force in the South because it expressed anxiety about real changes in progress, primarily the decline of the old system of white supremacy. Historian Joy Ann Williamson-Lott is correct to conclude that the "southern brand of academic McCarthyism was informed by fear and anxiety about social change as much as concerns over communism." She argues that anti-communism cannot be reduced to a simple "disguise" for racism. "Instead," Williamson-Lott writes, "in the South fervent anticommunism and racism were inextricable."[32] The Alabama legislators who created the ALCPP frankly acknowledged that their purpose was to criminalize dissent, to "hold a new club over race agitators."[33] The second conclusion is that the anti-communist hysterics, while exaggerated, contained a grain of truth. There was a radicalization among young people in the civil rights movement that did lead many of them to explore communist ideas. While the governor and the ALCPP imagined that local people were mere dupes or puppets of an international conspiracy, the truth of the matter is that activists—Tuskegee students included—were inspired by global events and took cues from them, but they also developed ideas and acted on them in ways that were entirely resonant with their own experiences in the US South.

Radicalization on and off Campus

At Tuskegee, the student movement did radicalize quite quickly, although it did so largely in the absence of any local communist organization or any "line" to follow. The generation of young black people who went to college in the 1960s confronted a contradiction between raised expectations and a power structure (white and black) resistant to change. At Tuskegee, the largely middle-class students came to campus with high hopes that change was possible without any radical rupture with American ideals and structures. By the end of the calendar year 1965, such a rupture seemed both inevitable and, to some, desirable. For the first two months of the year, however, the future still appeared bright.

At the start of 1965, Macon County was enjoying the fruits of the national and regional economic boom, which contributed significantly to the sense that progress was inevitable. In the summer of 1965, Governor Wallace boasted that $406 million worth of new industry came into Alabama. Businesses were seeking out Alabama, he said, because they "appreciate our stand for free enterprise and local government."[34] In 1965 the Department of Labor reported that 16 percent of the county's population was self-employed, as opposed to 13 percent in the state and 12 percent in the nation.[35] Macon County's residents' household income in 1964 had increased, on average, by $500 from the year before. That was a 10 percent increase, higher than the average household increase in the state (8 percent) or in the nation (5 percent).[36] Remarkably, 25 percent of that income was provided directly by the federal government in the form of salaries or subsidies.[37] By 1965, Macon County residents consumed a remarkable 34 percent more goods and services than they did just one year before.[38]

Nationwide, the number of black students continued to climb, contributing to a sense of possibility and change among young people and their families. In the mid-1960s, college enrollment for black people reached unprecedented heights—more than 100,000—boosted by civil rights activism, the Civil Rights and Higher Education Acts of 1964 and 1965, and the growing availability of federal scholarships.[39] Tuskegee enrolled a record-breaking 700 freshman in 1965.[40] President Foster expressed the hope that Tuskegee would provide students with a unique opportunity for personal development. In February, at the mandatory weekly Sunday service at Tuskegee Institute's chapel, Foster optimistically boasted that the "strength and happiness of Tuskegee is its people." He said that the school would strive to "find the ways to encourage every student, faculty, and staff member to involve himself truly in this exciting educational enterprise which goes on here on this campus."[41] One of the students in attendance was Melvin Todd, who had just started his career at Tuskegee in January. "The feeling that I got when I first went to campus was that I'm stepping into history," he said. "There have been many, many great souls that have walked these sidewalks and these pathways, and I have to do well."[42]

By the start of 1965, however, for many black college students, optimism lay in their hopes for social change, not merely personal growth. Michael Wright, who also started as a freshman that year, was introduced to protest politics right away. In his first few days on campus, he saw a group of female nursing students on a picket line. He discovered that one of their classmates had been expelled for violating curfew. "I was the only guy on the picket line, but it made perfect sense to me," Wright said. The following day, athletes were picketing on campus about not receiving financial aid, Wright recalled, and he supported them, too. Wright quickly fell in with students associated with SNCC, as well. Because of the campus's location—a highway that traverses the Black Belt counties runs right through campus—SNCC activists in the Deep South frequently used the campus "as a place for rest and rehabilitation and socialization," Wright recalled. In his first semester he joined the staff of the student newspaper (the *Campus Digest*) and became acquainted with SNCC people, including Sammy Younge.[43] Younge was one of the two hundred Tuskegee students who marched peacefully in double-file lines through downtown Tuskegee in February in sympathy with the voting rights movement in Selma, Alabama, where activists had recently been attacked by police.[44]

Tuskegee student activists sensed that they were in a position to make independent contributions to the movement. In addition to collaborating with SNCC, Tuskegee's leading student activists decided to create an organization of their own. In February 1965 the Tuskegee Institute Advancement League (TIAL) reemerged.[45] One of the first actions of the new TIAL was to lead a second march of three hundred Tuskegee students into the downtown area, also in solidarity with the Selma activists.[46] TIAL worked with and remained independent of SNCC. Patton in particular was wary of northern activists coming into the South through SNCC. "We didn't like people coming to liberate us," Patton said, comparing the dynamic to a condescending benefactor who would come in order to "civilize the noble savages," as she put it. "It was insulting."[47] Instead, TIAL members sought out a formal relationship with the faculty-led Tuskegee Civic Association; the TCA declined the offer.[48]

It was a time for getting serious about making social change. Less than two weeks before he was assassinated in Harlem, Malcolm X spoke at Tuskegee Institute, expressing a sense of political urgency to the three thousand students in attendance. Phillips recalls that Malcolm, sitting in his office before the speech, said, "Well, Dean, I want to tell you that people think I'm down here to try to incite some type of riot or something. I'm not, I'm just simply here to speak some truth to your students."[49] Having recently broken with the Nation of Islam (NOI), Malcolm was now committed to a program of social action, and he challenged the students to get involved. When asked about his relationship to NOI leader

Elijah Muhammad, Malcolm said, "Elijah believes that God is going to come and straighten things out. I believe that too. But whereas Elijah is willing to sit and wait, I'm not willing to sit and wait on God to come. If he doesn't come soon, it will be too late. I believe in religion, but a religion that includes political, economic, and social action designed to eliminate some of these things and make a paradise here on earth while we're waiting for the other."[50]

The hope in peaceful change that had animated SNCC's first gathering was quickly transformed by bitter experience. Malcolm's message resonated with that experience, and in many speeches he was giving that month, he predicted that violence against the black movement would increase.[51] Melvin Todd remembers that Malcolm spoke about his life being in danger. "He said that if anything were to happen to him, that it would not be done by white men," Todd recalled.[52] Malcolm X was assassinated by members of the NOI on February 21, 1965. Five days later, the young activist Jimmy Lee Jackson was murdered by state troopers raiding a mass meeting for voting rights in Marion, Alabama.[53] The quick succession of bloodshed shook the optimism of Tuskegee students. James Farmer of the Congress of Racial Equality was the next guest speaker on campus. He suggested that the movement was entering a new phase that would go beyond the issue of civil rights.[54] Citing Malcolm's assassination, attacks on marchers in Selma, threats on Martin Luther King's life, and war in Vietnam, Tuskegee student Peter Scott II wrote in the *Campus Digest* that "Malcolm X was right when he said that this would be the longest, hottest, bloodiest year ever."[55]

Marching on Montgomery

Tuskegee students would experience a small dose of this violence the next month. In March, they marched on the capital building in downtown Montgomery, and then tried to meet with the governor; instead, they were attacked by police and some were briefly arrested. After Jimmy Lee Jackson's murder, King and other civil rights leaders began planning a march from Selma to Montgomery. When marchers were beaten by state troopers in Selma on the Edmund Pettus Bridge ("Bloody Sunday"), TIAL started raising money from Tuskegee students to join the march in Montgomery. Sammy Younge even telephoned some of his former classmates at Cornwall Academy to ask for donations.[56] "This is a time for sober reflection," the *Tuskegee News* editorialized after Bloody Sunday, "a time for learning from hard experience." The paper didn't hesitate to point out the difference between Tuskegee and Selma: "Tuskegee can be thankful that it has been spared the agony which has characterized voter registration efforts in Selma."[57]

The Tuskegee administration forbade students to go to Montgomery, "invoking the doctrine of in loco parentis," and King balked at violating a federal judge's injunction against the march, but a mass meeting of Tuskegee students chose to go to Montgomery anyway.[58] Ruby Sales, a freshman, decided to go to the march because Gwen Patton came to her dorm to talk to students about it.[59] In general, Tuskegee's adults were concerned that the youth were moving too fast. George Paris remembers that they cautioned his classmates to "slow down." The students were undaunted. "Yeah, we never listened to that," Paris recalled. His peers' attitude was, "We're going to solve this problem, this afternoon."[60] Despite threats of expulsion, roughly seven hundred Tuskegee students—including Edith Washington O'Neil, Booker T. Washington's great-granddaughter—boarded buses and cars to travel to Montgomery on March 10, 1965.[61]

Stepping outside the Tuskegee "bubble," student activists caught a glimpse of the real dangers surrounding them. When the students arrived in Montgomery, the city and state police blocked the entrance to the capitol and threatened to arrest anyone who didn't leave. The governor refused to meet with a student delegation, and troopers intervened in the ensuing standoff. They used horses to disperse parts of the crowd, and arrested two students (who were later released). After a while, about five hundred left and roughly three hundred stayed, refusing to leave the capitol, singing freedom songs.[62] "A hard core of about 300 students vowed to sit-in in front of the Capitol until Governor Wallace decided to meet with them," Patton later wrote about how the incident radicalized Tuskegee students. "The pilgrimage had started out with naive, idealistic students marching for freedom. Fourteen hours later on a chilly March night, the 300 emerged as insurgents."[63] Police surrounded them. Anyone who left wouldn't be allowed to return, so those who remained were forced to relieve themselves on the spot. They did so in a circle blocked by picket signs, until a steady stream of urine ran down the capitol steps. "Thus did the great 'pee-in at the Alabama Capitol' join the civil rights lore," Patton wrote.[64] Tuskegee student Ruby Sales remembered this as the first time she was "confronted with white terrorism," and "the understanding that I was not my mother's daughter,—I mean that somebody would really hurt me."[65]

The march ended in frustration, which provoked a heated debate among the students. At two in the morning it was raining and they decided to seek shelter in the Dexter Avenue Baptist Church.[66] Much to their surprise, the deacons wanted the students to leave. They cut off the heat and turned off the water. "They knew the terrorism of the south. . . . They were terrified," Sales surmised.[67] Some students actually blamed SNCC leaders for prolonging the action in Montgomery, an idea also promoted by some professors. George Ware recalled that, in class, "instructors would say that TIAL was being manipulated by SNCC, . . . that students should be very wary, first of SNCC and second of that little radical core in TIAL."[68] Gwen Patton described the march as a breaking point. "After the march, a lot of people couldn't take Tuskegee anymore," she said. "They had come to a realization within themselves; they had seen what their education was doing to them. But some of them weren't strong enough to deal with it—defying their parents, defying the school, defying the whole society."[69]

At the same time Tuskegee students were questioning their upbringing and education, unbeknown to them President Foster appealed to the governor in their defense. One week after the student march, the governor received a four-page memo from Foster, which he had written in preparation for an in-person meeting (which Wallace indefinitely postponed). Foster's memo communicated that he and his colleagues at Tuskegee had been "deeply troubled . . . as we observed the slow progress in this State toward full democracy for all citizens." Foster called on the governor to ensure equal voting rights, appoint black people to positions in his administration, desegregate the schools, and speak out against police brutality. "We call on you urgently as the Governor of all the people of Alabama to speak out against injustice and to use every resource of your office to assure that this state moves forward," Foster wrote.[70]

Wallace apparently didn't reply, but took the opportunity instead to publicly insist that the marchers were the real problem. "Any preconceived 'march' along the public highways of this state is not conducive to the orderly flow of traffic," he wrote in a prepared public statement. "Such action would not be allowed on the part of any other group of citizens, or non-citizens, of the State of Alabama and will not be allowed in this instance." He concluded by noting the importance of education in solving the problem. "These matters will be solved best by increased educational opportunities and by the growth of the economic standing of all of us. We have a concentrated program in Alabama to further the education of all our citizens and to provide jobs for them."[71]

The march was taken seriously by students, administrators, and the legislature's anti-communist commission. "At last Tuskegee students are no longer apathetic to civil rights!" the *Campus Digest* editor-in-chief boasted.[72] The Montgomery march produced a core of organizers. Some of Tuskegee's marchers later became full-time SNCC workers, including Jimmy Rogers, Jennifer Lawson, George Ware, and Simuel Schutz. Others remained active while still enrolled in school, including Gwen Patton, Wendell Paris, Warren Hamilton, and Sammy Younge.[73] Despite his prior admonitions, even Foster had praise for the marchers. "I am impressed by the growing interest of students in this crucial current issue of civil rights," he told an all-Institute assembly. "You make us proud."[74] Some argued that the march had larger results. Gwen Patton thought that the student "march that wouldn't turn around" helped to pressure

King to complete the Selma to Montgomery march.[75] To the governor's anti-communist commission, the arrival of King and several thousand others in Montgomery symbolized the strength of the communist threat. The commission collaborated with local law enforcement officials to film the final march when it arrived on March 25, and to analyze the footage in order to document the attendance of communists and "revolutionary forces" there. The commission noted James Forman's presence. "He is a vicious revolutionary with a violent hatred for all whites," the commission reported. "This feeling he makes known freely when talking with Negro groups, including our own agents."[76]

Despite the commission's fears of Forman's influence, the radicalization at Tuskegee that month had more to do at that point with questioning the Tuskegee administration's rules and regulations. While Foster praised the student marchers, he also insisted on sending home a permission slip to all parents to allow (or prohibit) their children to participate in any further movement activity.[77] "[At] Tuskegee we [still] had parietals," Sales recalled, referring to the strict in loco parentis rules that had long governed student life on campus. "You couldn't even have a man in the dormitory. You couldn't even go downtown without your parents' consent," she said. "They had a curfew. If you were not in by 9 o'clock you could get expelled from school." Yet suddenly, the old rules no longer seemed to apply. "To go from that [old system], to make the radical move to going to Montgomery, and also people going out into the county without any parental consent," Sales said, "and then coming into the lobby of the dormitory to make speeches,—it really changed the social landscape at Tuskegee."[78]

The change was intellectual and deeply emotional. Sales recalled, "I think something else is going on that is very significant here, you are being opened up and realizing how much you don't know, and how much you'd like to know."[79] Forman began spending more time working with Tuskegee student activists. Many of them, he wrote, "simply could not deal with the contradiction between Tuskegee Institute and the life for which it was preparing them, and the events which had taken place only thirty minutes away in Montgomery." Tuskegee, as Forman put it, said to students "Get an education and you won't be a nigger." The movement, on the other hand, said to them "You're a nigger no matter what you do." In the process of trying to decide which was real, Forman reported, four students had nervous breakdowns that spring.[80]

Red scaremongering threw students back on the defensive. The issue reemerged when students invited the Marxist historian Herbert Aptheker to speak on campus on March 17, 1965. His topic was "Communism: Menace or Promise?"[81] That same day, the ALCPP warned members of the Alabama's House of Representatives that "today is a day of rather unusual events." The "unusual" in this case was Tuskegee students protesting on the steps of the state capitol, the president sending a voter registration bill to Congress, and Herbert Aptheker speaking at Tuskegee. The report quoted the CPUSA's newspaper, the *Daily Worker*, which called Aptheker a "communist spokesman."[82] A Tuskegee resident sent a letter to the *Campus Digest* warning the students about the "strategies and tactics [communists] use in order to manipulate people, especially impressionable and uninformed minds." George L. Knox Jr., student chairman of the lecture series, responded. "When the alarms are sounded and bells are rung, every time an 'agent of the communist conspiracy' is invited to speak on a college campus, there is one point . . . which seems constantly to be overlooked," he wrote. "It is this. We are not afraid of communism. We have faith enough in the free enterprise system to believe that it can stand toe to toe with communism, exchange blows and emerge unscathed."[83] In fact a minority of students—those working most closely with SNCC—were beginning to ask questions about the free enterprise system. Sales remembered when veteran SNCC activist Willie Peacock came to Tuskegee as a graduate student. "He was the first person that I ever knew who mentioned the word, 'Capitalism,'" she said. "It was one of those 'Aha!' moments that just began to open the floodgates for me."[84]

TICEP and TIAL

For the rest of the semester, students explored various ways to channel their activist energies. In April, Gwen Patton ran for president of Tuskegee's Student Government Association. She won with 75 percent of the vote, becoming the school's first female elected president.[85] "She was a real fireball," Melvin Todd recalled. "I was very impressed with her. She was a little short girl, very good speaker."[86] "I'd never seen a Black woman in a position that Gwen Patton was carrying out," Ruby Sales remembered. "I mean she had some authority,—she had some real clout on campus." Furthermore, "she had clout not because she was a beauty queen but because she was talking about issues."[87] Melvin Todd took photographs for the main newspaper of the southern civil rights movement, the *Southern Courier*, and helped Caroline Hilton get work there as a freelancer, too.[88] TIAL grew more ambitious, taking aim at the local economy and beyond. Student members picketed a local A&P market for four days, then halted their pickets when the manager conceded to hiring black people "on a non-discriminatory basis."[89] Meanwhile other TIAL members traveled to Lowndes County to participate in a "Freedom Day" voter registration drive alongside SNCC workers.[90]

Several hundred Tuskegee students were also radicalized by their participation in Dean Phillips's service program. In the summer of 1965, Tuskegee received a $500,000 federal anti-poverty grant to fund Phillips's "domestic peace corps," now called the Tuskegee Institute Community Education Program (TICEP). With that money, TICEP was able to pay seven hundred Tuskegee students to work as tutors in a dozen Black Belt counties.[91] The tutoring was meant to supplement public schooling, but Phillips hoped it would raise the consciousness and expectations of people in the Black Belt. "Most importantly," Phillips told an interviewer, "the program helped kids and their parents to become critical of the education they can get in Alabama now." Most people, Phillips said, "had no idea before this summer that they should want or expect anything better."[92] Given the long history of Black Belt activism, this was certainly an overstatement.

For many Tuskegee students, the tutoring program took them out of their sheltered lives and put them in direct contact with people in the Black Belt. For Lucenia Dunn, it was a life-changing experience. "I learned about the Black Belt and I learned about what it meant to be really poor," she said. "You walk into a house and the dirt floor with children with the extended bellies and mucus running out of their noses. Just abjectly poor. I had never seen anything like that." Working as a teacher had a profound effect on her. Teaching English one day, she heard one of her adult students shout, "Lord have mercy, lord have mercy! I can finally write my name!" She recalled that everything stopped "and chills just went up all over my arm." The man no longer had to write "X" to sign his name. "That right there said something to me about what I had to do," she said. "That cemented my commitment to black people."[93] Tuskegee student Cozetta Lamore remembers that her students had "joyous smiles" and exuded confidence. As Phillips had hoped, the program raised their sense of expectations—for themselves and for their schools. Lamore remembers that the attitude was "We're finally doing something to get out of this."[94]

Through tutoring, Tuskegee students also learned about the bravery of rural people in the face of racist terror. In May 1965 Todd joined the TICEP program. "I was deeply moved by the courage and passion and hospitality of the people that lived in the White Hall community of Lowndes County," he said. "They embraced us Tuskegee kids, and we did our best to plug gaps in the education of their children." TICEP placed him in the middle of one of SNCC's most radical projects— building a political organization called the Black Panther Party. Todd was housed for part of the time with the Jackson family. Matthew Jackson Sr. was one of the founding members of the Lowndes County Freedom Organization, which later became the Black Panther Party. "Matthew Jackson, Sr. basically lost his life coming from a voter mass meeting one night," Todd recalled. "His truck ran off the road and they found him dead the next morning in his truck," he said. "We assumed that was an accident."[95]

TICEP students learned about such "accidents" firsthand. Dunn picked up a car full of children in her car to take them home from tutoring. When everyone stopped talking at one point, she recalled saying to herself, "Oh-oh." She looked in the rearview mirror. "There was a truck full of white men," she said, "it was right on my tail and they had guns." She thought, "Oh god, I'm on a dirt road. Ain't no houses, nothing around in case something happens." The murder of Emmett Till flashed through her mind, and she stepped on the gas pedal. "I was shaking," she said, "the children were shaking. That's terror. . . . I had never had that sense of terror, and here are people who have it every day of their lives."[96] A few months later, a white civil rights worker, Viola Liuzzo, was killed on the same road that Tuskegee students used to travel to their TICEP appointments in Lowndes County. On the way there, Melvin Todd recalls passing the spot where her car had come to rest. "The tire marks still looked fresh," he said. "There was a fresh flower funeral wreath placed on the site." All of the students in his van "became silent for the rest of the trip," he said. "We were scared."[97]

For some students, the TICEP experience propelled them into direct action and confrontational protests, while for others, it cemented a commitment to providing direct service. Chester Higgins Jr. was the business manager of the *TICEP Journal*. For a time, he viewed TICEP as basically fitting the agenda of the civil rights movement, "just like hand to a glove." However, he concedes that the exposure to danger in the Black Belt had a radicalizing effect. "Perhaps," he said, "this combination of civil rights mission and the activism of the students who put their lives in sometimes precarious positions encouraged the questioning that later would lead to the confrontation between the students and the administration."[98] Some students concluded that direct service, not protests, would be more effective at making change. Writing in the *Campus Digest*, student Edwina Hayes argued that protesting and "handing out pamphlets" wouldn't accomplish much. The only way to promote genuine freedom, equality, and democracy, she wrote, was through "the unselfish and relentless efforts of our students." Echoing Phillips's call for a "domestic peace corps" (and perhaps speaking from her experience in TICEP), she suggested that the "agricultural majors could teach the farmers. . . . Nursing majors could aid in the attending of the young unwed mothers of children . . . and sociology majors could meet with destitutes and alcoholics and try to point out hidden qualities of worth."[99]

In the spring and summer of 1965, a small but influential group of students turned their attention away from service and toward civil disobedience. In particular, they targeted the town of Tuskegee, and pushed for immediate and complete desegregation. King—who now, five year later, in a changed political moment, was welcomed on campus—no doubt contributed to their confidence when he spoke to Tuskegee's graduating class that May. The civil rights struggle in Alabama, he said, "has suffered not so much from the violence of bad people as from the silence and indifference of good people." Echoing the students' sense of urgency, he continued, "The timid will say, 'Don't push too hard. Let's cool off awhile. Time will solve the problem.' The forces of bad will have often used time better than the forces of good will."[100] Tuskegee's most militant students—mostly members of TIAL—adopted this perspective.

Not unlike Patton's grandmother, TIAL members were not concerned with "integration" as such. Rather, they sought desegregation, the removal of racial barriers proscribing the use of all community facilities. For them, desegregation protests were a means of peeling away Tuskegee's façade, of "challenging racism in supposedly interracial Tuskegee," Forman wrote. "They were a way of exposing the lie of 'the model town.'"

Yet Tuskegee's middle-class leadership continued to cling to the façade and defend it. Boycotting the A&P for not hiring black people raised the ire of middle-class black people in town. To the black middle class, Forman wrote, TIAL activists "were just 'wild,' 'irresponsible,' dungaree-wearing 'kids' who threatened to rock the Model Town boat"; some community members even accused TIAL of being a communist group.[101] "Folks didn't like the way we dressed," Wendell Paris remembered, "and they would tell us that."[102] Undaunted by the opposition from elders, TIAL launched a series of protests over the summer that led it into conflict with Tuskegee's black middle-class leadership: Gomillion, the TCA, and the Tuskegee administration.

Sammy Younge and other TIAL students decided to desegregate the city swimming pool at the end of May. When black students showed up to swim, all of the white people fled, and the activists swam alone. The next day someone put a baby alligator in the pool. Soon after, students found glass shards sprinkled on the diving board, followed by manure and acid in the water. The city drained the pool on June 2 and refused to refill it. The next week a delegation of white people appeared at the city council asking for the pool to remain segregated.[103] Younge directly confronted Gomillion in a public forum for not supporting the effort to desegregate the swimming pools. "Gomillion, you're supposed to be the leader of the Negro people. What are you doing?" Gomillion didn't respond.[104]

TIAL also clashed with the TCA and the Tuskegee administration on voter registration. So as not to frighten white people, Gomillion and the TCA wanted to "go slow" on voter registration. Despite their majority (in 1964, there were 3,733 black voters and 3,479 white voters), the TCA only supported running two black people for the city council (out of five available seats), and it sent limited numbers of people to register at any one time so as not to give the impression that it wanted to take over.[105] "If it is evil to have all-white government," Stanley Smith, a Tuskegee sociologist who was one of the two black people elected to the council, said, "then it is also evil to have all-Negro government."[106] TIAL thought that everyone who was eligible should register to vote immediately, and let the chips fall where they may. When TIAL activist Wendell Paris heard that the TCA had agreed to bring no more than twelve people per day downtown to get registered to vote, he thought, "What kind of craziness is this?" TIAL also came into conflict with the Tuskegee leadership. "Needless to say, we bumped heads with the administration on the campus a lot of times," Paris recalled. He understood that TIAL might be messing with Tuskegee's image and ability to fundraise, and was of course concerned with student safety, "and so [Foster] really was kind of skeptical about Tuskegee students just leaving campus, going all over every which way to do voter registration when our parents thought that we were at school studying."[107]

In the context of growing pressure from activists and from the federal government, some of Tuskegee's white leaders decided to head off the growing civil rights movement in the town and retain their "model city" image. Several local businesses began hiring black people ahead of the deadlines for the imposition of federal mandates.[108] The Tuskegee Chamber of Commerce took out a full-page ad in the *Tuskegee News* stating that "in light of recent developments in ALABAMA," the organization felt an obligation to proclaim "what it believes to be right." "First," the ad read, "we believe in the full protection and opportunity under the law of all our citizens, both Negro and white."[109] Ever since Neil O. Davis, a white newspaperman known for racial liberalism, purchased the *Tuskegee News* in 1964, the paper repeatedly editorialized against Governor Wallace's attempts to obstruct voting rights for black people and against his use of violence against protesters.[110] These shifts illustrate the fact that the black movement successfully created a split among white southerners. Their struggle cracked the "solid South"—in Tuskegee, as in the region—but could not yet claim total victory.

As much as they denounced Tuskegee's middle-class leadership, TIAL was itself led, predominantly, by middle-class youth. "Tuskegee's budding young adult-children came home from the New England prep schools," Gwen Patton wrote of her newly radicalizing peers. "It became abundantly clear that rubbing shoulders with upper-class white kids activated their thirst for Black freedom."[111] Forman described Sammy Younge's political trajectory as a process of "rejecting middle-class standards and affirming" his "identity with blackness."[112] The activists in TIAL gave themselves elaborate titles—Younge was chairman of voter registration, Simuel Schutz was chairman of direct action, Wendell Paris was project director—which, Wendell Paris conceded with a smile, "didn't mean a whole lot," but spoke of the activists' sense of themselves.[113] Melvin Todd joined some of TIAL's demonstrations, but felt that the group was somewhat elitist. Todd said that the leadership "were mostly kids from Tuskegee, who were in that cluster of middle-class Tuskegee families." They had an "air," he recalled with a laugh, "of being a little bit more advanced than the rest of us, you know, who came from other parts of town." He included Younge in that characterization. He was not easy to get to know, Todd remembered. "He had an air about him that, you know, he had gone out, he had done a little time in the Navy, and I think he felt that he could do stuff and get away with it, that we couldn't do, the average guys couldn't do," Todd said.[114]

TIAL essentially was led by middle-class youth who were explicitly criticizing the class politics of their elders. In the pages of its newsletter, the *Activist*, George Ware wrote that TIAL had to "take to the streets" in order to get results, but the established leaders hesitated to do so because of their class position. "The middle class Negro views with disdain any fight for rights which occurs in the streets, however," Ware wrote, "because he associates 'the streets' with rabble-rousing and believes that the correct way to obtain justice is through the courts." But the court victories didn't come out of thin air. Rather, Ware asserted, they were movement victories: "We all know that this is a guise because the major decisions which have come from the courts are a result of outraged Negroes projecting issues into the public eye by taking the issues into the streets."[115] TIAL member Patricia Bailey assumed a leadership role for middle-class black people, even if they were reluctant to accept the part. "The lower-class Negroes are waiting for the middle-class Negroes to lead the way for them," she wrote, "but the middle-class Negroes do not like our methods of solving the problems in Macon County."[116] Wendell Paris further developed a class analysis by discussing the fact that the county contained poor people "of both races." However, he argued, "Macon County is so busy trying to help the middle class Negro to enjoy total equality that it has forgotten its under-privileged brother." Poor black people are "continuously exploited by the white man," and poor people "suffer humiliation from both races, by economic pressure from the white man and social pressures from the Negro."[117] The social pressure to conform to middle-class norms is part of what students rejected. Forman thought that Younge was drawn to SNCC because he found a group of people whose purpose was "real," not like "the Tuskegee world with its concern for status and status quo."[118]

Entering the House of God

In the summer of 1965, no campaign was as effective at pricking Tuskegee's self-image as TIAL's effort to desegregate local churches. On June 27, twenty-two students and some faculty split up into groups to desegregate three churches in Tuskegee.[119] Not one church admitted them; some activists faced mean shouts and taunts; others just had the doors shut and locked in their faces.[120] At the First Methodist Church, an usher told the group that they would "break up the congregation" if they entered. "If as Christians you deny other Christians the right to enter the house of God," George Ware replied, "then your congregation is already broken up."[121] When the service was over at the Southern Presbyterian Church, the Reverend Steve Bacon came out with another minister. "He seemed shocked to hear that we had been unable to come inside. He came over and shook hands with us and said that he was truly sorry that we had not been able to worship, and that he hoped some day, we would be able to worship together. He then led us in prayer." He did, however, concede that the lockout represented "the will of some in the congregation."[122]

After the church demonstration, TIAL declared its aims in writing. That week, TIAL published its first issue of the *Activist,* and the *Tuskegee News* reported that the new group distributed eight hundred copies around the campus.[123] "There is a strong, unyielding, but more important, fairly unconcerned white power structure in Macon County and throughout the South," the opening editorial, written by Elizabeth

Shields, stated. "TIAL intends to break this power structure in Macon County—not because it is white, but because it does not represent the majority of the people."[124] Shields pointed up the growing contradiction between American ideals and the reality for black people. "As Americans we learned to value and to expect certain hopes and dreams," she wrote, "but as Negroes we learn that these dreams can never be realities. . . . Hence, the present revolution." The *Activist* declared TIAL to be nonviolent. "But non-violence does not imply moderation," Shields cautioned. "Our philosophy is based on action. . . . We hope to mobilize Macon County's Negro population so that it can become an effective voice in this community and continue to be so on its own momentum."[125]

An article by Sammy Younge, titled (with intentional irony) "The Great Society," highlighted what he saw as the contradictions in the town. "Tuskegee isn't what its [*sic*] published to be," he wrote. "If Tuskegee is so great, why can't we go to church together? Why was the city pool closed? Why wasn't anyone prosecuted for throwing acid and rubbish in the city pool?"[126] Through direct action and its newsletter, TIAL increased pressure on city leaders to move quickly—and they did. During the same week the newsletter appeared, Tuskegee's city council, following the "letter and spirit of the 1964 Civil Rights Act," voted to create a special advisory committee to "facilitate further changes and improvement" in the city, especially the desegregation of public accommodations.[127]

The church desegregation campaign escalated quickly. The next Sunday, TIAL returned to the First Methodist Church with roughly five hundred people and the media. They went early, so some of their people actually got inside, but were still thrown out violently.[128] One white churchgoer who had been locked out along with the demonstrators commented, "These people have no interest in getting into church. It's a communist conspiracy."[129] The next week, July 18, Sammy Younge, Wendell Paris, and Simuel Schutz were the main leaders of the third attempt at First Methodist.[130] A mob of two dozen white men was waiting for them. Several of the activists were beaten, and some were hospitalized. Wendell was hit in the head with a Coke bottle and needed six stitches.

Sammy and George were chased away by a man wielding a .32-caliber pistol.[131] George and Wendell's father swore, George recalled, that "a white man would never again harm a child of [his] and live." George Paris, who at this point had graduated and joined the military, returned from basic training in time to participate in the church protests. He remembers that on the Sunday he arrived, his father was standing on the corner near the church, "with his overcoat on, in August"—concealing a shotgun.[132] This was no department store prank; Sammy and Wendell were now risking life and limb in open defiance of Tuskegee's Jim Crow traditions.

The church desegregation campaign led TIAL directly into conflict with the school's administration. "The administration asked us to ease some of our civil-rights activity," Patton remembered. "White/Negro interaction was approaching model human relations, we were told."[133] Later Patton claimed that Dean Phillips threatened to expel any TICEP student who participated in the demonstration, on the grounds that by joining a federal program, they could not participate in protest activity.[134] Phillips claims just the opposite, saying instead that he was, in discussions with President Foster, defending students' right to participate in protests, as long as TICEP students didn't do so "on the clock."[135] Patton wrote later that she was summoned to Foster's office. Foster allegedly told her that she "was not to encourage nor to lead the next Sunday's march to the churches." Patton replied that "the march would go on with or without me, and that the administration had overestimated my control over students." For safety, TIAL sought out assistance from an armed defense group, the Deacons for Defense and Justice from Bogalusa, Louisiana (it is unclear whether or not they actually came).[136] The violence at the protest (and, perhaps, the administration's stance) cowed the students. Only seven TICEP students participated on the next Sunday.[137]

The students were proved right. Church desegregation hit a nerve, especially with the established black leadership. Patton recalled that on many occasions Sammy Younge tried to appeal to older black leaders.

"They couldn't understand Sammy and the others at all," Patton said. "They began calling [TIAL members] communists. Sammy was ostracized." Forman later wrote that Younge's parents received death threats and that the Deacons for Defense came to guard his house for a few weeks.[138] The students may have alienated some black people, but Tuskegee's white power structure felt pressure from TIAL. Remarkably, three white men identified from the church incidents were arrested and charged with assault and battery.[139] TIAL succeeded in provoking a crisis, but never gained admission to white churches. The *Tuskegee News* issued a front-page editorial appealing for calm in July and admonished citizens "not to take the law into their own hands."[140] The *Tuskegee News* also printed letters from white citizens calling on fellow Christians to open their hearts. "How many children do you suppose watched the peregrinations of their parents and friends who ran from door to door at the Baptist Church in a concerted effort to see that no 'niggers' gained entrance?" one letter from Mrs. Wilhelmina R. Jones asked. "How can they come to terms with God in churches filled with hate and injustice?"[141] A hundred demonstrators gathered at Tuskegee's Methodist Church a week later for another attempt. With a large contingent of police looking on, they were told to "leave church property." And they did.[142]

"The Campus Revolution Is Here!"

As the summer came to an end and the 1965 fall semester approached, the United States continued to seethe. That August, in yet another confirmation of Malcolm X's prognosis, black residents of Los Angeles took to the streets by the thousands for the largest urban rebellion to date.[143] At the end of the month, Jonathan Daniels was murdered in Lowndes County, Alabama, as he and other civil rights workers were being released from jail. A Tuskegee senior, James Rodgers, reported that he had witnessed Tom Coleman shoot Daniels with a shotgun. A few minutes later, as Rodgers knelt over Daniels's corpse, some white men approached him and said, "Nigger if you don't leave here, the same thing will happen to you."[144]

That fall, the Tuskegee administration tried once again to embrace the students' sense of urgency for social transformation. In September, Tuskegee welcomed its largest freshman class ever: more than seven hundred. In an address to faculty and staff, President Foster encouraged the community to embrace change, warning that "this is no time to be timid, complacent or procrastinating."[145] The *Campus Digest* published an op-ed by Foster entitled "No Cliches, Just Facts." Foster made the case for reimagining the role of Tuskegee in the context of America's "crucial struggle within itself." In some ways anticipating the sentiments of students who would hold him hostage in less than three years' time, Foster argued for reimagining higher education as an instrument that could "reach into our big city slums and rural areas to bring distressingly vast numbers of ill-trained, socially rebellious, and negatively motivated young and middle-aged adults into a positive relationship with their society."[146] Two weeks later he emphasized to the arriving freshmen that "loyalty to self—a respect for one's identity and an abiding insistence on personal integrity" were the key to understanding the complexities of life.[147]

Students, however, increasingly felt that "change" wasn't happening fast enough, especially on campus. In a strident editorial indicative of the new mood, Peter Scott II argued that students needed to seize the opportunity to participate in transforming college life. "All students who are satisfied with 'just going to college' should stop and think!" he wrote. "All administrators who are bent on the fascistic or dictatorial rule should stop and evaluate! The campus revolution is here!"[148] Among other policies that were slow to change, students resented being mandated to attend religious services in the chapel. "I think that no administration should be given the right to make up a college student's mind," student Grace Gilmore told the *Campus Digest*. "I don't believe in compulsory chapel."[149] The rule never made sense to Caroline Hilton. "I didn't see any reason why I should have to go there," she said.[150] And even though only a small minority of students had participated directly in the campaign, anger over TIAL activists being shut out of Tuskegee's segregated churches lingered, too.

The barrier between on- and off-campus politics began to break down. That fall, Tuskegee students voted 3–2 against routing their homecoming parade through downtown Tuskegee, an old tradition that was stopped during the TCA boycott and had never been resumed. The mayor had hoped that the parade could "contribute very much to a better understanding and unity of everyone." But Peter Scott, a Tuskegee student, responded that if the city wanted to improve relations, "it can prosecute the men who beat Tuskegee students attempting to attend church services at the all-white First Methodist Church this summer."[151] Soon afterwards, the student assembly voted to present a series of demands to the administration, including the end of compulsory chapel, and the placement of students on curriculum, entertainment, and other committees, with voting rights.[152] As 1965 drew to a close, students' expectations for change, in their town and in their classrooms, were rising.

Tutoring the Tutors

From 1960 to 1965, Tuskegee students began to take action, and, through a series of successive approximations, tried to break out of their comfortable middle-class "bubble" and come to terms with the reality of their society and their place within it. Some volunteered their time in Black Belt counties, hoping to effect change as tutors, and ended up being tutored by the rural families they met. All were bothered by big questions: What would it take to transform the conditions of the Black Belt? Why should black people in Tuskegee and beyond continue to submit to the humiliation of segregated public facilities? If American society needed to change, didn't that mean Tuskegee Institute had to change, too? As Tuskegee students began to question Tuskegee Institute, they inevitably had to confront the legacy of Booker. T. Washington.

Not since the student strikes of 1903 and 1940 had Tuskegee Institute seen so much agitation among students. At the end of the fall 1965 semester, Tuskegee's administration still held out hope that dialogue with students could smooth things over and reconcile the two parties. In December, two thousand Tuskegee students, faculty, and administrators gathered at a forum entitled "Student Unrest and Its Implications." The event was prompted by a wave of protests over everything from bad food, to compulsory chapel, to teaching methods. In a single week, students dumped their food trays in the cafeteria, boycotted chapel, or walked out during the service, and some marched on the president's residence. "We want to be involved in governing the campus," student government president Gwen Patton said, admitting that the administration's refusal to let the Supremes sing on campus was "the straw that broke the camel's back."[153] Professor Paul Puryear praised the students, and TIAL in particular, for their courage, and called on the administration to follow their example. Dean Phillips said that mistakes had been made on both sides. "We're a very good college on our way to greatness," Phillips said. "But we won't get there unless we change the climate on campus."[154] The "climate" was, at this point, comparable to well-publicized protest movements on other campuses nationwide. A photo essay in Tuskegee's *Campus Digest* about the recent protests on campus was titled "No Berkeley, but a Tuskegee."[155]

Tuskegee's movement was not yet "on the map" as Berkeley's was at the time. But this was about to change. As the calendar year 1965 drew to a close, two men who would play a large role in shaping the southern black student movement—and consequently, national and even global politics—met in Lowndes County, Alabama. When black people were evicted from their homes for trying to register to vote in that county, Sammy Younge was one of many young activists who leapt into action, helping to set up tents as temporary housing, which became known as "tent city." SNCC activist Stokely Carmichael was there, too; he was surprised to see Younge. Younge was failing his classes and had taken a break from the movement to try to get his grades up. "What's happening, baby?" Carmichael said, greeting him. "I can't kick it, man," Younge replied. "I got to work with it," he said, referring to the movement. "It's in me." On New Year's Eve, Carmichael and Younge were together again, discussing Younge's idea for creating an independent political party in Macon County, modeled on the Black Panther Party SNCC had built in Lowndes County.[156] Younge's instinct was well-founded: the turn toward the ideas of Black Power was just around the corner, mere days away, accelerated by the first, bloody days of the new year, 1966. Stokely and Sammy, in life and in death, would leave their mark on the next phase of the struggle.

3

A Center of Black Power, 1966–1967

"We Will Fight until We Die"

This is what we know. Running an errand for cigarettes during a late-night SNCC meeting on January 3, 1966, Sammy Younge Jr. spied a Standard Oil service station near Tuskegee's campus on Highway 80. Younge pulled his car into the station and asked the white attendant, sixty-nine-year-old Marvin Segrest, if he could use the restroom. Segrest told him to use the one in back of the station. Younge said that he refused to use a segregated bathroom, and according to a bus driver eavesdropping from the depot next door, a shouting match ensued. Segrest brandished a pistol and chased Younge off the premises. Younge went to the police station on foot to report the incident and then returned to the Standard Oil station to retrieve his car. A second shouting match began, but this time Segrest fired a shot at Younge and missed. The bus driver approached Segrest to try to de-escalate the situation, while Younge hid behind his car. Younge found a golf club near the bus station and approached Segrest a third time. Segrest fired another shot, at approximately 11:45 p.m., hitting Younge in the head and killing him instantly.[1]

When a cab driver discovered his body just after midnight, news of Younge's death traveled swiftly on campus. "I was the one that was called at 2:00 in the morning to come down to the station, the gas station, and identify his body," Bert Phillips recalled.[2] George Paris remembers his father getting an early-morning call as well. Paris and his father "loaded for battle" and went to the bus station, where they, too, saw Sammy's body.[3] "Sammy Younge's death really was a key turning point for us in terms of how we were going to move," Wendell Paris said. "Simuel

Schutz that same night said, 'We will fight until we die. We will be fighting injustice in the United States and around the world until we die as a result of the death of Sammy Younge.'"[4]

From Civil Rights to Black Power

Beginning with the murder of Sammy Younge, Tuskegee student activists began organizing under the banner of Black Power. Younge's murder destroyed any veneer of progress in the town of Tuskegee and created a sense of urgency among Tuskegee students that greater changes were needed. What kind of change did "Black Power" mean in a Black Belt town like Tuskegee?[5] In the first place, Black Power meant democracy, a demand for immediate and full black participation in local political life that was resisted by municipal leadership and, to some extent, by Tuskegee Institute's leadership. Second, while the global context of decolonization and national liberation—especially in Africa—gave black students in all regions of the country the inspiration, the language, and the tools of analysis to understand their situation, in the Deep South the colonial analogy was particularly apt, especially in Macon County, where black people outnumbered white people four to one. If black people could take over and run their own nations, why not the county? Hence, Black Power meant political power. Third, given Tuskegee's origins as a site of colonial educational practices with connections and influence in global colonial enterprises, the anticolonial linkages made by Tuskegee students in this period represent quite a significant reversal of the school's traditions. Black Power at Tuskegee, in these ways, meant the sharpest confrontation to date with the legacy of Booker T. Washington.[6]

In the context of so much change on so many scales, Tuskegee students began to feel that the "normal" operations of their school were oppressive and antiquated. As they experienced success wresting concessions from the town and the county, students eventually turned their attention to Tuskegee Institute. Their political movement also became an

educational one. Beyond the cultural dimensions of self-love and affir-
mation, "Black Power" demands for self-determination and democracy,
applied to the campus, meant greater student power to shape their curriculum and instruction. For this reason, both Alabama segregationists
and Tuskegee administrators found "Black Power" too frightening, too
much, too fast. The issue for Tuskegee Institute's leadership (as it had
always been) was how much to accommodate (or "go slow") because
of the fears of powerful white people. The new slogan, "Black Power,"
communicated—far more than the old slogan, "Freedom"—the idea that
black students were no longer willing to wait for white people to accept
their demands, on campus or beyond.

"Tuskegee Came Unglued"

After Younge's murder, Gwen Patton wrote years later, "Tuskegee came
unglued."[7] However, for the first few months that followed, the tragedy
seemed to actually bind the campus community closer together. Nearly
3,000 people marched downtown the day after he was shot, January
4. The *Campus Digest* noted that this was "almost the entire Tuskegee
Institute student body (2,700) and faculty, staff, and community persons."[8] Students who previously felt protected from the worst effects of
racism experienced, in the aftermath of Younge's murder, a sensation
of vulnerability. "That really brought it close to home," Caroline Hilton
remembered. "We read about things and saw it on the news that things
happened in other campuses, but that was Tuskegee, that could have
been any one of us."[9] Cozetta Lamore called it a "wake-up call." Referring to a well-known fictional sleepy community, she thought, "Maybe
we're not as insulated as we thought we were and this is not the May-
berry town that people might like to think."[10]

Tuskegee's administration, led by President Luther H. Foster, and the
students, led by Gwen Patton, each sought to take advantage of Younge's
death to create changes in town, although by different means. At the
very moment Patton led the marchers to City Hall to demand an audi-

ence with the mayor and the city council, Foster was already meeting with the city's political leaders.[11] Student activists felt that Foster was attempting to wind down their movement (by, among other things, inviting the already exhausted student leaders to long meetings with him), while they were trying to escalate it.[12] At the steps of City Hall, Patton directed her words to the mayor: "You (the city and the press) have told us that this is a model city where white [*sic*] and Negroes get along together. . . . You have told us how good the Tuskegee image is, . . . yet you closed the city swimming pool and barred us from your churches. . . . Now, we want to know what you are going to do?"[13] The *Southern Courier* quoted Patton as also saying, "The students at Tuskegee Institute will tear this town to bits, if justice is not sought."[14]

Younge's life and death were an inspiration to activists to redouble their efforts and their commitments. "Sammy was a dedicated civil rights worker," Michael Wright recalled, explaining that his death marked a moment of escalation. "At that point I never went back to class for a couple of years." Instead, he began working with SNCC full-time doing voter registration work in Macon County and pushing for desegregation.[15] Singer and activist Harry Belafonte praised Younge in a fundraising letter for SNCC. "Many Americans believe the battle for racial justice is won," Belafonte wrote. "Sammy Younge's death proves how far we still have to go."[16] Activists searched for ways to "go" further. "Here is my bosom buddy killed," Wendell Paris said. "What do you do? Do you just give up? Do you roll over? Do you do something foolish? Do you try to come forward with some constructive way of combatting, of addressing the issues that led to his death? I still wrestle with that. We knew we needed to defend ourselves. We just didn't plan to roll over and die."[17]

George and Wendell Paris were traumatized by the death of their close friend, but James Forman felt responsible for Younge's murder, Wendell believed, since Forman had done so much to bring Younge into the movement and to work with him. "He really did feel the weight of the death of Sammy," Paris said.[18] Two years later, Forman published a book-length tribute to his fallen comrade, *Sammy Younge, Jr.: The First Black College Student to Die in the Black Liberation Movement*.[19] Walking from Younge's memorial service to his car, Forman wrote that he was "crying as I never cried before."[20] Forman wasn't the only civil rights leader to feel the weight. While mourners gathered in Macon County, representatives from SNCC and the Southern Christian Leadership Conference gathered for a funeral service for Younge at the Lincoln Memorial in Washington, DC.[21]

For the next week several hundred Tuskegee students held a consistent schedule of protests. Funeral services at Tuskegee were held on January 5, and all classes were canceled. The Tuskegee Institute Advancement League led 250 students on a January 6 march to City Hall, where Patton presented a fourteen-point desegregation proposal to the mayor. On January 7, 300 people marched against segregation downtown; Wendell Paris spoke, explicitly rejecting Booker T. Washington's policy of moderating black people's demands. "We got this statue out here of that man who's supposed to be lifting up the veil," he told the crowd. "Man, he's putting it back on!"[22] On January 8, 400 students started to march downtown but were stopped by police, so they sat-in to block the road. After an hour they were allowed to continue along their route. Students also picketed City Hall on January 10 and 11. On January 12 TIAL held a teach-in in the town square on the city's segregation practices.[23] In Melvin Todd's view, "the student body was like 100 percent unified. They were really behind the student leaders."[24]

The students were united among themselves, and felt, for a time, that they were united with Tuskegee Institute's administration, too. In addition to the tensions that emerged on campus at the end of 1965, the murder of Sammy Younge shifted Tuskegee's leadership into a posture of pressing for immediate desegregation downtown. On January 6, before nearly the entire school, President Foster reaffirmed the right and responsibility of Tuskegee Institute members to participate in civil rights activities. This statement was "an event of considerable symbolic significance," Tuskegee professor Arnold Kaufman wrote, for it "completed the break with the Booker T. Washington philosophy that had been in process since Rosa Parks decided to stay put in a Montgomery bus some 30 miles away and more than ten years ago."[25] A fourteen-point desegregation proposal was drawn up by an ad hoc committee (led by President Foster) in collaboration with TIAL. It included demands to establish an open employment policy (especially in the public sector), prohibit segregation in public facilities, and desegregate public housing in Tuskegee.[26] "We . . . do not share the view that the killing of Samuel Younge was the isolated act of one individual," Tuskegee professor Paul Puryear, a member of the committee, said. "It is our firm belief that Mr. Younge's murder is symptomatic of much deeper and more pervasive evils in our community."[27]

The deeper evils were never far from sight. On Saturday, January 15, at another protest in the city square, a police officer tried to arrest a Tuskegee High School senior on an unrelated, previous charge. A crowd of Tuskegee students gathered around the officer as he began beating the high school student with a blackjack. Other officers arrived and shouted, "Get back!" The *Campus Digest* reported that this "melee" (the *Southern Courier* called it a "riot"[28]) lasted for about five minutes. Word traveled back to campus quickly, and 1,200 Tuskegee students immediately marched downtown. White men in unmarked cars with no license plates circled the protesters until students chased them away, hurling bricks and bottles. In the process, students broke windows in eleven downtown buildings.[29]

In these volatile days the "glue" was strained, but held. The *Campus Digest* editors praised Foster for standing with students and not calling for a moratorium on protests, despite the fact that property damage put him in a "dubious position." "Dr. Foster is closer to more students now than he has been for quite some time," the *Campus Digest* editors wrote. "This is how it should be." Seconding Foster and TIAL, the editors also called for students to "follow the principle of non-violence or decline to participate."[30] A Tuskegee faculty member wrote a letter to the *Campus Digest* praising the moderation of student leadership at the protests. "As long as they show this type of deliberation, consideration, and responsible thinking," he wrote, "we need not fear how and where this student leadership will go and act."[31] Meanwhile, *Tuskegee News* decried the violence of bottle-throwing students and called for a return of the "intelligent, dedicated" leadership of the Tuskegee Civic Association. "If Tuskegee is fortunate, the TCA leadership will exert itself again in these trying times," the editors wrote.[32] Some black citizens let it be known that they, too, thought the students were in the wrong. Decrying "SNCC-type" people who were coming in from "outside," one woman wrote a letter to the *Tuskegee News* supporting "equality of opportunity" and adding, pointedly, "but we are not radical street demonstrators."[33] Two weeks later, the ad hoc alliance of administrators, faculty, and radical street demonstrators scored a victory: a desegregation ordinance passed the council by a five-to-one vote after a particularly stormy session.[34]

"One Big Classroom"

For the next several months, joining "the movement" was still primarily an off-campus calling, and Tuskegee student activists essentially sought further desegregation and democratization. Reforming the structure of power in town, however, did not yet imply a similar overhaul on campus. On January 31, participants in a student-faculty roundtable event debated whether or not civil rights activism interfered with academic goals.[35] Gwen Patton was the only speaker to challenge the terms of the discussion, defending both sides of the "scholar-activist" identity.[36] "Civil rights is part of the educational process," she said. "It can't interfere with it. I have learned more from my civil rights activities than in any class."[37] The next month Jennifer Lawson dropped out of school to work for SNCC full-time. "To me, this is just a big classroom right here in Alabama," Lawson said. "In a classroom, you hear all about the great theory of democracy and you swear that it's working. Out here, you know it isn't."[38] By the end of the year, Patton and other Tuskegee students would extend Patton's and Lawson's argument further, no longer fearing "interference" with their present education, but increasingly finding its form intolerable.

As students and their allies racked up some victories in 1966, President Foster defended student activists behind the scenes, while the governor's ire grew. The appearance on campus of Communist Party leader Gus Hall in February spurred a heated correspondence between George Wallace and his supporters about what could be done to stop the spread of communism at Tuskegee.[39] Foster and his administration stood by the students. The university defended one of its student teachers who was not accepted in a field training assignment in a local school because of her civil rights activism.[40] In April Foster presented a report to Tuskegee's board of trustees, noting concern over "intra-group conflicts" and "students' frustrations that result from racial barriers." In his report to the trustees on civil rights activism in Tuskegee, Foster defended the school's policy of allowing students to express themselves within the boundaries of law and democracy, and argued that the incidents involving property damage did not "reach truly riotous proportions."[41] To some extent, the Tuskegee community had successfully isolated the white segregationists, and, as desegregation proceeded, white and black leaders hoped that student activism would wind down. In mid-July, twenty-five years of segregation at the city swimming pool ended quietly, the *Southern Courier* noted, "without a splash."[42]

Taking Sides on Vietnam

Among the ripple effects of Younge's murder was the increasing willingness of civil rights individuals and organizations to speak out against the war in Vietnam. For a long time, many civil rights organizations operated within the ideological limits of Cold War liberalism. Both the Congress of Racial Equality and the NAACP purged communists from their ranks to prove their loyalty to the United States in the war against communism.[43] The NAACP's president, Roy Wilkins, argued that "civil rights groups [do not] have enough information on Vietnam, or on foreign policy, to make it their cause." The Urban League's Whitney Young agreed. "Johnson needs a consensus," Young said. "If we are not with him on Vietnam, then he is not going to be with us on civil rights."[44] For all its fiery rhetoric, even the Nation of Islam censured Malcolm X when he described the assassination of US president John Kennedy as an example of America's violence in Vietnam ("chickens") reverberating domestically ("coming home to roost").[45] But as the war expanded, so did critical views of it. There were 25,000 US troops in Vietnam at the start of 1965, rising to 184,000 the next year, and to more than half a million in the three years to follow. Black soldiers were only 10 percent of all of the armed forces, yet they were concentrated in frontline units that faced combat, such that they were 22 percent of all Army casualties by November 1966.[46] SNCC members on the front lines of battles for democracy and human rights in the Deep South were, by the mid-1960s, drawing connections between such domestic and international conflicts, and, as a result, were breaking from the Cold War liberalism of their elders.[47]

Tuskegee students were well acquainted with the war. At least twenty-two people from the town and campus combined were killed in Vietnam, including two TIAL members, Laurence Dudley and William Boone.[48] Tuskegee Institute's long-standing mandatory ROTC program meant that students were in a pipeline to Vietnam—as officers. George Paris graduated from Tuskegee Institute in 1964 and went to Vietnam as a second lieutenant. For him, though, spending time in the military meant preparing for a global revolution. "I had fifty men, five thousand pounds of ammunition, a set of mortars, two Jeeps, and full combat gear, on one C-141 Air Corps Troop Carrier," he recalled. "That was one of the reasons that I went, and some more of my friends went. We were convinced that there was going to be a shooting revolution in the United States. Where best to learn how to fight than in the United States Army?" Whether from their experience in Vietnam or their experience fighting for democracy in the US South, SNCC and TIAL activists' skepticism about the war was quickly turning into outright opposition.

FIGURE 3.1. Sammy Younge Jr. in his Navy uniform. Tuskegee Institute Archives.

Sammy Younge's murder resonated on multiple levels. Younge spent two years in the Navy after high school, and received a medical discharge before enrolling in Tuskegee. He was not just a Tuskegee student, and not just an activist at the cutting edge of the struggle for democracy in the Black Belt. He was also a military veteran. The murder of Sammy Younge was, in George Paris's view, "the straw that broke the camel's back."[49]

SNCC's next move represented a more radical break from Cold War liberalism. In November 1965 SNCC leaders had agreed to make a statement on Vietnam, but nothing came of it until Younge's murder. "Release of that declaration was triggered by the murder of Sammy Younge, Jr.," Forman wrote in his autobiography.[50] The statement, released two days after Younge's murder, marked the first time a civil rights organization spoke out against the Vietnam War. It was a rejection of the liberal protest paradigm, expressing solidarity with the official enemy. SNCC positively identified its struggle with that of the Vietnamese, comparing it to the work of Sammy Younge. "The murder of Samuel Young [*sic*] in Tuskegee, Alabama, is no different than the murder of peasants in Vietnam," the statement read, "for both Young [*sic*] and the Vietnamese sought, and are seeking, to secure the rights guaranteed them by law. In each case, the United States government bears a great part of the responsibility for these deaths."[51]

The ripples of Younge's murder spread all the way to the halls of the US Congress. One month earlier, in December 1965, the twenty-six-year-old SNCC leader Julian Bond had been elected to the Georgia legislature from Atlanta. Since Bond was one of the principal authors of SNCC's anti-war statement, the legislature refused to seat him in January of the following year on the accusation of being disloyal and "un-American."[52] Bond took his case to federal court, and ultimately to the Supreme Court, which ruled in his favor, finally allowing him to take his seat nearly one full year after he was elected.[53] Appearing at Tuskegee Institute soon after his court victory, Bond defended the rising militancy of southern activists and their use of the term "Black Power." "Black means us," Bond said. "Power is the ability to influence others toward your desires."[54]

What We're Going to Start Saying Is "Black Power!"

Newly elected SNCC president Stokely Carmichael popularized the slogan "Black Power" in June 1966 while continuing the march through the South that had been started by James Meredith (and halted while he recovered from a gunshot injury).[55] The linking of those two words, "Black" and "Power," struck a chord with young people nationwide, and became an enduring way of framing new developments in the student movement and beyond.[56] "Black Power" marked a shift from self-description as "Negro" to a self-description as "Black," signaling a reversal of attitudes, refusing to accept the denigration of—and further, taking pride in—the very thing that had been stigmatized for so long:

blackness. "Black" was no longer to be associated with degradation, but with a proud political and cultural stance.[57] In this new, militant race consciousness, black identity itself was "the soul of a new radicalism."[58] The slogan has been associated with urban insurrections in the North and armed self-defense organizations in the West, although recent historical scholarship has broadened our understanding of the scope of Black Power activities by including the work of women, schoolteachers, welfare rights organizers, health care activists, educators, and more.[59]

From the perspective of activists at Tuskegee Institute, the new attitude had already taken root before Carmichael raised the slogan in Mississippi. "When you look at it," Wendell Paris commented, "the death of Sammy Younge is what ushered in the Black Power movement."[60] Younge was dead less than a month when national civil rights leaders told the *New York Times* that they were "watching current racial unrest in Tuskegee" and interpreting it as a sign that "coalition" governments with white people might no longer work. The NAACP continued to defend the ideal of biracial political leadership, but after Younge's murder SNCC leader John Lewis was quoted as saying that "it might be necessary to have all-Negro government before you can have a workable interracial government."[61] By the time Stokely Carmichael shouted "Black Power" on a Mississippi highway, some white people in Tuskegee had been bracing for escalating conflict for six long months. Two weeks before Carmichael raised the slogan, the *Tuskegee News* warned about the danger of black nationalism to "race relations" in Tuskegee. "The Negro leadership in Tuskegee has feared and fought against such a reactionary approach to the problem of equal rights," the editors wrote.[62]

A new leadership, however, concentrated among Tuskegee students, was already embracing Black Power and debating its meaning.[63] Several leading activists described the goals of Black Power as essentially a realization of democracy and self-determination in the Black Belt. Michael Wright highlighted these themes in notes he drafted to explain the concept to Tuskegee students. "Black Power is simply a process whereby Black people can unite to control the resources, both politically and economically, in their areas and make the decisions upon matters which affect them," he wrote. "Every other ethnic group has done this, so why not Blacks in America?"[64] Gwen Patton felt that TIAL had "absolutely" sought Black Power all along. "If we want to control it, we're going to control everything," she said. "The supermarkets. We want a theater downtown. If they had listened to us, they would have a thriving community. We didn't want to have to come in contact with white folks first, [but,] if we did, it would have to be on a fair basis, a fair basis of negotiation. . . . That was the difference between TIAL and TCA."[65] The idea that Black Power might represent basic fairness was lost on most media accounts of the movement, but avoiding misunderstanding was no longer a priority. "For once, black people are going to use the words they want to use," Carmichael wrote, "not just the words whites want to hear. And they will do this no matter how often the press tries to stop the use of the slogan by equating it with racism or separatism."[66]

For some students, words they wanted to use included "revolution," causing significant alarm in the corridors of power. One Tuskegee graduate student, Ernest Stephens, believed that the urban rebellions were a harbinger of a deeper social transformation. He argued that black students could form the leadership of a coming Black Revolution. In order for black students to "formulate a program of action on black campuses and implement the bread and butter fight of black Americans," he wrote, they would have to "fight the administration, the faculty, and, yes, even the student body for the right to pursue this course."[67] Tuskegee students were spreading this militant attitude across the state of Alabama, or so the governor's anti-communist commission, the ALCPP, believed. In September, the commission sent a confidential memo to George Wallace warning that several Alabama towns, including Tuskegee, were "at a point where trouble of considerable proportions could erupt." As the "rumblings grow louder," the memo concluded that they seem "to eminate [sic] from Tuskegee campus."[68] In his fall 1966 convocation address to the Tuskegee Institute community, President Foster tried to quell the rumblings, arguing that violent revolution was outdated and that the nature of change going forward would be largely technocratic. "Problems of this day are essentially those of know-how," he said, "and of the strategies and techniques required to make a better world society."[69]

The technocratic ideal, however, was losing its grip on the political imagination of students. The Black Power movement represented an intellectual awakening. Students—especially activist students—read, discussed, and debated widely, and mostly outside class. In these years, students circulated among themselves books and articles by Amiri Baraka, Nikki Giovanni, Stokely Carmichael, Sonia Sanchez, H. Rap Brown, Frantz Fanon, Che Guevara, Martin Luther King Jr., W. E. B. Du Bois, Booker T. Washington, Kwame Nkrumah, and Malcolm X.[70] "Everybody had a copy of *The Autobiography of Malcolm X*," Wendell Paris recalled. "You just had that in your back pocket."[71] Some of the faculty encouraged the ferment among students. One Tuskegee professor, writing in the *Campus Digest*, argued that black people were more and more divided between assimilationists and revolutionists. The assimilationists (who were "usually educated, middle-class Negroes") sought to enter white society and maintain the status quo. The revolutionists, on the other hand, "are tired of maintaining a system of near slavery," he wrote. "They are Negroes with self respect and who wish to end the great white brainwash."[72]

The message of self-respect and militancy was echoed repeatedly by a series of guest speakers who came to Tuskegee in the mid-1960s. Tuskegee students didn't only read Martin Luther King, James Forman, or Malcolm X, they met them in person.[73] Chester Higgins believes that Tuskegee's status as a privately funded school gave it more leeway to invite controversial speakers. "Politically, we were exposed to the kind of things that were not available at a publicly supported state school like the nearby Alabama State University," he said.[74] One of the biggest events on campus was the appearance of the young man perceived to be the national leader of the black student movement: Stokely Carmichael.

Carmichael's arrival in the fall of 1966, at the invitation of students, was also an opportunity for Tuskegee activists to address the campus

FIGURE 3.2. Media coverage of Stokely Carmichael's address at Tuskegee Institute. *Southern Courier*, October 22, 1966.

as a whole. Two thousand students, faculty, and staff packed into a hall to hear him. Wendell Paris, who had recently graduated, and Oscar Sykes, a freshman, gave opening remarks.[75] Sykes used the opportunity to speak out against mandatory chapel. "What gives Tuskegee the right to make students attend religious services when Jesus himself didn't compel anyone to hear him?" he asked. Paris riled up the audience by comparing "good niggers" and "bad niggers"—the former being those who wait politely for change, the latter being those who "stand up to the white man and tell him he doesn't care about him." The *Campus Digest* reported that the audience "burst into applause," adding, "Paris urged the students to 'be a bad nigger.'"[76]

Carmichael, the featured speaker, explored the personal, political, and educational implications of Black Power. "In order for us to be free we must accept our blackness and force the white man to accept it," he said. Carmichael had traveled to at least two dozen other colleges and universities that year, and made a point of addressing the connection between politics and education.[77] Carmichael challenged the idea that the purpose of education should be individual career advancement. Rather, he suggested that black people should stop trying to prove themselves by success in traditional professions, but instead should "go back to the ghettos and black communities where there is much work to be done. What good is an education if you are going to use it as a ticket into white society?" Rather than asking for acceptance, Carmichael argued, black people must recognize the actual power relations of society and act accordingly. "This country is not run on love, brotherhood and non-violence but on power," he said, "therefore the Negroes [sic] must overcome his fear, and he must stand up and fight for power."[78]

The Postcolonial Roadmap

Tuskegee Institute had always been concerned with power. In its origins, however, the campus was bound up with another kind of power: that of European and North American colonialism in the late nineteenth and early twentieth centuries.[79] Like many other black thinkers and educators in those years (including W. E. B. Du Bois for a time), Booker T. Washington believed that bringing "civilization" to Africans would benefit them.[80] The mid-twentieth-century anticolonial revolutions changed the way black Americans saw Africa. For some Tuskegee students in the 1960s, their view of who was civilizing whom transformed.

As national liberation in Africa became a tidal wave, it was inevitable that black people in the United States would not only draw inspiration from it, but also begin to see the transition from colonialism to independence as a roadmap for their own struggle. "The American Negro shares with colonial peoples many of the socio-economic factors which form the material basis for present day revolutionary nationalism," the iconoclastic scholar Harold Cruse wrote in 1962. "From the beginning, the American Negro has existed as a colonial being."[81] In 1966 Stokely Carmichael went further, from "sharing factors" with colonized Africans to black neighborhoods being identical to colonized African nations. "The colonies of the United States—and this includes the black ghettoes within its borders, north and south—must be liberated," he wrote.[82]

Tuskegee student activists began following national liberation struggles closely. Chester Higgins admired the African students on campus because of their study habits, and they exposed him to anticolonial literature. Higgins's African classmates showed him books by Nnamdi Azikiwe, the first president of Nigeria, and others by Kwame Nkrumah, the president of Ghana. "Then somebody turned me on to [Jomo] Kenyatta," he recalled. "It's not somebody that African Americans would read, and want to be seen with a book with a funny name."[83] Gwen Patton remembers that it was South African exiles teaching at Tuskegee who encouraged students to read Kenyatta's book *Facing Mount Kenya* and Frantz Fanon's *The Wretched of the Earth*.[84] Melvin Todd got access to global literature through writing for the school newspaper. In the office of the *Campus Digest* "we would get newspapers from all over the world," Todd recalled. "We would get papers from Cuba, from the

Communist Party, everything that you can imagine. I read everything that came because I wanted to be knowledgeable about the world."[85] Some student activists began writing about global politics. To spread an understanding of the connection between black people in the United States and African national liberation, Michael Wright drafted a series of in-depth essays for SNCC. He explained the historical origins of colonialism and capitalism, tracing the growth of major corporations, their investments—and consequent political commitments—in colonial and neocolonial regimes all over the world.[86]

As they looked to anticolonial, national liberation struggles for theoretical and practical guidance, some students were breaking from the outlook of one black middle class (in Tuskegee) and embracing the outlook of another black middle class (in Africa). In the 1960s, nationalist leaders in Africa and Asia came from the same milieu: middle-class, college-educated students and young professionals. The Black Power movement in the United States drew its leadership from the same set.[87] Che Guevara, Kwame Nkrumah, and Frantz Fanon shared this class position with Gwen Patton, Samuel Younge, and Michael Wright. The pattern was the same across black campuses in the United States. Although the ideas of Black Power were adopted by all classes of black students in the United States, Jeffrey Turner notes that "private campuses tended to foster the most militant versions of Black Power." Elite black schools with wealthier students, he concludes, "were more likely to pursue separatism and educational goals influenced by black nationalism."[88]

Some of the new heads of state in the so-called Third World advocated for the ideas of socialism, but as they attempted to survive in a hostile capitalist world, this meant using the existing state apparatus to nationalize industry for the purpose of reform and development.[89] The Black struggle in the United States shared similar impulses, as had global revolutions for more than a century.[90] The ideas of social revolution and anti-capitalism were "in the air," but not translated into immediate strategies as Wallace and his advisors feared. More sympathetic observers understood that, under the banner of Black Power, insurgents in the

United States were most immediately fighting for an expansive conception of democratic reform.[91]

From their perspective at Tuskegee Institute in 1966, the meaning of
the events in Africa was clear to Tuskegee students: black people were
fighting the Europeans and winning. Wendell Paris's local activism was
inspired by events in Africa. "Black Africa, sub-Saharan Africa, now, is
standing up," he said, describing the time. "You needed to understand
that folk were rising up, not only in your local community, but all over
the country and all over the world." Paris furthermore believed that
these developments had urgent implications for Macon County. "It was
necessary to have an international perspective, a global perspective," he
said, "but more importantly, you needed to understand what was going
on in your local community and how you could impact what was happening there. That's how we spent the majority of our time, just trying
to bring our people to the point where they would move, in spite of their
fears, to make constructive change."[92]

Working toward constructive change, however, frequently brought
Tuskegee students face to face with armed agents of the status quo.
Tuskegee activists working in the Black Belt reported being followed by
FBI agents.[93] Even the ostensibly nonpolitical Tuskegee Institute Community Education Program (TICEP) volunteers found themselves subject to intimidation, followed by white men with guns, their cars run
off the road.[94] Melvin Todd admired SNCC workers because he saw
that they were risking their lives to register people to vote. Stokely Carmichael introduced him to the rural family that housed him when he
joined the campaign. Todd was impressed with the generosity of people
in the Black Belt, but he also encountered mortal danger. In Lowndes
County, two black men approached him one day and asked him what he
was doing. Assuming that, as black people, they would be sympathetic,
Todd explained the voter registration drive. One of the men pulled out
a revolver and put it to his head, saying, "Nigger, if you don't get out of
here, I'll blow your head off."[95]

Intimidation, terror, the threat of violence, and violence—especially the murder of Tuskegee student Sammy Younge—drove home the idea that black people in Macon County were in a situation perhaps more than analogous to that of colonized Africans. In a county where black people outnumbered white people by nearly four to one, democratic voting could only mean the rise of black political power.[96] In Macon, some black people began thinking that the problem of violence and power could be overturned together in one stroke: by electing a black sheriff.

The First Black Sheriff Elected in the South since Reconstruction

Military veteran Lucius Amerson attended Tuskegee Institute on the GI Bill, and worked long hours in the school's housekeeping department to support his growing family. One night the police hauled him to the Macon County jail on a domestic disturbance charge, where he had an epiphany. Noticing the disorganized, inefficient, and cluttered atmosphere of the jail, Amerson had an idea: "If I was sheriff I could run this place 100 percent better." Amerson thought of Sammy Younge's "blood-soaked body lying on the ground in the rain," and then, according to his memoir, he had "a revelation that I could run for the office of sheriff and win!"[97] Although he had no political experience and few law enforcement credentials to speak of, the Tuskegee student was correct—Younge's murder did, in fact, propel Amerson into public office.[98]

Amerson's victory is evidence of a shift in political clout and leadership, from Tuskegee faculty assembled in the TCA to Tuskegee students affiliated with TIAL. Charles Gomillion believed that the office of sheriff should be the last one for black people to seek, given its power to arouse white fears. Meanwhile, students from TIAL and SNCC teamed up to campaign aggressively for Amerson.[99] Hostility between Amerson and the TCA leadership came out into the open, Norrell noted, when students rigged a sound truck for Amerson and drove around Tuskegee decrying the failed leadership of "middle-class niggers."[100] With the help

FIGURE 3.3. Lucius Amerson in 1966, shortly after he was sworn in as the first black sheriff elected in the South since Reconstruction. Photo by Jim Peppler. Alabama Department of Archives and History, courtesy of Jim Peppler.

of student activists from Tuskegee Institute, Amerson narrowly defeated his challenger in the Democratic Party primary in June 1966 and then prevailed in a landslide (3,868 to 2,002 votes) in the general election in November.[101] The students reveled in their power. "We elected the first black sheriff in the South since Reconstruction," Wendell Paris remembered with pride.[102]

Amerson's election was widely recognized as a watershed event. "One chunk of Alabama soil is no longer the political province of the white man," a *New York Times Magazine* article declared.[103] The election echoed in headlines nationwide, reporters converged on Macon County, and Amerson received a congratulatory telegram from Vice President Hubert Humphrey and an invitation to the White House.[104] In 1970 Hollywood released a feature film starring Jim Brown, based on Lucius Amerson's story.[105] As the news spread, others followed in Amerson's footsteps. In the years immediately following his victory, black sheriffs were elected in several other Black Belt counties.[106] Thus, it is not surprising that Macon County in general and the city of Tuskegee in particular were on the minds of two activists who sat down to lay out a book-length explication of the meaning of Black Power.

"Tuskegee, Alabama, could be the model of Black Power," Stokely Carmichael and Charles Hamilton wrote in what became one of the most influential books of the era, *Black Power: Politics of Liberation in America*.[107] Carmichael, who later changed his name to Kwame Ture, had plenty of opportunity to observe the political dynamics of Tuskegee in person. Carmichael had spent a great deal of time working with Tuskegee student activists, and Charles Hamilton had been a Tuskegee professor.[108] Seeing firsthand the acceleration of events after Sammy Younge's murder, including the election of Lucius Amerson, the authors devoted an entire chapter in this short book to an analysis of Tuskegee's potential as a center of Black Power. "It could be the place where black people have amassed political power and used that power effectively," they wrote.[109]

The Black Power movement is, in the popular imagination, associated with guns and incendiary rhetoric. The month before Amerson's election, two community college students in Oakland, California, Huey P. Newton and Bobby Seale, borrowed the feline symbol from the electoral campaign in Lowndes County, Alabama, and founded the Black Panther Party for Self-Defense. The vision laid out in *Black Power*, however, had more to do with ballots than bullets. Furthermore, recent historical research has unearthed a broader tapestry of Black Power activism by the Oakland Panthers and others, including electoral campaigns.[110] Carmichael had discussed with Younge—the week before his murder—the idea of creating a new political party in Macon County. "The black people of Tuskegee could play a major role in building an independent county political organization which would address itself to the needs of black residents along lines we have already indicated," Hamilton and Carmichael wrote. Carmichael had tried to raise this idea with other

civil rights activists but met with resistance.[111] In Tuskegee, some student activists were ready to break from the Democratic Party, whose
emblem in Alabama was a rooster and whose official slogan remained
"white supremacy."[112] Wendell Paris spoke out at a forum on campus to
say that black people should not "vote for the white rooster" anymore
because "the whole thing is corrupt."[113] In *Black Power*, the authors
stressed that figures such as Amerson alone could not make significant
change without an independently organized party. "Such an independent force would give greater meaning to the election of Amerson by
creating a genuine, organized base of power," they argued, "not merely
putting one black man, however valuable, into office."[114]

The expectations for what could be achieved in Tuskegee by electoral
means were measured. "It would be naïve to expect that the operation
of Black Power in Tuskegee could transform Alabama state politics,"
Hamilton and Carmichael wrote. "But it could establish in that one area
a viable government based on a new and different set of values—on
humaneness—and serve as an example of what civilized government
could be in this society." In this way, "pockets of Black Power" could
become "illustrations of what legitimate government really is—a phe-
nomenon we have not experienced to date in this society."[115] But even
these modest expectations immediately ran into resistance from white
officials. Civil rights activists charged Tuskegee's white mayor with deliberately demoting black police officers to open up space for more white
officers in order to undermine Amerson.[116] Amerson disputed the inadequate allocation of funds to his office by the Macon County Board
of Revenue, alleging a pattern of discrimination.[117] The newly elected
Alabama governor, Lurleen Wallace, also apparently attempted to thwart
the black sheriff by appointing white people as special constables in
overlapping jurisdictions.[118]

The independent power base that Hamilton and Carmichael imagined in Tuskegee did not come together, and Amerson did not see himself as accountable to the movement that put him in power. Amerson
explicitly challenged the idea of building an independent political party.

"The Democratic Party has the best policy," he said, "and I don't think the other party will get very far."[119] Amerson had actually been clear with Tuskegee students from the beginning of his campaign that he was not a "Black Power candidate" and that he wanted them to help him as individuals, not as TIAL.[120] Still, in the months and years to follow, the black students who supported him pointed proudly to the fact that Amerson arrested a white man accused of raping a young black woman, and in an even more spectacular reversal of the social order, arrested a police chief and a state trooper for threatening and brutalizing a black man.[121] Wendell Paris believed that Amerson's presence meant that "we have police powers here," and that black citizens finally had cause to believe that "their voices had to be heard."[122]

The results of the movement in 1966 and 1967 were, at best, mixed across the Black Belt. While some black sheriffs were elected, they did not entirely end police brutality, as some had hoped. Even more modest efforts to desegregate Tuskegee stumbled and struggled. Tuskegee students and faculty continued Younge's effort to desegregate Tuskegee's white churches, but after three attempts in the summer of 1966, the doors remained shut to black worshippers.[123] Under court order, Tuskegee high schools were set to be integrated in the fall of 1966, but the reality of student allocation remained predominantly segregated.[124] In their strongest Black Power demonstration project to date, activists built popular support for an independent black-led political party in nearby Lowndes County, but widespread voter fraud, terror, and intimidation explained why, in a county that was 81 percent black, their party failed to gain a single seat in the November elections.[125]

The election of Lucius Amerson is a twist on the story of Black Power and the tradition of armed self-defense in the South. Given their overwhelming numbers in the county, Tuskegee student activists sought to seize control of the state apparatus—including its monopoly on "legitimate" violence—by electing a black sheriff. Black Power civilian activists in Oakland wielded weapons openly to police the police, while in the Black Belt their counterparts wanted to become the police. Although

Tuskegee students saw his election as a step toward the kind of decolonization that was sweeping the African continent, Amerson saw himself as part of the mainstream of American law enforcement, not as a Black Power activist or agent of decolonization.[126] In his memoir, Amerson claims that Stokely Carmichael once asked him how he would use his position to support the Black Power movement. "I am too busy performing my duties as sheriff to be concerned with black power," Amerson replied.[127] Before the twentieth century's first black sheriff swore the oath of office, however, the legal system delivered another blow to the student movement at Tuskegee: a verdict for Younge's murderer.

"To Hell with Alabama!"

Like the defeat in Lowndes County, the trial of Marvin Segrest showed that Alabama's white power structure was far from beaten. In November 1966, Segrest's lawyers successfully petitioned to have the trial moved to Opelika in the majority-white Lee County. The defense argued that protests had created a feeling of resentment against Segrest, and the judge agreed.[128] "What the attorneys were really saying," the *Southern Courier* editorialized, "is that no white man accused of killing a Negro should have to face a jury of independent Negroes."[129] Indeed, Segrest stood before twelve white jurors who, in mid-December, found him not guilty of murder after only seventy minutes of deliberation.[130] A SNCC member in the courtroom kicked the floor and stormed out, shouting, "To hell with Alabama!"[131] "There is a rotten and foul branch of this community that must be uprooted before we can have a just society," wrote one member of the Tuskegee Institute community in a letter to the *Tuskegee News.* "We see roads paved, city limits extended, police integrated, more Negroes registered to vote and sitting on juries, even anti-segregation ordinances adopted, and all accompanied by something that looks like white benevolence and black accommodation," he continued, adding, "But you can still get yourself a nigger in Tuskegee."[132] "Let us ask ourselves seriously," Tuskegee student Ernest Stephens wrote in his self-published broadsheet, *Black Thesis*, "is it against the law for white folks to kill niggers in this country?"[133]

Gwen Patton's assessment of the aftermath of Sammy Younge's murder was more true after the acquittal of his murderer: little was left of Tuskegee Institute's "glue" following the verdict. Three hundred students gathered in Logan Hall for an impromptu meeting, then decided to march into the town, and as they did, their numbers grew.[134] The headline of the December 19 edition of the *Campus Digest* read, "Slayer Goes Free; Students Riot" and the article reported that 1,500 students protested downtown.[135] Students smashed windows of thirteen downtown businesses and mounted the statue of a Confederate soldier in the town square, painting the face black. They put a yellow stripe down its back and painted the words, "Black Power" and "Sam Younge" on its base.[136]

President Foster immediately chastised the students, saying that "the struggle for human rights must go on," but it is "serious" and won't progress through "flippant discussion, careless planning, or precipitous action."[137] Following the protests, Foster gathered the entire Institute community for a meeting. Activists were angered that he failed to say anything about the verdict, directing his comments only to student actions.[138] While the school administration did not oppose peaceful protest, Foster said, "Tuskegee Institute does very definitely oppose and counsel against any protest which grows out of careless planning, confusion as to purposes, and disregard of orderly processes." Demonstrations and marches "had their place at times in the past," Foster continued, but going forward, more "sophisticated strategies" are needed; he added that Tuskegee was an educational institution, "not a place for the professional civil rights advocate." The *Tuskegee News* editors called it a "wise statement."[139]

For a time, the legacy of Tuskegee's founder and that of its fallen student martyr appeared to be in direct competition. To some, Younge's murder gave urgency to the calls for Black Power and sweeping change, and the acquittal of his murderer revealed the true nature of White Power. To others, the militants had simply gone too far. An anonymous

The Campus Digest

VOLUME XXXV   TUSKEGEE INSTITUTE, ALABAMA, MONDAY, DECEMBER 19, 1966   NUMBER 10

Slayer Goes Free; Students Riot

MORE THAN 1500 STUDENTS converged upon the business district of Tuskegee Friday, December 9, 1966. The marchers ended their vigil with a rock-throwing finale. Storefronts and other properties underwent damages from the angry students. Coming in the middle of the demonstration, a historic statue received a change of dress. Students are shown seated on the lawn of the Square before the statue was painted. See the complete story on page 3.

U-M Exchange Students Enroll Next Semester

MAJ. ROBERT L. FAIRCHILD (l.) has been recently awarded the Bronze star. Lt. Col. Reginald Crocker, head of the local Army R.O.T.C., pins the medal on Fairchild. The Bronze star was presented Maj. Fairchild for his outstanding efforts during his tour of duty in Viet Nam.

ANN ARBOR—Ten University of Michigan students have been selected to participate in the academic exchange program with Tuskegee Institute for the winter semester. The students will enroll at the U-M for the winter semester but attend regular classes at The Institute in Tuskegee, Alabama. Academic work taken at Tuskegee is considered an extension of residence rather than a transfer of credit; grades and credit hours earned there will be recorded at the U-M.

Juniors selected include Daniel Darrah, **Livonia**; **Linda** Hawkins, **Harvey, Illinois**; Diane Renver, **Detroit**; Charlene Richardson, **Detroit**; and Kenneth Siegel, **Flint**.

Sophomores chosen include David Bianco, **Dearborn**; Joyce Cain, **Bay City**; Julia Moore, **Whittaker, Michigan**; Charles Tyler, **Flint**; and Steven Unger, **Ferndale**.

This is the second year in which U-M students have enrolled for courses at Tuskegee. Last winter seven students participated in the program.

Currently Augustine X. Nicholas, Gwendolyn L. Hester, Charles L. Hayden, Barbara J. Mahone, Larry J. Jones, Lee D. Packer, Ruffer Johnson, David D. Godfrey, and James E. Green are enrolled at the University of Michigan for the fall semester. Eight of them are students in the college of Literature, Science, a n d the Arts and one is a student in the School of Education.

The students chosen represent a wide cross section of academic pursuits including psychology, philosophy, microbiology, speech, anthropology; education, pre-law, linguistics and English.

Selection was made by a committee headed by John Chavis, coordinator of special projects in U-M's Office of Academic Affairs.

Students Respond
"Open Season On Negroes"

The CAMPUS DIGEST asked students of the Institute to comment on the verdict rendered in the Sammy Younge killing. Replies were lucid and freely given. A segment of these replies follows.

Jimmy Jacobs—Physics Major—Tampa, Fla.
"If it is coming to a time when the white man can kill and go scott free then what is going to be the outcome?"

Whitehead—Grad. Student—B'ham
"It is a typical case, a White man killing a Negro. The results of the case were not surprising. The events that are to follow will also be typical—protests and criticisms.

Walter Gross—Physics Instructor
It is the criticism of 300 years racism in this country. I am not surprised that this murdering of oppressed Non-white people is typical of American policy both at home and abroad. Both Governor Wallace, who has instigated this sor of actions and President Johnson have done nothing to prevent it and are equally responsible for this travesty of justice. Johnson is more interested in killing people in Viet Nam."

Fritz Latham—Interior Decorating—Jackson, Miss.
"It is saying that the white man is just ruling the South."

George Harp Gadsden—Industrial Ed.—Charleston, S. C.
"This is one example of Southern justice and until the Negro learns to stand tall and walk like a dragon what happened will happen again . . . again and again."

Demetrius Clifton—Vet Med.—Statesboro, Ga.
"I think it is an injustice to the city of Tuskegee for allowing the trial to be moved to Opelika. I think that the citizens of Tuskegee should have put forth more iniative and effort in seeing that the trial remained here.

Richard Powell—Grad. Student—New Orleans
"It proved one thing, it is open season on Negroes and you don't need a liscense to hunt . . . just be a white man."

Eugene Johnson—Counselor in Res. "D"—New York
"I would rather be in Viet Nam if this is justice. Why send Negroes to Viet Nam when they can get killed here? I know that there are a lot of advanced R.O.T.C. cadets who are scared to express their candid opinions on the Viet Nam issue—well, that's too bad."

Earnest Fields—Physical Ed.—Natzreg, Miss.
"I can't say nothing about that, is is unbelievable, American Justice is pathetic."

James Stewart—Electronics—B'ham
"It ain't nothing to say about it. The trial was nothing but a formality no matter what county it was held in."

FIGURE 3.4. Front page of the *Campus Digest*, December 19, 1966.

white Tuskegee merchant, invoking the proud legacy of Booker T. Washington, ridiculed Black Power as essentially a slogan of vandalism and burglary. "Are the officials of the Tuskegee Institute going to sit quietly by and thus show their approval of this Black Power jaunt?" he asked.[140] The next month the biracial city council rejected a proposal from Tuskegee students for a permit for a downtown march to commemorate the first anniversary of Younge's murder.[141] The black sheriff who owed his office to the students agreed. Amerson let it be known that, in his opinion, "no worthwhile purpose is going to be served by continuing demonstrations and uproars in the city."[142] In truth, the uproars were just getting started.

A "Freak Factory"

The political transformation of many of Tuskegee's young people during 1966 and 1967 led them to question the nature of their education. They were changed as people and as students. When Sammy Younge was murdered, they saw the school as culpable—Tuskegee's historic policy of accommodating white supremacy had resulted in the murder of one of their own, they believed. "Sammy was killed, and we blamed the school," Patton said.[143] Also, as students gained experience challenging and changing city and county politics, their expectations for change on campus grew as well. In the wake of Sammy Younge's murder, students "started making much more demands on the administration to change some of those Neanderthal practices that were still in place," Wendell Paris recalled. "People weren't accepting the old Tuskegee practices that we had."[144] Students simply stopped going to chapel, a trend that was later ratified by the administration: attendance ceased to be mandatory.[145]

Sammy Younge's murder coincided with a shift in black student activism nationwide. Historian Robert Cohen notes that, while black students were crucial to initiating, in 1960, the mass phase of the civil rights movement, they were slower than white students to take aim at their own campuses.[146] It wasn't until the spring of 1966 that black student unions began to appear, for example.[147] Tuskegee played a leading role in developing a conscious movement of students thinking about their role as students. In April 1966, Tuskegee hosted the first annual Student Human Relations Conference, attended by students and professors from ten Alabama colleges. Featured speakers included Bettina Aptheker, Stokely Carmichael, William Kunstler, Howard Zinn, and Gwen Patton, with performances from Joan Baez and Judy Collins. Attendees decried the state of black colleges, criticized heavy-handed administration, and strategized about how to democratize higher education.[148] The next semester Patton took her campus organizing skills on the road, resigning from student government to accept a position as a "campus traveler" for the human relations project of the United States National Student Association.[149]

Tuskegee was both ahead of the times and behind them. Tuskegee Institute had promoted change off campus but not on campus. Tuskegee faculty had led the charge for voting rights, and the administration signed off on the TICEP program, sending students into the Black Belt as tutors just as civil rights activism was heating up, but the educational experience in classes and on campus went unexamined.[150] "Tuskegee was so backwards," Michael Wright said, that "in 1966 there was only one 'Negro history' class in the entire college. And the students had to fight tooth and nail for that."[151] The kinds of ideas that flowed freely in the SNCC-sponsored Freedom Schools were, for the most part, not yet available in Tuskegee classrooms.[152] In the summer of 1966, Wright addressed an "Open Letter to Black Youth," to advertise what they would learn in Freedom Schools, especially the history of Africa. "We really have something beautiful to identify with," he wrote, "and I ain't talking about the white man's history that we study in Social Studies in school."[153] In 1966 and 1967, students began expressing the desire for similar changes in Tuskegee's classrooms.

In these years, students, faculty, and even trustees reevaluated Tuskegee's historic role in relation to white supremacy and to the larger society. "Is it our role to assume the qualities of the white educational structure, or must we direct our development along different lines?" Ernest Stephens asked in the *Campus Digest* in the fall of 1966.[154] In their own way, the trustees were asking themselves the same question at the same time: how could Tuskegee prove itself invaluable to southern society in a moment of turmoil and change? One white trustee suggested that Tuskegee Institute needed to "show the South what it could do educationally and socially" before tapping southern donors.[155] For many students, what Tuskegee "could do" was clear: it could help them to "make it" in society.[156] Professor Arnold Kaufman thought that most Tuskegee students were "apathetic" because "they fear that civil rights militancy could endanger their future career success."[157] At the end of 1966, Gwen Patton was part of a minority of students who wanted black colleges to focus more on social change and less on training students to climb the American ladder. In an op-ed for the *Southern Courier*, Patton argued that the future of black colleges was in doubt if they didn't "wake up" and "start thinking BLACK."[158]

By 1967, however, Patton's sentiment had become an organized current. Seventy-five students, SNCC workers (including H. Rap Brown, Courtland Cox, and George Ware), some faculty (Nathan Hare from Howard), and Tuskegee deans gathered for a National Student Association conference at Tuskegee Institute in February to discuss the state of black colleges. Students debated whether black colleges were just "service stations for white society," or whether white people needed to be "kicked out" in order to reorient the school toward teaching black people about their own interests.[159] LeRoi Jones came to Tuskegee that month and told an audience that college is "a freak factory" and that black colleges produce students who are "half white."[160] Jones's visit prompted protest in the pages of the *Tuskegee News* for his use of coarse language ("gutter talk") when reading his poems about life in Newark. A Tuskegee student replied, poignantly, that it would make more sense to be "shocked at the fact of the obscene ghetto, not at the words a poet might use to describe the experience of being caged there."[161]

The political state of Tuskegee's student body in the spring of 1967 is probably best described as polarized. Warren Hamilton was elected student body president by a margin of only forty votes out of roughly one thousand cast, squeaking by an opponent who tried to hurt him by playing up Hamilton's association with "outside" influences, especially SNCC.[162] At the very moment that black students at Alabama State College were marching in large numbers, boycotting a new student center building, and presenting the administration with demands,[163] some Tuskegee faculty and students complained of student apathy, that classmates "glide[d]" through four years without becoming "excited" by Vietnam, the draft, or "tyrannical administrative policies."[164] A visiting student, Tony Mohr, reported that the atmosphere was neither academic nor radical, that there were "undercurrents" of black nationalism and civil rights activism present at Tuskegee, but that they were "buried in the frenzy of student government activities, parties, fraternities, sororities."[165] Mohr's piece provoked a debate in the *Campus Digest* about Tuskegee and what it could or should be. One professor argued that the entire freshman year should be "scrapped" and replaced with "Negro-African studies."[166]

As similar ideas began spreading among black students nationally, one of the first comprehensive proposals to reformulate the role of black colleges as educational institutions was published in the spring of 1967 in the civil rights journal *Freedomways*, by a Tuskegee graduate student (and friend of Sammy Younge), Ernest Stephens.[167] Stephens may have been inspired by a manifesto produced at Howard University that semester calling for the "overthrow of the Negro college" and its replacement by a "militant black university."[168] Thinking along similar lines, Stephens asked, "How long will it be before black leaders and educators take hold of Negro colleges and transform them from 'training schools for Negroes' into universities designed to fit the real needs of black people in this nation?"[169] The problem with black colleges, he argued, was that they "programmed" students "in white supremacy and self-hatred," with "little or no emphasis" on a "realistic analysis of the Negro's plight."

Furthermore, "compulsory religious and military activities are examples of indoctrination, not education," Stephens wrote. Black colleges suffer, he argued, from the fact that they are controlled by white-dominated boards of trustees. "If the tone of education at Negro universities strays too far from white sanction," he wrote, "the university will suffer financial loss."[170]

Stephens proposed an education that would help students to grapple with the realities of black life. "The black university should speak to the needs of the nation by speaking first to the needs of its oppressed black population," he wrote. This meant rethinking the curriculum to include 350 years of oppression, since, as he put it, there "can be no realistic solutions to black oppression until the problems are clearly understood." Trustees, administrators, and faculty were not likely to push through this program, Stephens believed. "If these changes are to become a reality in the black university, students themselves must initiate them." Students should not be surprised, however, to find that their "struggle for liberation is suppressed within the very framework of our own black educational institutes."[171]

In the September issue of *Negro Digest* Tuskegee students could read another landmark proposal for revising the paradigm of black colleges, written by their former professor Charles Hamilton.[172] Black students are not like other students, Hamilton argued. They have been shaped by their deliberate exclusion from the benefits and services of society. "In our haste and quest to make middle-class people out of black students," he wrote, "we have probably overlooked the fact that those black people have insights that we should heed." Hamilton laid out a proposal for a different type of college. "I propose a black college revolutionary in its purposes, revolutionary in its procedures, revolutionary in its goals." Instead of a college oriented toward the technocratic, dominant white society, "I propose a black college that would quickly understand that Western technology is not the criterion of greatness." Instead of a college mired in self-hatred, "I propose a black college that would deliberately strive to inculcate a sense of racial pride and anger and concern in its students." Hamilton even suggested that "one of the criteria for graduating summa cum laude would be the demonstrated militancy of the candidate."[173] Michael Wright endorsed Hamilton's "Black University" idea in a letter he drafted to Tuskegee students, indicting Tuskegee as a symbol of the "sickness" that plagued higher education.[174]

Students continued to debate the meaning of Black Power for Tuskegee Institute in the pages of the *Campus Digest*. "There is a revolution going on," *Digest* editor James Norton Jr. wrote in November 1967. "This revolution is a change from a white-conscious environment to one which exemplifies black consciousness or consciousness of self." Norton cited the tendency of black people to imitate white people. But now that was changing, he wrote. "There is a growing awareness of Negro culture. Negroes are beginning to realize the greatness and beauty which surrounds their culture." Norton concluded with a call to fashion: "So black brothers and sisters, wear your afros, African clothing and whatever that exemplifies the culture which we have been deprived of for so long a time."[175] Thomas Schmidt wrote a letter the next week in reply, arguing that Norton only described the "external trappings" of the revolution. The deeper meaning of black culture, Schmidt argued, is to not separate intellectual and emotional elements of experience, but to unite them.[176] While only a minority of students engaged this debate, it was undoubtedly an influential minority. And one Tuskegee student (Ernest Stephens) and one former Tuskegee professor (Charles Hamilton) authored two foundational texts of what became a movement to transform black colleges nationwide. For these activists, applying the ideas of Black Power to higher education meant rejecting the dominant "white" perspectives focused on individual advancement and encouraging educational forms that reinforced the collective goals of social change on a global scale. This radical internationalist perspective was an essential aspect of the black movement of the 1960s and 1970s.[177] At Tuskegee, students who adopted this perspective clashed with the school's long-standing tradition as a center of military training.[178]

A Global Struggle

At the start of the calendar year 1967, Sammy Younge had been dead for one year and his murderer had recently been acquitted. Younge's death prompted SNCC to come out against the Vietnam War, and Tuskegee students successfully campaigned to elect the first black sheriff in the South since Reconstruction. As Black Power seemed to sweep across the continent of Africa, Tuskegee students had begun thinking about what a "postcolonial" society in Macon County would look like. As the year progressed, however, the international perspectives of student activists collided with Tuskegee's historic collaboration with the American government and its proud military history. The war in Vietnam and the resistance to apartheid in South Africa both became central issues on campus.

Tuskegee retained its military training program in these years, but the "hearts and minds" of students and faculty were in doubt. In 1967 Tuskegee's annual ROTC parade was interrupted by half a dozen student protesters, including Michael Wright and Chester Higgins Jr., who joined the crowd carrying signs that read, "We Protest the Draft" and "No Viet Cong Ever Called Me a Nigger"—the latter slogan a reference to Muhammad Ali's famous defense of his own refusal to fight in Vietnam.[179] As Higgins mingled with the ceremony crowd, two young women in attendance saw he was holding an anti-war petition and stopped to sign it. "For my brother," one woman said, "he's in Viet Nam."[180] The next month a full-page ad ran in the *Campus Digest* with a headline quoting Martin Luther King's bombshell speech in Harlem calling the United States the "greatest purveyor of violence in the world today."[181] Amazingly, 140 faculty and students signed their names to the ad, protesting the "oppressive" war in Vietnam and calling for a ten-minute silent vigil on campus.[182]

Some Tuskegee student activists became directly connected to national and even international anti-war forums. Back in 1965, Gwendolyn Patton told the *Digest* that she did not know enough to comment on the

Vietnam War.[183] Just two years later she argued that it was a "racist war," that black people should be on the side of the global revolution (the Vietnamese side!), and that "this country was built on racism and imperialism."[184] Patton later signed on as a full-time worker for the Student Mobilization Committee (affiliated with the Young Socialist Alliance) to organize students nationwide against the war.[185] Patton wasn't the only Tuskegee student activist making such global connections. George Ware was one of two SNCC members to travel to Havana with Stokely Carmichael to speak about Black Power and the Vietnam War.[186] The Tuskegee administration could not stop alumni like Ware from speaking out, but they could try to give equal time to pro-military voices on campus.

Anti-war activists and pro-war US officials debated American policy in person before audiences of Tuskegee students in 1967, particularly in reference to US government support for apartheid in South Africa. South African activists spoke at Tuskegee Institute that year on more than one occasion, encouraging students to make connections between political situations an ocean apart, and calling out the US role in propping up the South African regime. Dennis Brutus, who later shared a jail cell with Nelson Mandela, came to campus and indicted the US government for helping to preserve apartheid.[187] Reporting on a Tuskegee forum on Africa and Afro-Americans, the *Campus Digest* editors summed up the connections: "Our causes are identical," they wrote. "We are united, united as one against a common oppressor." They called for Tuskegee students to "throw off the psychological veils of misconceptions" and "see for ourselves what this African heritage is about."[188] In late November, Forman led a symposium on South African politics attended by three hundred Tuskegee students. Calling the US policy toward South Africa "racist," a South African exile told the crowd that "economic and political power . . . is the answer." "We're not Americans, brother," Forman said, echoing the previous speaker. "We are victims of the US force which has colonized black people all around the world." In a sign of shifting attitudes on campus, the State Department representative G. Edward Clark, also an invited speaker at the forum, tried to defend the US position, but received only boos from the audience.[189] At no other point in Tuskegee's history could such a response to a white guest speaker have been conceivable.

The Governor's Revenge

The radicalization of Tuskegee students over these two years did not go unnoticed or unopposed. In published accounts and interviews, some of the activists have stressed the role of the Tuskegee administration and of President Foster in trying to retard the student movement.[190] Guy Trammell, Ernest Stephens's brother, took a more sympathetic view. Foster excelled at finances and budgeting, Trammell said, but wasn't as well equipped to respond to the students' requests for educational change on campus. He suggested the analogy of a child wearing a formal suit. "If you're thinking about keeping the same suit on junior and he's grown up," Trammell said, "it just doesn't fit anymore."[191] Indeed, although Foster had broken with tradition by supporting civil and voting rights activism on the part of faculty and students, he seemed determined to keep students from outgrowing that particular "suit." However, there is evidence, presented above, that, in 1966 and 1967 Foster continued to work behind the scenes to defend students' right to take part in protests. Foster's management of students, trustees, and politicians meant that Tuskegee Institute was not completely "unglued" in these years, and may explain the late emergence of a movement to transform the campus.

In 1966 and 1967 the most intense pushback came not from within the campus community but from without. In these years, in a historic reversal, Tuskegee Institute came to be perceived by the governor of the state of Alabama as an enemy of the status quo. George Wallace and his wife and successor, Lurleen, openly despised the school. Lurleen Wallace followed in her husband's footsteps, staunchly opposing desegregation, creating greater tension with Tuskegee Institute, whose administration, faculty, and students were increasingly visible as desegregation advocates. The voting rights struggle described in chapter 1 was the first break between the state leadership and the school. School desegregation was the second. In March 1967 a federal court ordered all Alabama schools to desegregate.[192] Lurleen Wallace opposed the plan, while Tuskegee community members—including student Chester Higgins and others—gave public testimony in favor.[193] Two months later, in May 1967, Governor Lurleen Wallace proposed a budget for the following year that did not include an appropriation for Tuskegee, rupturing an eighty-six-year tradition of state support.[194]

Lurleen Wallace's attitude did not necessarily reflect that of Alabama's elite or that of other sections of the American ruling class, who continued to support Tuskegee Institute. George Wallace made a name for himself in national politics as a staunch segregationist, a position he clung to long after other southern leaders had decided that segregation was expendable. On a personal level, Wallace was known for meting out harsh reprisals against anyone who crossed him.[195] The *Southern Courier* editors believed that the move to defund Tuskegee Institute was George Wallace's way of seeking "revenge" because the school had broken away from its historic relationship with the state, allowing oppositional people and ideas on campus.[196] The liberal *Tuskegee News* editors agreed that "evidence of reprisal is clear" in the governor's education budget.[197] The appropriation in question was about $650,000, or 5 percent of Tuskegee's $13 million budget.[198] Foster estimated the state appropriation at 11.6 percent of Tuskegee's total budget, claiming that it subsidized 53 percent of the student body.[199] The Wallaces' disapproval did not seem to be widespread among their class. Tuskegee continued to receive support elsewhere. In 1967 the Ford Foundation gave $300,000 to Tuskegee to advance scientific research on "race relations."[200] Southern elites had not yet abandoned hope in the school, either. The Wallaces were unable to convince Alabama's politicians that Tuskegee was a threat. The Alabama State Senate voted almost unanimously (26–1) in early August 1967 to restore $470,000 a year in funding to Tuskegee for two years.[201] Governor Lurleen Wallace signed the bill, though she did succeed in stalling the payment for one month.[202]

While Tuskegee Institute won a reprieve, the student movement faced new and challenging obstacles in the years ahead. The intellectual ferment of the movement was exciting, but the brutal reality of racist violence was chilling. Sammy Younge's murder and the acquittal of his murderer deepened the sense among Tuskegee students that they could not trust the system to protect them. This was especially true for students who had been close to Younge. Earlier in the same day that Younge was murdered, a voter registration official in Macon County had pulled a knife on Younge and threatened to "spill [his] guts." Younge's friends promptly reported the incident to the FBI. The *New York Times* reported that FBI officials did enter Macon County soon afterwards—to investigate Younge's murder.[203] Student activists had fought continuously for local white people to comply with federal desegregation orders, but began to realize that federal agents might not be on their side. Gomillion and the faculty built their movement on the basis of appealing to the federal government for intervention, but Tuskegee students increasingly saw themselves as participants in a global struggle, and one that the US government was, at best, unwilling to join and, at worst, opposing. As they radicalized and made common cause with global revolutions, the students demanded democracy in the county and on campus. To carry out that struggle, one could not call upon the FBI, or even the black sheriff of Macon County. To truly make Macon County a center of Black Power, or to transform Tuskegee into a Black University, student radicals could only count on themselves.

4

A Black University? 1968

In 1968 Martin Luther King's prophecy that the bombs in Vietnam would "explode at home" seemed to be coming true, as Tuskegee activists bore witness to the murder of student protesters on a nearby campus. Soon afterwards, the fate of their movement became bound up with the nation's reaction to King's assassination. But even before that moment arrived, Tuskegee's inflexible leadership brought matters to a head. All of a sudden, in 1968, Tuskegee's long-standing political-educational paradigm was turned upside down from the inside. Those most associated with Booker T. Washington's emphasis on practical education—engineering students—took the most militant actions. And Tuskegee's military history and traditions, long a source of pride, became a source of controversy, threatening a relationship with the institution's most important sponsor, the federal government. When students spoke of making Tuskegee Institute a "Black University," their administrators knew that they meant a wide range of on-campus reforms, some of which challenged their priorities. But when the state of Alabama heard the phrase, it took it to mean "revolution," and sent men with rifles and bayonets to Tuskegee's campus for the second time in its history.[1]

The 1968 revolution at Tuskegee Institute began in an unexpected place. By the 1967–1968 school year, leading "scholar-activists" like Gwen Patton and Wendell Paris had graduated, creating an opening for a new crop of leaders to seize the political initiative on campus. On December 12, 1967, Tuskegee's engineering students did just that; they sent a five-page letter to the dean of their department, laying out a series of complaints and recommendations (both in great detail) for improving their course of study. The missive discussed inadequate equipment and the need to upgrade facilities, but circled back again and again to one central problem: poor instruction.[2]

The professors, the engineers wrote, were chronically underprepared, assigning textbooks that they did not use and giving exams that did not match the material discussed in class. For some instructors, the failure rate was "unusually high," and often there was clear "lack of preparation" to teach.[3] In a section called simply "Mandate," the students outlined "directives for immediate implementation," including removal of chronically ineffective instructors; they also demanded that deans conduct classroom visitations, exams be aligned with course material, and the department make necessary equipment available to students. The students demanded an answer to the mandate from the dean by December 14, 1967.[4] That date, and many other deadlines, would come and go before the engineers decided to do more than write letters.

Mandatory participation in the Reserve Officer Training Corps program for male students, meanwhile, was another bone of contention on campus. It was Tuskegee's second president, Robert Russa Moton, who initiated the organization of ROTC on campus, beginning in 1919.[5] The implementation of a fully funded program was part of a political battle for equal treatment of African Americans in the armed forces.[6] Armed black student soldiers bearing the nation's uniform were a provocative sight in those years, particularly in the southern states. ROTC students were a proud part of Tuskegee's legacy, and had even defended the campus from the Klan.[7] Student soldiers remained quite visible in the 1960s, drilling in uniform on campus every Wednesday. "If you went to Tuskegee on a Wednesday," Ronald Hill recalled, "you would think it was a military school."[8] George Geddis, a senior and a leader of the protest movement in 1968, had hoped to advance to the Air Force through ROTC (the Air Force lost interest, he said, when he switched his major to English from engineering).[9] Warren Hamilton came to Tuskegee in 1964 from a black community that had rallied to introduce a Junior ROTC program to its high school. It was a basic question of fairness.

"We didn't have it, and they had it at the white high school," he said.[10] That black students, just a few years later, protested against ROTC is a sign of how far their ideas had traveled.

Massacre in Orangeburg

As in Tuskegee, Alabama, there was a large black middle class in Orangeburg, South Carolina, due to the presence of two historically black college campuses in town: South Carolina State University and Claflin College. At the start of 1968, after several years of bitter desegregation struggles, the only bowling alley in town (and the only one within a forty-mile radius) remained off-limits to black people. In late 1967 the "For White Only" sign was tactfully taken down and replaced with one neatly printed in the new lingo of segregation, "Privately Owned." In early February students from South Carolina State University began protesting the establishment by entering, being denied service, and then repeatedly finding themselves ejected. During a week of protests beginning February 6, police defended the owner's decision to keep black people out, responding to the students in numbers and with violence, swinging clubs and sending several students to the hospital. Students retaliated by smashing windows at white-owned businesses in town and throwing bricks and bottles at police. One student, Henry Smith, an advanced ROTC aspirant, called his mother to explain the violence and the protests. "Sit tight on the campus," his mother advised. "But if you have to go, pray."[11]

On the evening of Thursday, February 8, hundreds of frustrated students built a large bonfire from wood scraps. They hurled more insults than projectiles at police, who surrounded them in great numbers: more than one hundred state patrolmen and National Guard troops gathered nearby, some shouldering their weapons. The troops pushed the students back away from the bonfire, and one of them began to fire on the students, followed immediately by several others. In approximately ten seconds of shooting, bullets hit thirty students, three of whom would soon die of their injuries: Samuel Hammond, Delano Middleton, and Henry Smith. "Who's laughing now?" one policeman said in passing to injured students in the hospital emergency room.[12]

Although white officials insisted on calling it a "riot," among black people the framing of the event matched the divergent response to what had actually happened: it became known as the Orangeburg Massacre.[13] In the aftermath, the presidents of five black colleges (Atlanta University, Clark College, Morehouse College, Morris Brown College, and Spelman College) and of the Interdenominational Theological Center sent an open letter to President Lyndon Johnson, the attorney general, state governors, and local police, calling on them to stop "storm troopers" from invading college campuses.[14] The governor of South Carolina was burned in effigy on black college campuses in Virginia, South Carolina, and North Carolina.[15] A Howard University campus demonstration of sympathy with Orangeburg victims drew almost five hundred students.[16] SNCC decided to send members to Orangeburg from Tuskegee Institute, who, for their own safety, traveled as representatives of their Student Government Association (SGA) instead. Faculty and students raised $112 on campus to send the Tuskegee delegation, which included Melvin Todd, Michael Wright, and Warren Hamilton.[17]

The trip to Orangeburg both terrorized and radicalized the Tuskegee student delegation. "We were on the way to Orangeburg, and we were on a two-lane road, driving kind of fast," Melvin Todd recalled, "and a car comes behind us and pulls right up on the bumper and would not back off." The students had a .38 pistol in the car for protection, and debated when or whether they might need to use it on the road. They wondered, "If he tries to pass, do we shoot at him before he can shoot us? If so," Todd said, "which one of us is going to do it?"[18] When the delegation arrived safely in Orangeburg, there were troops and armored personnel carriers in the streets. Hamilton saw small planes flying low over the Orangeburg campus; it seemed to him "like a military occupation."[19] He also told the *Southern Courier* that he had the opportunity to view the body of one of the slain students. "He had been shot in the chest and the back," he said. "Another boy's back was almost blown out."[20] Local students told him they heard someone shout "Shoot the niggers!" before the police opened fire and that local black people in Orangeburg believed that the KKK controlled the state National Guard.[21] Michael Wright recalled that, when they returned from Orangeburg, the Tuskegee delegation decided to start a new campus organization called Unity. "We realized that the same thing could happen at Tuskegee," he said, "and we had to protect ourselves."[22] Orangeburg "may well be the site of a future racial war," Melvin Todd wrote in a report for the *Campus Digest* that was reprinted in other regional newspapers. The delegation's reports were so shocking that some Tuskegee students reacted with disbelief. After reading his *Digest* article, one classmate asked Todd why he would print lies.[23]

Still, other Tuskegee students were making connections between armed conflict abroad and at home. In mid-February, several representatives of the Nation of Islam (NOI) came to speak to what was reported as an "enthusiastic crowd" on campus. The Vietnam War heralded the end for white rule, NOI minister Louis Farrakhan told Tuskegee students. "The wars are not going to stop until the white man's power to rule is completely broken down," he said.[24] Michael Wright and several other students decided to make this connection more concrete in an act of theatrical solidarity a few weeks later. On February 29, four officials from the US State Department came to Tuskegee to defend the Vietnam War in a campus forum. The first had just begun to speak when Michael Wright rushed to the front of the hall with a sign and a brown bag full of raw eggs. Several white professors called out from the audience accusations that the panelists were "murderers."[25] Wright shouted the words printed on his placard: "Inasmuch as our Vietnamese brothers don't have adequate . . . air force to do their bombing, we black brothers will help them." Four or five other students then helped him pelt the panelists with eggs before dashing out of the room.[26] The administration began proceedings to have Wright expelled, giving Unity its first call to action.[27]

Unrest

In March, Tuskegee student grievances reached a boiling point. That month, the administration was unable to isolate the relatively small group of students who pushed the movement forward, primarily because those leaders wisely hewed closely to the demands supported by the largest number of their peers: ending compulsory ROTC participation, granting athletic scholarships, increasing student power in governance, and supporting the engineering students. That there needed to be more Afro-American- and African-oriented curricula rapidly became common sense, also. This combination of demands, some to effectively upgrade Tuskegee's offerings and increase student decision-making power, and others that linked the university's curriculum to the broader concerns of the global black movement, is what student organizers began to call the "Black University concept."

As administrators moved to take action against Michael Wright and his fellow protesters, Unity leaflets tacked between affirmations of politicized blackness and attempts to defend students' rights and student power. A March 1 leaflet (unsigned, but presumably issued by Unity) called administrators "indigenous uncle Toms" for attacking anti-war protesters as they challenged an attempt by the State Department to "brainwash" black students. The authors resolved, in the very masculine language of many Black Power activists in those years, that they "as Black men" would "carry on the struggle for Liberation of all oppressed and exploited people," asking students, "Which side are you on?"[28] Two days later another leaflet registered a new approach, calling for students to specifically defend Michael Wright on the premise that his case represented an assault on students' rights. The authors acknowledged that "many students believe that the actions of Michael Wright (and possibly others) were wrong but don't justify being expelled from school." The administration's charging of Wright and others with "conduct unbecoming" of a Tuskegee student set a dangerous precedent by using such an "elastic" criterion, the leaflet argued.[29] This temporary strategic retreat from attacking the broader issue of the war to the narrower issue of student expulsions was probably a wise move; it may have reflected a recognition that the February 29 egg-throwing action was a few steps ahead of what "many students" were ready to support, and displayed tactical savvy on the part of student activists interested in building the broadest possible base for future actions.

No doubt sensing the gathering storm, on March 7 the administration arranged for an all-Institute meeting where students would be allowed to air their grievances, provided they submit them in writing in advance. Unity threatened an all-student boycott without "free-flowing" dialogue, but called it off after the acting chair of Unity had the opportunity of "conferring with the President."[30] The all-Institute meeting proceeded as planned, but there is no record of the discussion. It is likely that no amount of talking could overcome the basic problem: students wanted to move as quickly as possible, and the administration tried to move as slowly as possible. Each day student demands went unmet, the student movement's resolve deepened and strengthened. The underlying issue of power—who would decide the content and pace of reform at Tuskegee Institute?—was just below the surface. And then Stokely Carmichael returned to campus.[31]

Bringing Carmichael to campus offered an opportunity to once again assert the connection between student power and the ideas of Black Power. Unable to successfully move the administration on other issues, student activists asserted their control in an area where they had greater autonomy: the selection of outside speakers. Carmichael, then at the height of his fame, naturally drew a flock of reporters. Student organizers, however, decided that Carmichael's speech would be for black people only, and white people (in this case, all of the journalists who arrived) would not be permitted to enter. This decision immediately raised alarm bells; white visitors had never been barred from Tuskegee's campus in its entire history. A local television news program featured an on-camera editorial, "Monday Night's Incident at Tuskegee," claiming that reporters and photographers were "bodily ejected" by non-student

SNCC members; campus officials briefly got them in, only to ask them to leave moments later, fearing that "the militant attitude of some SNCC leaders would lead to a confrontation," the editorial stated. The broadcast attempted to frame the issue of power as originating in the presence of outside agitators: "The general impression of the reporters who were there was that SNCC and not the Student Government group or the Tuskegee Administration . . . was in control and running the show."[32] The editorial may have falsely posed the "outsider" issue, but the matter of control was very real.

March 20 was a day of reckoning: Foster met with a delegation from the Ad-hoc Committee for the Advancement of the School of Engineering (ACASE), although the content of the discussion is unknown; separately, five students were placed on probation for participating in an "unauthorized meeting"; roughly three hundred students marched to Foster's home on the outskirts of campus, and someone threw a projectile through his window.[33] The *Campus Digest* and Unity leaflets both reported that student leaders Michael Wright and Warren Hamilton worked to prevent further "hot-headed" actions at Foster's house by organizing students into discussion groups on the spot.[34] Those groups voted to endorse five resolutions: ROTC should be voluntary, curfews for juniors and seniors should be eliminated, restrictions on student living arrangements should be removed, health services should be improved, and students should be allowed to make up lost time on work-study assignments.[35] Meanwhile, another collection of students showed up at the faculty meeting that day and tried unsuccessfully to present a petition of clemency for students penalized for protesting. The students listened to faculty deliberations about how to deal with the student movement. One instructor was heard to say that the activism was the result of a "malignancy" in the student body. He warned that they needed to "take action now" to "get rid of the cancer."[36]

Foster apparently concurred. On March 21 he issued another stern missive to the entire Tuskegee community. Events were becoming "increasingly serious" and "threaten the continued operation of Tuskegee's program for the remainder of the year," he wrote. Foster cited unauthorized meetings on campus and the projectile—a piece of concrete—thrown through his window. For the first time, he mentioned that he was thinking about closing the school entirely.[37] That morning, two students—Burns Machobane and Chester Higgins Jr.—witnessed the swirl of protests: "students from the school of Engineering had placards raised high and were marching in front of Huntington Hall," and "determined and adamant young ladies with 'natural' hairdos sat blocking the entrance in a manner that indicated there would be no classes that day." Higgins decided to create an archive of the tumult by systematically collecting the daily flood of documents. The resulting 166-page documentary volume, *Student Unrest, Tuskegee Institute: A Chronology*, published in 1968, is the most comprehensive record of the textual evidence available: every memo, leaflet, letter, and transcript he could find.[38]

One thing that comes through quite clearly in *Student Unrest* is the role of the engineering students in pushing forward a cause that was widely perceived by the broader student body to be just: raising the standard of education. On March 21, the day after it met with President Foster, ACASE issued a "to whom it may concern" letter essentially stating that it had tried to go through "due process" and gotten nowhere. Now, the engineers declared, they were willing to boycott and picket classes, and contact the press.[39] Interestingly, they insisted that their militancy was not to be confused with radicalism. On the same day, in a separate letter from ACASE to the faculty, the engineers emphasized, "We are not part of any other organization. We do not follow any leaders except our own elected officers, we are not a subset of any Black Power organization."[40] Thus, the students essentially disavowed the context that gave their protest force. At the same time, their department's leadership refused to concede any ground. The *Campus Digest* reported that Dean Dybczak, head of the School of Engineering, appeared on a local TV show the following day (March 22) and claimed that the engineering students were led by outside agitators and were trying to "lower" the school's standards.[41]

Engineering students, if they received adequate preparation and actually graduated, had promising futures ahead of them. AT&T, General Electric, IBM, Xerox, Bell System, Ford, Western Electric, Pan American World Airways (Guided Missiles Range Division), Pan American Petroleum (division of Standard Oil), and other corporations paid frequently for advertising space in the *Campus Digest* to recruit students.[42] While most 1960s black student activists were concentrated in humanities departments, it was Tuskegee's engineering students who systematically escalated their actions in 1968, and provided an anchor for the broader student movement. The engineering students were not, in the first instance, motivated by broader social justice aims. Rather, they were fighting for Tuskegee to live up to the promises of its existing educational program. In the context of heavy corporate recruitment, this was a high-stakes struggle, and one that led them into coalition with leftward-moving students.

The "cancer" continued to spread over the next few days. Of course, there were "outside" agitators (from SNCC especially), but by the spring of 1968 their focus was mostly elsewhere; Tuskegee's spring was a home-grown revolt. On March 22 the administration cancelled all classes to arrange more discussions.[43] In the evening, twenty-seven students and faculty members met to forge a consensus for common action. They agreed to focus on two issues: ROTC and athletic scholarships.[44] No self-appointed leaders could stop other demands from circulating, however. In the context of a mobilized student body, making demands and seeing some of them met, other students began thinking about what they would like to see changed, too. A student from the Electronics Division wrote to the *Campus Digest* complaining of the high student-faculty ratio, the scarcity of laboratory equipment, and the generally dirty and "deplorable" conditions of the division. The piece was titled, "What about Us?"[45] For Bert Phillips, the man who had, more than anyone else, always worked to reconcile the students' right to protest with the priorities of the administration, the situation on campus became increasingly untenable. On March 23, the student paper reported that Phillips was

FIGURE 4.1. A typical full-page corporate recruitment advertisement aimed at Tuskegee students. *Campus Digest*, October 19, 1968.

resigning his post as dean of students.[46] He was leaving, he said, "because of actions, inactions, and reactions of the students, faculty, and administrators over the past few weeks."[47] His resignation would take effect in two and a half weeks, on April 10. In 1968, however, two and half weeks was a very long time.

The student movement gained strength day by day, transgressing beyond the administration's expectations of what was reasonable or necessary. On March 25, activists were able to mobilize broader layers of the student body. They called for a boycott of classes; students who were reluctant to participate encountered picket lines blocking their entrance to at least three buildings.[48] An unsigned leaflet explained that although "we appreciate the effort of Dr. Foster to suspend classes last Friday," those discussions were insufficient, so "we will remain out of class until all problems are resolved."[49] A possibly apocryphal scene capturing the clash between faculty and students was relayed to visiting professor James Torrens, a white Jesuit who arrived at Tuskegee to teach in the fall. "Ada Peters was an elegant, brisk schoolmarm," he wrote, describing one of his colleagues, a black woman from Maine. When Peters arrived to teach her class one spring day, she was blocked:

> "You can't go in there, Miz Peters," one of the militants told her, "I'll lay right down here in front of the door." "Lie!" she corrected him indignantly, and walked in.[50]

No class meant mass meetings in the open air, a show of force that got results. Warren Hamilton spoke to a crowd of a thousand students who gathered in front of the administrative building: "We want our education to be relevant to us—that's what this is all about," he said. Foster was correct that the activists indeed were "a relatively small fraction," but for a time they connected with a much larger group of students. Mary Ellen Gale reported for the *Southern Courier* that senior class president William Clark elicited "wild applause" from a crowd representing roughly one-third of the student body when he said, "Viet Nam is someone else's war—our war is here!"[51] Foster was no doubt aware that he could not isolate the "fraction" and that further discussions were useless. By the end of the day he granted several concessions to the students, including the immediate reinstatement of the student judicial system, extended library hours, and the availability of all syllabi at the beginning of each semester. Remaining issues were deferred to other bodies: Foster recommended that all departments consider whether faculty should be required to have research publications; acknowledged that students would hold a referendum on athletic scholarships; and said that students should be invited to the April 6 meeting of the trustees to make a presentation on ROTC.[52]

With some victories under their belts, most students returned to class on March 26.[53] That day a TV editorial agreed that Tuskegee student demands were valid, but only up to a point. It warned viewers of the danger that a "militant minority" might try to take over.[54] In March, however, the most militant minority was not the students gathered around SNCC, but those enrolled in the School of Engineering. On March 27 they boycotted all classes, physically barred faculty from entering the department building, and left the administration's latest reply to their demands burning in a nearby trash can.[55] Their militant stance earned respect and support from their fellow students. Non-engineering students joined demonstrations outside the building they occupied. The engineers drew praise and admiration for methodically pursuing their demands, at each step willing and able to escalate. "It is impossible," James Norton Jr. editorialized in the Campus Digest, "to not admire the cool, professional and dead-serious attitude that they have shown during the period of protest."[56]

The Death of Nonviolence

In the first eight days of April 1968, the conflict between students and administrators on Tuskegee's campus became a matter of life and death. Not since Sammy Younge's murder two years earlier had the stakes seemed so high. On their own, the issues yet unresolved were not lethal. The call to make ROTC voluntary flowed from growing animosity toward the brutal war in Vietnam. Athletic scholarships would help to secure a place on campus for many students who otherwise would have difficulty affording tuition. Engineering students dug in their heels over the replacement of professors because without new ones they felt unable to succeed in courses, and consequently, in the field. Underlying these concerns was the question of who was in charge, the students or the administration. The students never proposed themselves as a replacement for the faculty or the administration, but they insisted on the power to have a say in the matter of their education. The first eight days of April were the highest expression of this long-standing tension on Tuskegee's campus, rivaled only by the student strikes of 1903 and 1940.

The events at Tuskegee might not have been so dangerous, however, had it not been for the assassination of Martin Luther King on the fourth day of April, 1968. His death, and the uprising of black people that followed in 125 American cities, meant that any collective action by black people in Alabama, even on a private college campus like Tuskegee Institute, was treated by the state as a mortal threat. The students wanted reform, but the state of Alabama responded like it was revolution.

The very first day of April 1968 began with threats and defiance. President Foster wrote a letter to the engineering students expressing satisfaction that they were close to an agreement on all issues except one. In his view, the reasonable thing now was for classes to resume. He explained that he would conduct a referendum among engineering students, asking, Will you come to class on Tuesday April 2, yes or no? If no, he threatened to take steps to suspend the engineering program for the rest of the year. The students replied the following day to say that they did not want their department closed, but rather wanted the issues resolved, particularly the problem of ineffective faculty. The engineers sought broader support, writing an open letter to their fellow students. They repeated Foster's threat, and warned that students should "be aware of the fact that at any time he could decide to close your school too." Engineers called for students to assemble outside Moton Hall at 11:00 a.m. to show their support.[57]

While the engineers rallied, a group of approximately thirty students gathered separately to plan next steps for the broader movement. "We weren't getting anywhere with Foster," George Geddis recalled, so the discussion shifted to what to do with the upcoming meeting with the trustees on April 6. Geddis was the president of the student theater, so he was able to make that space available for "plotting" and as a "staging area" for the protest.[58] Michael Wright was there, and spent much of the time drafting what became known as the "Mandate" document, including its preface, outlining the Black University concept. The "Mandate" was far from "revolutionary," Wright recalls, but included reforms that the students felt were realistic. "They were concessions that we knew they could make without harming any of the operations," Wright said. "It would just harm the reputation of the place of Tuskegee's elite with the political class that runs this country," he continued. "But that's their problem."[59] According to his handwritten affidavit, Wright stayed in the theater overnight in early April for several days.[60]

The document that emerged from the theater (the "Mandate") was an eighteen-page catalog of proposals for reforming Tuskegee.[61] Some were more far-reaching than others. As Wright indicated, many of the items were easily actionable. Other, more philosophical points raised in the "Black University Concept" in the first two pages would have required greater revision of Tuskegee's political-educational paradigm. In fact, there is a significant political distance between pages 1–2 and pages 3–18. The first two were unsigned, although participants agree that they were written by Michael Wright.[62] At the time he was probably the most politically active undergraduate student on campus, and the text expresses his vision of connecting the Tuskegee student movement to a broader struggle for democracy and justice. The remaining sixteen pages are also unsigned,[63] but they come across as less political and more like a wish list for students who have personal ambitions that go beyond the limitations of their school's offerings.[64] The meaning of "Black Power" and the idea of a "Black University" at Tuskegee in April 1968 are contained in the merger of these two tendencies.

The Black University concept, as Wright defined it in this document, meant a "re-direction of the goals" of Tuskegee such that, ideally, the school "benefits and carries on a perpetual reciprocal relationship with the entire Black community." The purpose should be to speak from and to the black experience, not to "hand America a carbon copy of itself." Wright contrasted "individual concerns" with a "collective ethos," emphasizing that "survival of the Black population is of primary concern." The document continues by briefly outlining two types of "mandates" addressed to "inter-Tuskegee" problems: policies regarding outside speakers and political activities on campus; and academic "revisions" to implement. The text indicates that students and faculty had voted to approve revised policy guidelines, but that "final official endorsement" by the administration was not yet forthcoming. The academic revisions were "major academic and programatic [sic] considerations" for which the students demanded "immediate or as nearly feasible attention as possible." These included a general emphasis on Afro-American history and culture, and specifically the addition of an Afro-American history course as a general requirement, as well as the addition of specific black-oriented tracks of study in sociology, psychology, and "all of the social sciences." Wright also proposed a new African Studies Program, and mandatory Ibo and Swahili courses as foreign language requirements.[65] In this way, some of the "mandates" were actually aimed not at administrators but at students; ROTC would be voluntary, but Ibo and Swahili would be mandatory!

As they gathered in the student theater on April 2, perhaps taking turns at a typewriter, the twenty or thirty students assembled dreamed up their ideas for how to reform Tuskegee Institute. They came up with demands in thirteen domains: faculty research, education, ROTC, the School of Mechanical Industries, engineering, fine arts, music, speech and drama, John Andrews Hospital, a free student theater, withdrawal from courses, checks and balances, and assigning of names to nameless dormitories. Of these, only three were written up to express explicit connection to the "Black University" theme: education, a free student theater, and nameless dormitories.[66] Pages 3–18 lack the philosophical flourish of the first two pages, but make up for it with often (but not always) greater levels of detail and specificity. The document overall feels like a collection of proposals drafted independently of each other. The document also reflects the pressures of the moment, trying to maintain broad support among students and seize an opportunity to make substantive changes.

At Tuskegee Institute in April 1968, invoking the Black University concept served to connect local demands to the global context. With the Black University concept came the Black Power movement and the uprising of black people around the world. Thus the proposal to reform the School of Education stated that professors needed to "be aware of the special problems that are peculiar to Black people, and to provide the essential proficiency in the techniques of dealing with Black people."[67] The page explaining the call for a free student theater proclaims, "Since the theater has chosen to address itself to the expression of *Black* needs, *Black* ideas, and *Black* talent, and since the administration has not [seen] fit to provide us with these things, and has, indeed, attempted to suppress such expression," what had been known as the Little Theater should become a free student theater, they wrote.[68] Without the specific demands for upgrading Tuskegee's academic offerings (research requirements for faculty, improving the Schools of Mechanical Industry and Engineering) and quality of student life (improved service at the hospital, the ability to withdraw from a course at any time), the movement would have lacked numbers on campus, but without the Black University concept, it would have lacked the moral force of the global movement. Tuskegee's students fought for reform under the banner of revolution. Some of Tuskegee's administrators and trustees came to understand this. The State of Alabama did not particularly care to interpret the difference.

By April 3 there was no going back. On that day, Foster offered to continue the student-initiated suspension of all engineering classes pending a settlement of the outstanding issues, on one condition: the engineering students had to relinquish control of their department's building. The students voted to turn down the offer and maintain their occupation. In response, administrators cut off all power and telephones in the building, so the students resorted to using candles and walkie-talkies for light and communication.[69] As the engineers plotted their next steps by candlelight, other students gathered in the Little Theater. They finished typing up their demands, but they prepared to confront the trustees with more than printed words on a page.[70]

Unlike the black elite or the southern segregationists with whom Tuskegee student activists had largely clashed thus far, Tuskegee's trustees were the liberal (and mostly northern) elite. Tuskegee had twenty-three trustees in 1968; five—president Luther Foster, former president Frederick Patterson, Dr. Montague Oliver, president of the board of education in Gary, Indiana, Federal Reserve member Andrew Brimmer, and millionaire businessman and civil rights movement supporter A. G. Gaston—were black and men; only two—congresswoman Frances Bolton of Ohio and Donna Salk, advisor to California's Fair Employment Practices Commission and wife of the famous scientist Jonas Salk—were women (and white).[71] In exchange for partial funding from the state, Tuskegee Institute had granted the governor the ability to appoint five trustees. In 1968 the most radical among them may have been Gaston, and the least was probably Walter Bouldin, president of the Alabama Power Company and member of the deeply conservative Alabama Chamber of Commerce.[72] In total, six were businessmen, six were public officials, three were bankers, and the rest were mostly a collection of lawyers and philanthropists. One notable exception was a retired four-star general, Lucius Clay, who had commanded American forces in Europe during the Second World War.[73] Gaston wasn't the only one left-of-center on the board, however. Melvin Glasser was the director of the social security department of the United Auto Workers, a position he used to advocate for a national health care program.[74] Investment bankers Richard Waddell and William Gridley had both financially supported civil rights activism, and Alexander Aldrich, executive assistant to then New York governor Nelson Rockefeller, had marched with Martin Luther King.[75] These, truly, were the country's liberal elite.[76]

This collection of powerful personalities could not have known that the mounting conflict on the nation's most well-known historically black campus was about to coincide with the assassination of the nation's most well-known black leader. When the trustees arrived on Tuskegee Institute's campus ("in Cadillacs," as Michael Wright recalled), the roughly twenty to thirty students assembled in the Little Theater decided that they should be confronted with protests from the overwhelming majority of students.[77] But the activists had a problem: how would they convince their classmates to come out in such numbers? It's not clear who arrived at the idea, but somehow the activists decided that if they physically locked up classrooms and buildings, students would have no choice in the matter; they would have to gather outside.[78] "That was my part; I had the locks," Ronald Hill remembered. "I locked up all the buildings."[79] Michael Wright remembered that they were thoughtful about which buildings to lock and which not to lock. "We left the cafeteria open, obviously, and we left the recreation room untouched, obviously, because we did not want to alienate 'the base,'" he recalled with a chuckle.[80] Preparations continued into the night and the next day, April 4. But that evening, the laughter stopped. "In the middle of that planning," George Geddis said, "we were watching TV and the news came across: Martin Luther King had just been shot."[81]

It is difficult to overstate the impact of King's assassination. King was murdered in Memphis, where he had traveled to support black sanitation workers who went on strike for union recognition. "African Americans everywhere recognized King's death as a watershed moment that required a massive response," historian Michael Honey writes. "King's death burst the dam of whatever patience held back the rage of Black America at Depression-level unemployment; job, housing, and school discrimination; pervasive police brutality; useless deaths of Black soldiers in Vietnam; and the plethora of ills that stalked the ghettos."[82] The state responded with an unprecedented mobilization of troops on domestic soil; the governor of Tennessee called four thousand National Guard troops to enter Memphis that night.[83] President Johnson ordered the same number to guard the nation's capital, and governors mobilized guardsmen in Chicago, Detroit, Boston, Jackson, Mississippi, Raleigh, North Carolina, and Tallahassee, Florida, to "stem disorders or guard against them."[84] It seemed that King's murder spelled the end of nonviolence as a strategy. In DC, Stokely Carmichael told reporters, "White America has declared war on Black America." There was "no alternative to revolution," and for black people, "the only way they will survive is by getting guns."[85]

"We were in shock," Michael Wright said of his reaction to the news of King's assassination. "My girlfriend . . . loved Martin Luther King beyond any level of love." She worried that Michael and the other student activists would be killed. "She had an existential meltdown," he said. King's death "entirely changed the tone" of the student movement, George Geddis thought. "We became much more sober and much more dedicated. . . . After we got through crying, we focused on the anger and on the dedication to our goals."[86] Cozetta Lamore remembered that after King was murdered, "a small group took charge" and made demands of Tuskegee Institute's administration. The attitude was, "Enough is enough; you killed our leader."[87] Polls published a few days later in the *Campus Digest* indicated the growing resolve: a majority of students agreed on the need to remove inadequate instructors, upgrade academic offerings, support scholarships for athletes, and stand in solidarity with the Unity movement.[88]

On April 5 Tuskegee administrators, faculty, and students were united in grieving and at odds in action. In the morning, many Tuskegee students did not go to class. Michael Wright, Eugene Adams, and a few other activists led flying pickets of roughly three hundred students combined that traveled around campus enforcing a boycott of classes.[89] Students sat-in in all of the administrative buildings. Some students gathered at Dorothy Hall—the site of the trustees' meeting—and demanded that the trustees act on the "Mandate." "Basically, as we're going up the stairs and to the second floor where the meeting was," Geddis recalled, "I was met by a bunch of people," including Dean Phillips, who told them they had to leave.[90] At some point during the day, a local court granted Tuskegee an injunction against student protesters.[91]

We know that some students did get through, however. The trustees recorded in the minutes of their meeting that they met with approximately thirty students that afternoon to discuss a "Mandate"; Foster was excused from the meeting to allow "freer student expression." Ten trustees were absent that day, which meant that only thirteen had arrived in the first place. With Foster out of the room, that left twelve trustees.[92] Thirteen other Tuskegee officials were in the room, however, including lawyers, accountants, auditors, other officers of the university, and two representatives of the Carver Research Foundation.[93] After listening to the students, the trustees argued that it was not fair to insist that they respond—as the students apparently demanded—in just four hours. The students replied that some items could be acted upon immediately, since they did not require additional funds. The trustees replied that they did not have a quorum and were therefore unable to vote. The meeting was adjourned at 7:15 p.m.[94] That evening, the combatants temporarily united, nearly three thousand people in total, by gathering in Logan Hall for a memorial service for King, featuring speeches and singing. The Reverend Raymond Harvey, who led the service, spoke about ongoing injustice in the state of Alabama, but made no mention of the student protests or demands.[95]

Although unspoken the night before, student demands were at the front of everyone's mind the next day. According to their minutes, the board of trustees reconvened the following morning, April 6, at 10:00 a.m. They rearranged their agenda in order to consider student grievances first and planned to hold further discussions with students that afternoon. Also, "by prior agreement," twenty students joined the meeting at 11:15 a.m. Two students laid out three central issues that represented the will of the student body. Bennie James explained the grievances of the engineering students. Albert Joyner discussed ROTC and athletic scholarships. The trustees promised to respond by 3:30 p.m. that day. The trustees reconvened at 2:00 p.m. and, at some point during their deliberations, they were informed that students had taken control of the telephones and switchboard and had locked the entrances to Dorothy Hall.[96] "I don't recall how the decision got made," Geddis said. "It was kind of one of those decisions. We decided that we weren't going to leave. We chained the doors to the guest house." There were roughly one hundred students inside.[97] Ronald Hill chalked it up to a failure of communication and a desire, on the part of the administration, to say to students, "no, stay in your place." As a result, "we just did what we had to do."[98] When the students refused to reopen the switchboard or leave the building, the trustees voted to call the sheriff. They adjourned at 5:00 p.m.[99]

Approximately three hundred students participated in the occupation of Dorothy Hall on April 6. For students like Michael Wright, this was the confrontation they had been building toward. For others, the moment swept them up and carried them along like a wave.[100] "I was always a quiet person," Lena Agnew admitted. "I would see and watch, but I didn't get involved as much as most people did."[101] Agnew's one and only participation in a protest during her years at Tuskegee was the April 6 sit-in at Dorothy Hall. Still, she understood the issues. "We heard that the trustees were coming for their annual meeting and we had some things that we wanted them to do," she said. "We wanted better food, better dorms. There were a lot of issues we were confronted with, and we thought the only way to get their attention was to have a sit-in where they were staying."[102]

Inside the building, as students confronted the trustees directly, face to face, their hopes of persuading them fell. At some point, one of the trustees called student William Clark a "communist."[103] In his disciplinary hearing the following month, Clark recalled that this comment made him "furious." "I told him we are not communists—every time a black man does something in this country," he said, "we are called communists."[104] For George Geddis, it was "my first confrontation with real power. I remember specifically, at that time, I spoke to one of the trustees, Melvin Glasser." Geddis misremembered him as a representative of General Motors (not the UAW). He said to Glasser,

> Do you understand what happens if these state troopers come onto a black campus? We are a bunch of ugly niggers. Somebody's going to get killed. He looked at me and said, "Well then, leave." That's when I realized nothing's going to happen. These guys have all the power and we can't move them.[105]

In the heat of the moment, the students were twice betrayed by people they had trusted. At some point, a local photographer, P. H. Polk,

FIGURE 4.2. Outside the occupation of Dorothy Hall in 1968. Photo by P. H. Polk. Tuskegee Institute Archives.

FIGURE 4.3. Inside the occupation of Dorothy Hall in 1968. Photo by P. H. Polk. Tuskegee Institute Archives.

entered Dorothy Hall. He was not a professor or employee of Tuskegee Institute, but he was known to the students and trusted (it was Polk who first taught Chester Higgins Jr. how to use a camera). Apparently no one complained as he began taking photographs of the occupation, and some may have even posed for him. Polk later turned the images over to the administrators, who used them to identify and prosecute student activists.[106] The trustees also contacted the sheriff, Lucius Amerson. In the aftermath of the massacre in Orangeburg and King's assassination, this was a perilous move. Amerson, in turn, escalated matters further by calling in the Alabama National Guard. The students who had worked so hard to get him elected didn't quickly forget, and referred to him as an "Uncle Tom" in the weeks and months that followed.[107] Finally, at 6:30 p.m., the trustees announced to students inside and outside the building that, for the first time in its history, Tuskegee Institute would close its doors for an indefinite period of time.[108]

Striking Back

Challenging white supremacy in Alabama was a dangerous business, but no one faced physical harm from the students. Major General Lucius Clay had a plane to catch. He explained his situation to the students, and they let him leave. Presumably Clay knew danger when he saw it, and in the occupation of Dorothy Hall, he didn't see it. "This is simply a group of rebellious young students who want to run the university," he told *Tuskegee News*. "There was no threat of violence."[109] There actually was a threat of violence, but not from the students. With the Orangeburg massacre on his mind, Michael Wright suggested that the students protesting outside Dorothy Hall should come inside for safety.[110] "We had no intention of hurting anybody . . . but we were not going to just get shot down like the students at South Carolina," he said.[111]

Day gave way to night, and morale gave way to hunger and exhaustion among the students, who struggled to maintain a unified stance on their aims and means. "It was a very emotional situation," Michael Wright recalled. "To carry out a consensus meeting was becoming more and more difficult."[112] Between two and three o'clock in the morning, the committee of students leading the occupation decided to let the board of trustees go, conceding that their lack of quorum meant that no decisions would be made on the spot. Wright disagreed with this decision, and a group of students continued to confront the trustees as they came downstairs to leave. Still another group refused to let Foster go, so the president stayed in the building and continued to respond to their questions. Michael Wright went into the bathroom and cried.[113]

Around 3:30 a.m., Sheriff Amerson led roughly three hundred National Guardsmen and seventy state patrolmen to the gates of Tuskegee's campus.[114] As word of the troops' presence reached Dorothy Hall, the bulk of the students still occupying the building "vanished."[115] Lena Agnew and her friends lied to their classmates who were blocking the exits. The young women claimed that they needed to retrieve pillows so they could be more comfortable, and never came back.[116] At one point Dean Phillips ran over to Michael Wright and told him, "If you've never listened to me in the past, listen to me now. Let the President and myself go out because the state troopers are coming."[117] The news also spread to the dorms, where Caroline Hilton remembers that some of her classmates braced themselves for battle. "I didn't realize how serious it was until the girls would say, 'The National Guard's coming, the National Guard's coming,'" she recalled. "They took mattresses and put them across the doors in the dorm, and they all pulled out their guns. They were getting ready to shoot it out. I couldn't . . . I said, 'No, no, no, I have to get out of here.'"[118]

Perhaps nothing illustrated the contradictory position of Tuskegee's students—simultaneously recruited into the corridors of power and affluence as graduates and feared and punished as protesters—as much as this: Tuskegee Institute, itself a military training ground, was facing a military invasion. As they did twenty-eight years earlier, troops gathered near Tuskegee Institute's gates, preparing to enter the campus. And just as President Patterson did in 1940, Dean Phillips (once again) acted to protect students. He approached the gates with some other campus officials, and noticed that the troops had bayonets affixed to their rifles. Phillips asked them not to cross the gates, but the soldiers said they were coming anyway. One of them told Phillips, "Well, you know, you all at Tuskegee have been too uppity for a long time."[119]

Somehow, the dean did convince the soldiers not to go to Dorothy Hall. Amerson, however, led troops to the Engineering Building, where he presented a copy of an injunction against their occupation and successfully persuaded the engineering students to leave in order to avoid being arrested.[120] Fortunately, there were no injuries and no lives lost, but the armed forces of the State of Alabama had finally accomplished at gunpoint what neither the trustees nor the administrators could: dislodging the student movement and its leadership. This was a bitter ending, one that exposed divisions and tensions about who stood where and who was on whose side. For example, as they crossed the campus in the early morning hours, Sue Pendell, a professor, recognized some of her students among the National Guardsmen.[121]

The closing of the campus brought this phase of the student movement to an abrupt end. All students were ordered to leave campus and thus, physically removed from the school community, the activists were unable to organize. The bus and train stations were instantly jammed with suitcases and boxes.[122] One Tuskegee student who owned a small private airplane—a Cessna—gave Caroline Hilton and some friends an airlift out of town.[123] Meanwhile the administration took the opportunity to get more organized. Administrators successfully sought police warrants for charging sixteen students, including Ronald Hill and Michael Wright, with disturbing the peace.[124] They also began openly making plans to use the shutdown to permanently expel the main organizers of the movement. Parents were sent a letter explaining that all students were dismissed and would have to apply for readmission—an unprecedented step in the school's history. "Tuskegee officials . . . hope to weed out the troublemakers by carefully screening the new applications," a local television editorial segment reported. "These moves are drastic, but they are necessary."[125] Two weeks later, on April 22, Tuskegee Institute reopened, with approximately 90 percent of the former students applying for readmission.[126]

For the rest of the semester, Tuskegee student activists—those who returned—spent most of their energy defending themselves and their comrades in court, on and off campus. Thirteen students took Tuskegee to federal court for not readmitting them. They claimed that they were exercising their right to protest, and were trying to win "modern educational programs . . . rather than merely training Black students in obsolescent technical skills designed to keep the Black people relegated to second-class status."[127] Judge Frank M. Johnson, who had repeatedly ruled in favor of the Tuskegee faculty in their bid for voting rights, now ordered both parties (the students and the administrators) "cross-restrained," meaning that the administration had to reinstate students who had been summarily expelled, and at the same time, those students were prohibited by the court from doing anything to "disrupt" the process of schooling at Tuskegee Institute.[128] The judge ruled that students' right to due process had been violated, so the administration organized on-campus trials for student activists. With perhaps unintended irony, and seeking a means to protest what they called "kangaroo courts,"[129] student defendants wore chains with padlocks around their necks as they traveled on campus, both evoking the accusation that the administrators was serving as "overseers" on a "plantation" and displaying the very tools they were accused of using to shut down the school.[130]

Student activists maintained a defiant stance, and their anger at the administration deepened. As the trials proceeded and some students began receiving suspensions, the *Campus Digest* shared their outrage. A familiar refrain was the idea that administrators were acting as servants of the white trustees. "The Administration is not Black; it is white," a May 18 editorial argued. "No matter what reasons are given, the only real reason that the Black brothers and sisters are being 'executed' by the Administration is that the students offended the Administration's WHITE BROTHERS!" An accompanying cartoon portrayed a menacing figure in a white pointed hood labeled with the president's initials, "LHF."[131] Dean Phillips, perhaps sensing his inability to reconcile the antagonists, abstained from the campus judicial process.[132] The results of these trials are not clearly recorded, but there is evidence of a wide range of outcomes. Some, like Michael Wright, were expelled.[133] It seems that many others, such as George Geddis, were permitted to return to campus.[134] Still others, like Warren Hamilton, were allowed to graduate early. "I felt really hurt by that," he said. "It was like they just got rid of me."[135]

Victory in Defeat

Returning to campus after the shutdown, Caroline Hilton thought that she had been through a "time warp," as though the occupation of

Dorothy Hall "wasn't really real." It seemed as though everything was back to "business as usual."[136] George Geddis felt the difference, though. The "tone" of the campus had changed. "There were more instructors doing African American history," which felt like an accomplishment.[137] The *Campus Digest* remained an outlet for the angriest students, although the lack of bylines suggests that the anger was mixed with fear. One anonymous front-page editorial attacked the administration (alternating capitalization of "Black"):

> Your white National Guard allies didn't have to pull the triggers of death on black students as they wanted to because your whitewashed minds had already and still are pulling the triggers of suspensions, suppression, and extermination of Black Souls, Minds and Bodies. Your whitewashed minds have already pulled the triggers which snuff out the lengths, breadths, and heights of Black students in a black institution. Forgive our whitewashed Black Judases for they know not what they do.[138]

Something had changed on campus, but it was more diffuse and intangible than a well-organized movement of students might demand. The militants on campus now commanded few forces, if any. The ALCPP incorrectly predicted that Tuskegee Institute would be the "head" of black student protest in the year to come.[139] But everyone was aware that the global movement was gaining steam, which seemed to validate the militants. The day after Tuskegee Institute reopened, students occupied five buildings on Columbia University's campus in New York City, only to be dislodged by police attack a week later. The next month, a protest movement that had begun in Parisian college dormitories spread to workplaces; on May 22, nine million people were on strike in France, the largest general strike in world history at that point.[140] Undeniably, Tuskegee students had contributed to this great wave of global protest. Frederick Patterson, former Tuskegee Institute president and one of the trustees held hostage in the prior month, actually paid homage to the activists in his 1968 commencement speech to the campus. Patterson said that the student movement was part of a "larger context of rebellions involving college students all over the United States—and, in fact, over most of the world." Revolution, he said, "is long overdue" in American society. He cautioned against separatism, however, arguing that black people could get their fair share of America's resources without going "off in a corner for blacks only to get it."[141] Patterson essentially outlined the administration's new stance (now that the crisis had passed): they would praise the militants as forward-thinking, but draw the line at separatism.

When classes resumed in the fall with a record enrollment,[142] students turned to the pages of the *Campus Digest* to assess what, if anything, had been accomplished, and what the future held.[143] In a letter to the incoming class of freshmen, an anonymous student author warned, "If you are willing to walk the straight and narrow, and not do or say anything 'unbecoming to a Tuskegee Student,' welcome to the right place."[144] Some students feared that Judge Johnson's temporary injunction against student protests would continue as a tool for punishing future demonstrators.[145] "At this moment, with the threat of reprisals for any, and every action hanging over our heads," Caroline Hilton wrote, "we are not free people."[146] Confirming their worst fears, Judge Johnson did just that. He extended the injunction, making the temporary ban on protests a permanent one.[147]

Radicalism was replaced with caution. Two elections—one on campus, one off—may be interpreted as a backlash, or at least a move away from a radical posture. In August, Tuskegee's first black candidate for mayor, Thomas Reed, failed in his bid. Although black people were more than 80 percent of Tuskegee's registered voters, Reed captured less than half of the overall votes. A white man, C. M. Keever, was elected in a landslide. Keever speculated that his election represented the will of Tuskegee's black citizens to not "control" or "segregate" the city.[148] Likewise, some students decided to keep their "heads down" and focus on graduation.[149] In mid-October, Lamont Isom was elected student body president, campaigning on a promise to improve "relations" between students and faculty. Caroline Hilton called Johnson's injunction "a big issue" in the election.[150]

But this was not a return to the past. The idea that Tuskegee had to change persisted, particularly in the area of curriculum. For their part, the faculty openly debated the merits of black speech patterns and whether or not they should teach "standard" English. Professor Torrens was told that the English department, which had a high proportion of white professors, was the object of much faculty resentment in part because of its campaign, "real or imagined, against Negro dialect," Torrens wrote. One black faculty member referred to them as the "Foreign Language Department."[151] Caroline Hilton, the new *Campus Digest* editor-in-chief, continued to defend the Black University concept. Lamenting that this aspect of the spring demands had been "lost in the mire," she argued, "Our curriculum must be made relevant to the total black experience."[152] Hilton wasn't alone. The "girls" of Rockefeller Hall sponsored a talk by history professor Aubrey LaBrie on the Black University concept. LaBrie stressed the need for independence from the government or from any white people.[153]

The next week, Hilton argued that a "new breed" of black students was coming of age at Tuskegee Institute. The philosophy of this new breed, she wrote, was "black: Black pride, black awareness, black self realization, and most of all, a black social consciousness." Whereas at the height of their power, activists on campus married individual and collective impulses, now they were counterposed. This group eschewed materialism and individualism, Hilton claimed: "Collective growth as a people must precede any and all personal aspirations."[154] This was a more radical stance, but in the last months of 1968 it inspired fewer followers.

From the pages of the *Campus Digest*, the most political students continued to imbue the concept of blackness with a radical critique of the status quo. Student Arthur Pfister published one of the most searing indictments of Tuskegee in a full-page poem accompanied by photographs of black students in military uniforms. In "Ain't That Sad," Pfister ridiculed the rituals of ROTC, marching, drilling, and wearing military dress, as "white." "'Skegee is Mean, so big—so mighty," the poem began, "But it still makes BLACK PEOPLE / into copies of whitey. / . . . ain't that sad?"[155] The Student Organization for Black Unity (SOBU), an organization quickly spreading across campuses nationwide, was officially chartered at Tuskegee Institute in November 1968. The purpose of the organization, according to an announcement in the *Campus Digest*, was to "unify the black students of Tuskegee Institute with the black community and all Black Student Organizations across the country, which are pertinent to the struggle for Human Rights of the Black Man in America, and all the colored peoples of the world." Through working in SOBU, a Tuskegee student would become "aware of his vanguard role in the liberation struggle, a struggle for which many are called but few answer." The founders were listed as nineteen students, including Cozetta Butts (later Lamore), Caroline Hilton, George Geddis, and Arthur Pfister, with Aubrey LaBrie serving as faculty advisor.[156]

Some students interpreted the presence of white professors at black schools as "inherently problematic." Ironically, in many cases white faculty members were among the most enthusiastic supporters of black student protests.[157] One student, Julia Ann Fuller, argued that all white professors should be removed from Tuskegee. "They are bringing white-oriented ideas on our campuses because they are white and those are the only ideas that they could possibly bring," she wrote.[158] Some, indeed, did leave.[159] Caroline Hilton described Tuskegee as a campus "in turmoil" on the one hand, yet also "a vanguard of revolutionary thinking among black colleges in the south." The students gathered around the *Campus Digest* and SOBU had, in fact, played a vanguard role on campus, and although their organized forces were smaller, their influence was still felt. The official theme for the homecoming festivities was "Mind Expansion through Black Awareness."[160]

There were also those in the campus community who reacted against the more radical meanings of blackness. Professor E. B. Henderson defended the idea of Black Studies, as long as it was not "propaganda" for separatism.[161] The newly elected SGA president, Lamont Isom, articulated support for the Black University concept, while echoing the arguments of trustees that Tuskegee should "place great emphasis on Black ideas and Black culture," but should not prepare students for a "totally Black society."[162] Outgoing student president Warren Hamilton felt torn between the two groups. As he walked across campus one day, someone threw a large rock at his head. "I was too radical for some people, and I was a Tom to other people, because, to the revolutionaries, I didn't go far enough."[163]

Social movements can't be measured only by their victories, but the changes Tuskegee students won in 1968 are impressive.[164] Late in the semester, the *Campus Digest* printed a full-page report from a special joint committee, detailing its recommendations and the Tuskegee Educational Council's actions on issues raised by students in the spring. The reforms resulting from student pressure included: student representation on all committees dealing with student affairs; abolition of the second year of compulsory ROTC; full scholarships for athletes; increased attention to black cultural and economic study, specifically fifty new course hours devoted to black culture and an African Studies program; principle of publication as a requirement for faculty; revised guidelines on outside speakers; upgrades to the School of Education; improvements to the School of Mechanical Industries; student majority control of the *Campus Digest*; an independent student theater; improvements in health services at John Andrews Hospital; students' ability to withdraw from courses at any time; and buildings renamed after famous black people. Only a few issues remained outstanding: the formation of a student-faculty committee to further deliberate on the issue of how to evaluate engineering faculty; the formation of a committee to evaluate the system of checks and balances in Tuskegee's administration; and the demand for a status of greater independence for the dean of students.[165] Winning such significant changes quickly, when added to the frightening near-invasion of state troopers, meant that only a small number of students remained convinced by the fall of 1968 that the movement hadn't gone "far enough." Whatever might be said of the hotheaded, rash, or impatient tendencies of student activists, all of these same qualities were essential ingredients for pushing through this sweeping reform agenda on Tuskegee's campus.

The 1968 shutdown threw the Tuskegee movement back on its heels, but the black student movement nationwide was just getting started. In November 1968, some two thousand people attended the "Towards a Black University" conference at Howard University, and black students at San Francisco State College initiated a strike that would rock the entire state of California and lead to the founding of the nation's first Black Studies department.[166] If more than 150 recorded black student actions made the 1967–1968 academic year tumultuous, the 1968–1969 school year was even more intense. Black students organized more than 250 protests that year in all regions of the country, occupying campus buildings, and facing hundreds of arrests (including 365 students arrested from Alabama State University alone), representing the apogee of the US black student movement to date.[167] Some of these actions (such as the occupations at Cornell, Columbia, and Howard Universities) are more vividly remembered, but in retrospect the movement at Tuskegee University was part of the vanguard, helping to translate in words and actions the ideals of Black Power in the context of one of the nation's most renowned campuses.

Looking back at their former selves of half a century before, Tuskegee student activist alumni said that in 1968, Tuskegee was a "haven for activists."[168] Yet they conceded that the core of the movement constituted fewer than two dozen students,[169] who, by the late 1960s (and unlike their predecessors), were relatively disconnected from the surrounding black communities,[170] and that while its means were militant, the late 1960s student movement's demands were not necessarily radical.[171] Ironically, their assessment echoes that of their former antagonist, Tuskegee president Foster. In December, Foster published his annual president's report, reflecting on the 1967–1968 school year. "There was a strong orientation of Tuskegee students to vital issues in today's society," he began. "It is a tribute to Tuskegee's philosophy and program that this place has nurtured student views and their frank expression." Faculty and students "were chagrined" by the "breakdown in orderly processes" that had been "led by a small cadre of militants bent on disruption," leading to the school's closure. But learning from the experience would lead to greater unity in the community, he concluded, adding that an "examination of the Student Mandate of last spring, along with the philosophical stance of the Institute on most of the issues, revealed that we were closer together than might have appeared."[172] Foster was correct in pointing out that the "Black University" concept as spelled out in the "Mandate" document was winnable, although he neatly obscures what it took to make those reforms a reality. Closer to the truth is that it took the threat of a revolutionary movement to win reform. By temporarily galvanizing the entire student body around a reform agenda and under the banner of Black Power, a small group of student activists successfully created enough force to break through their school's institutional conservatism, forging a new organizational and intellectual consensus at Tuskegee Institute, articulating ideas and aspirations that resonated far beyond their campus, and still do.

5

Conclusion

The Leadership of Black Students

Guy Trammel is a very busy man. He grew up in Tuskegee, Alabama, and although he did not attend Tuskegee Institute, his brother, Ernest Stephens, did. Ernest, I learned, had passed, but his brother Guy lived nearby and was willing to speak with me. Guy Trammel did not have time to conduct a sit-down interview, but he was willing to talk if I would do so on the road. I met him in Tuskegee's town square, where the Confederate statue attacked by student protesters in 1968 is still standing. I hopped into his van, turned on my recording device, and we zoomed off on a mission to pick up supplies from a statewide food bank distribution hub. Trammel was following in the footsteps of his mother, an activist with the Congress of Racial Equality in Philadelphia who found work as a teacher in Macon County. She took her son with her after school and on the weekends, loading up the car with clothing and books to take to rural families in the nearby counties. "When I got older, she had me sit down and read with the children," he said.

We paused the interview only to load up his van with nonperishable food, and later to unload it all at a community center back in Tuskegee, where it would be available to people who needed it. The difference between the town described in the chapters of this book and the town as it was at the time of my meeting with Guy Trammel was jarring. While Tuskegee University's campus seems just as pristine, immaculate, and impressive as ever, one has only to cross the street to be in a different world. It is no longer the case that Tuskegee Institute is surrounded by Alabama but not in Alabama, as George Paris said. As I drove around with Guy Trammel, it felt more accurate to say that Tuskegee University is surrounded by

Tuskegee, Alabama, but is not of it. Off campus, the official poverty rate in town is 27.6 percent.[1] Macon County's poverty rate, 32.2 percent, places it among the poorest counties in one of the nation's poorest states.[2]

On our return trip, Guy Trammel took a detour to show me the large, well-maintained mansions around City Lake—owned mostly by people who work for the city government, he said. Trammel and many people interviewed for this study explained the town's economic woes in similar ways: the result of white flight and corruption in city government. City managers are widely believed to be corrupt: they brought millions of dollars into Tuskegee through the "Model Cities" program and other federal initiatives, maintaining their salaries and standards of living, but never seemed to translate that into sustainable economic development and wider opportunities for the population.[3] Johnny Ford, a twenty-nine-year-old son of a VA hospital employee, was elected mayor in 1972, completing the capture of political power that had once been exclusively in the hands of white people.[4] "Black Power" was, in a sense, achieved, but it was not what many people expected.

In informal conversations with Alabamians, I frequently heard people connect the pattern of white flight to the events of 1968. This may explain why the dramatic story of the Tuskegee student uprising has gone untold thus far: for those who stuck around, it seemed to mark the end of the good years. Tuskegee University, for its part, understandably might hesitate to lift up a story about how its students became such harsh critics of their school, took such militant action, and were expelled en masse. Unlike the voting rights struggle, the Tuskegee airmen, or other chapters from Tuskegee Institute history that highlight the school's contributions to proud national accomplishments, the student movement seems to have led nowhere—at least, nowhere good. But one lesson of this study is that the events at Tuskegee were central to the broader black movements in the South, and share many dynamics of the black movement nationwide, including its outcomes.

Tuskegee is not the only municipality where the ascension of black elected officials who rode a social movement wave to power did not result in improved conditions for the majority of black people. What happened in Tuskegee, Alabama, also happened in Newark, New Jersey, and Chicago, Illinois.[5] "Practically everywhere black Americans attempted to steer liberalism from the late 1960s onward," N. B. D. Connolly writes, "they wound up trying to replace older forms of white paternalism or political patronage with only a fraction of the public and private resources local governments once enjoyed."[6] The twin ironies, as Norrell likewise points out, are that white people fled the town in fear of intrusions by the federal government, just as the government started to shift toward conservatism in the 1970s and 1980s. Furthermore, black people were seizing control of the local political machinery at the very moment that the local machinery was becoming less important.[7] Thus, depending on your perspective, one could conclude either that the black movements in the 1960s "went too far" or, alternatively, that they "didn't go far enough." To me, the latter framework makes more sense than the former.

The Students

For many Tuskegee student activists, their post-campus careers reflected a continued commitment to the project of social change. Wendell Paris contributed to the struggle to wrest control from segregationists of the farmers' aid organization, the Agricultural Stabilization Conservation Service, and to use its resources to help Black Belt farmers. His brother George traveled to Zimbabwe to work with farmers as part of the nationalist movement there. George Paris still lives a short distance from the university and has a small farm that some students help him to tend. As we walked among the neat rows of fruits and vegetables sprouting from the earth, I thought of the ways that the work of George and Wendell Paris resonated with the long struggle of black people to acquire and hold land as a means of economic and political independence and self-determination.

After leaving Tuskegee, Ernest Stephens lived for a time in New York City with George Ware. When their childhood friend Kathleen Neal came to stay with them, they spent countless evenings in intense political discussions and escorted her to her first demonstration. Ware—who had also traveled to Cuba with Stokely Carmichael—and Stephens were the first to introduce Kathleen Neal (later known as Kathleen Cleaver, a leader of the Black Panther Party) to radical ideas and politics. Kathleen Cleaver and I met in midtown Manhattan, at the City University of New York Graduate Center, where I had reserved a room for us to talk. The more she spoke about growing up in Tuskegee and the political education she received from Tuskegee student activists, the more I understood that this book would be, in part, about recovering the wide ripples of impact this movement made around the country and the world.

I met Chester Higgins Jr. at his home in Brooklyn. He spoke in gentle tones, eyeing me with curiosity and asking me many questions. This was my very first time interviewing someone who had been involved in the events of 1968 at Tuskegee Institute, so the project was just beginning to take shape, and I still didn't know so much about what I didn't know. Higgins stepped away for a moment and returned with a thick leather-bound volume, immediately placing it in my hands. The golden letters engraved in the cover read, "*Student Unrest, Tuskegee Institute: A Chronology*, by Chester Higgins, Jr." I was blown away by the fact that a Tuskegee student had the forethought to so systematically and comprehensively document the events of 1968, that Tuskegee Institute itself had published the documentary record, and that its author had now placed that history literally in my hands. Chester Higgins Jr., I learned, took up photography late in his career as a Tuskegee student. He told me the story of his first encounter off campus with P. H. Polk, how he was entranced by Polk's photographs, and how he convinced Polk to teach him the craft. Higgins turned that instruction into an award-winning and globe-spanning career documenting the beauty, strength, and humanity of Afro-Americans and people of the global African diaspora. For him, this has also been a spiritual journey through time. His latest work explores the role of ancient Africans in the origins of human religion.[8] "Your understanding of history," he wrote to me in an email about his new book, "and the role of African people in faith-making is about to change."

Tracking down former Tuskegee student activists, I was continually impressed with their lifelong intellectual curiosity and dynamic approaches to political engagement. After leaving the Tuskegee area in 1968, Michael Wright went on to study and work in the mental health field; though now partially retired, he continues to work as a counselor and consultant for clients with a wide range of needs. What is most important for him, he told me, is his commitment to his religious endeavors in the traditional West African-based Ifa religion and philosophy. He also counsels young people on the importance of spiritual culture to maintaining their personal and social stability and their continued growth as focused, productive, and pro-social young black men and women.[9] Though we never met in person, his enthusiasm for recounting the Tuskegee movement was palpable over the phone. I learned so much from those conversations, particularly from his tone: combining a radical critique with reverence for his alma mater. In 2000, Lucenia Dunn was elected the first female mayor of Tuskegee. She still lives there and I had the privilege of meeting her in her living room. I learned all about her time at Tuskegee Institute as a student, and how even today she is working on developing the local economy, hoping to develop the local farmers' market in a way that will be beneficial to both residents and farmers. Arthur Pfister became a well-known figure in the black radical poetry scene. His 1972 book *Beer Cans, Bullets, Things and Pieces* includes a foreword by Amiri Baraka. Pfister is known today as "Professor Arturo"—he has taught on many college campuses and is particularly celebrated in his hometown, New Orleans, for his contribution to artistic responses to the political crisis that followed Hurricane Katrina.[10]

Of all of the 1960s Tuskegee students, Gwen Patton's post-graduation activist career is probably the most extensive.[11] Apart from Sammy Younge Jr., she is the most well-known Tuskegee student activist and certainly is the most widely cited. In part, this is because she, more than any of her classmates, continued to work closely with organizations of

FIGURE 5.1. Gwen Patton in her home office, July 2015. Photo by Brian Jones.

the broader American left. She worked with SNCC and the Socialist Alliance, and collaborated with both the Black Panther Party and the Detroit Revolutionary Union Movement. She was a co-founder of both the National Black Antiwar Antidraft Union and the Black Women's Liberation Committee, pursuing them as vehicles for her internationalist and anti-imperialist politics, as historian Ashley Farmer notes.[12] Her trajectory appears to be similar to that of other radicals as the movement ebbed. She was one of nine national delegates in Jesse Jackson's Rainbow Coalition, a historic attempt to capture the Democratic Party with an insurgent electoral campaign.[13] She earned a doctorate and was a professor for a while before settling back in Montgomery. Patton is widely interviewed and quoted in civil rights and Black feminist literature, but has never herself been the subject of a scholarly study.

From Black Power to Black Studies

In a new afterword to the 1992 edition of *Black Power*, coauthor Charles Hamilton (by that time a professor at Columbia University) revised his ideas on Black Power. What he could see now, he wrote, was the rise of a conservative interpretation of Black Power as black capitalism. That strain of black nationalist thought, Hamilton noted, ran through Booker T. Washington, Marcus Garvey, and the Nation of Islam. "People could 'close ranks' and still have vastly different views about how to proceed politically," Hamilton concluded.[14] Racial identity was "necessary," he argued, but not "sufficient" for building a truly liberatory movement. There would have to be a political reckoning and a challenge to black capitalism. "The earlier edition of this book was not sufficiently attentive to this predictable dichotomy."[15]

These issues of identity and geography remain unresolved. In the Black Power movement, many Afro-American radicals identified their work with the global struggle of people in the Third World against colonialism. Despite Frantz Fanon's cautions about the important differences between these contexts, some harbored dreams that there could be a territorial or geographic solution to the problem of anti-black racism in the United States. In the 1960s, it was widely believed that territorial sovereignty in the Black Belt and racial autonomy in higher education could mean genuine liberation in both. But even nominal "independence" of an impoverished nation-state was actually not the dream that all African revolutionaries dreamed—some saw it as a new kind of trap.[16] Not unlike the first wave of black politicians to capture political offices in the 1960s, African activists who led newly "independent" nation-states in the same years faced similar dilemmas. And even on a much smaller scale still, decolonizing the campus would likewise prove to be a process full of pitfalls.

Attempts to institutionalize Afro-American studies in the United States did not begin in the 1960s; Du Bois, Hubert Harrison, Carter

G. Woodson, Arturo Schomburg—and at Tuskegee Institute, Monroe Work—are among the most successful progenitors of this effort.[17] By the time Tuskegee students got around to demanding a "Black University" in 1967, some of what they wanted was unofficially in place—the time, space, and other resources provided by relatively accessible and generous higher education systems were crucial to nurturing that generation of young black activists. Nearly every organization of black radicals in the 1960s and 1970s has its origins on a college campus.[18] Using the campus as a launching pad was one thing; overturning racist curricula and institutionalizing Black Studies was another.

In a twenty-three-page assessment of the Black Studies struggle, published by Tuskegee Institute in 1970, African Studies instructor James Preston argued that the effort rose and fell with the student movement that brought it into being. Curiously, he alternates in the text between calling it a "Black Studies" program and an "African Studies" one. After the student "revolution" was squashed, the African Studies idea continued to circulate on campus, he writes, and was formally proposed and well received by students, faculty, and administrators just one month after the showdown at Dorothy Hall. In the fall of 1969, the program was officially announced, and a leader was named, but the effort suffered from the start. The faculty who were qualified to teach the courses were already overstretched and couldn't dedicate time to it. The effort to recruit faculty was strained by a bitter debate over whether white faculty members with appropriate credentials should be allowed to teach some of the courses. Preston believed that this was a "psychological hangup" on the part of students, which endangered the program. Such students "would rather win the battle and lose the war," he wrote. The program required extra care and attention from administrators to make it successful, but none was forthcoming. "In the beginning of the struggle," Preston concluded, "all the pressure had emanated from students; and without their constant prodding, the program had little chance of survival." Fearing that the degree would have no relevance after graduation, few signed up. By the spring of 1970, the program had only one student majoring in it.[19]

The impact of the Tuskegee student movement, however, has to be measured beyond the rise and fall of a single program in a single institution. As the vision of an insurgent movement, Black Studies was about transforming the entire school institution on the way to changing the whole society. As the Black Power movement ebbed in the 1970s and 1980s, however, higher education proved resilient to change, able to thwart Black Studies or to incorporate it into the framework of other academic disciplines.[20] Since the society, too, was resilient, Black Studies as insurrection became untenable and unsustainable.

So what was the point, then? Since we know the outcome, it would be simple to read history backwards and therefore wonder what, if anything, had been accomplished. But the scholar-activists of the 1960s made the brave choice to not concede defeat. Despite half a century of hindsight, we would do well to remember that in 1968, because of the high level of social contestation, many different futures became possible, not exclusively the one we ended up with. To the extent that Tuskegee students contributed to pushing the boundaries of our educational and political imaginations—even if they ultimately failed to achieve all of their larger aims—they remind us that we cannot reduce the ideals of "black education" to the plans and philosophies of famous educational leaders, past or present. As they have been historically, and as they are at the moment of this writing, it is likely that educational systems will continue to be challenged and changed by black students awakening to their collective powers.

From the Tuskegee student strike of 1896, to the occupation of Dorothy Hall in 1968, through today, black student movements at Tuskegee Institute and everywhere have been leading for a long time, and have ever shown higher education its future. That doesn't mean that black student activists get everything right or are beyond critique or reproach. But on the whole, their struggles have been a necessary force for reform, pushing institutions and our society toward greater freedom and democracy, in the truest senses of the words. Black students transformed higher education in this country, and their impact beyond the campus has been profound. Historian Peniel Joseph argues that in the 1960s in particular, the "Black Studies Movement" represented "perhaps the greatest political and pedagogical opportunity to fundamentally alter power relations in American society."[21]

The Tuskegee student movement, like the Black Power movement in general, challenged and wrested concessions from centers of American wealth and power, but did not fundamentally alter power relations in American society. Establishing Black and other ethnic studies as legitimate scholarly pursuits was simultaneously an enormous achievement and a technology of managing difference and forging a new national multicultural identity, as Roderick Ferguson argues, to effectively contain the threat posed by the 1960s social movements.[22] Tuskegee, because of its integration with the US military, was more fused with this national identity than any other HBCU. The eruption of an anticolonial student movement on its campus was, therefore, a high-stakes affair. One of the trustees taken hostage by students in 1968 was a retired four-star general who had commanded American forces in Europe during the Second World War.[23] Another was former Tuskegee president Frederick Patterson, who, when invited to return the next month to give the school's commencement address, praised the student protesters for their contributions to the global revolt. It was, he said, "long overdue."[24] Once the wave of student protest had crested, the university was able to re-form.

Fifty years later, in a moment of crisis for higher education in general and HBCUs in particular, the legacy of the 1960s student uprisings can seem ambiguous. Postsecondary institutions live in a contradictory state where institutionalized victories from half a century ago share space with institutionalized defeats. Interdisciplinary fields of ethnic studies, Black Studies, and women's studies coexist on campuses alongside the casualization of labor, anti-black policing, and sexual violence. And increasingly, the latter proliferate while the former fall to the budget axe, so Black Studies is often underfunded or cut altogether. At the time of this writing, the nation was in the grips of partisan conflict over the supposed teaching of Critical Race Theory in American schools, although the real anxiety seems to be the teaching of history.[25] Thus, it does not make sense to conclude either that the victory of Black Studies is complete or that Black Studies has been completely co-opted and defanged. Rather, teaching black history remains a practice that is both essential and controversial.

We have arrived at another crossroads, and, not surprisingly, the concept of colonialism endures as a way to think about our predicament, as calls to "decolonize" various institutional spaces abound, and neocolonialism persists across the globe,[26] but we lack the sense of inspiration from someplace where liberation seems to have actually been achieved. Given that global landscape, and the difficulty of building institutions outside of compromises with power, less confrontational strategies endure.[27] In contrast to the contradictory results of Tuskegee students' brand of anticolonial internationalism, Washington's more cautious methods can strike the modern mind as more workable and sustainable. Between or outside Washington's golden egg laying and Michael Wright's raw egg throwing, however, there may be other paths and other strategies available to intellectuals, students, and members of the middle class who seek to contribute to the project of fundamental social change in the twenty-first century.[28] Try as we might, truly stepping outside institutional and liberal democratic paradigms is easier said than done. As Imani Perry puts it, "We are constrained and implicated by that constraint. That is our condition."[29] Now, as then, it is likely that securing new reforms, or more, from our present predicament will require a massive struggle.

Washington and Washingtonism

Booker T. Washington endures in our imaginations because the institution that he built endures in real life. It not only survived his death in 1915, it thrived. By the mid-twentieth century, Tuskegee, Alabama, was home to a large black middle class, even if not the kind that Washington imagined. Where he preached the value of tilling the soil, many of the black people in Tuskegee were more likely to be found mowing their lawns. Tuskegee's black middle class was an intellectual and professional set, many of whom were more equipped to interpret poetry than farmers' almanacs. But even if Washington's specific proscriptions were no longer practicable, he remained useful as a symbol. Washington's immediate successor, Robert Russa Moton, and the leaders who followed him learned to revise Washingtonism to fit each new age, in words and in deeds. As Tuskegee Institute raised its sights, increased its offerings, and became a university, it seemed useful to imagine that that had been what Washington had wanted all along. When Tuskegee professors respectfully and patiently asserted their right to vote, it was conceivable that they, too, were operating within Washington's long-term plan of using economic strength to gain political power. When students began to adopt the ideas of Black Power, some, like Gwen Patton, tried to interpret this step, too, as an extension of Washingtonism. But when Tuskegee students boycotted classes and took the mostly white trustees hostage, it was no longer tenable to conjure the founder on behalf of the movement.

Yet, Booker T. Washington and Washingtonism are still with us. Of course, we do have the option of admiring Washington and acknowledging his achievements without believing that his ideas are applicable to all times and places. But the impulse to apply his credits to the present and even to the future persists, perhaps because of the ways that his struggles rhyme with our own. The late twentieth century, beginning in the 1970s, saw a counterrevolution of sorts—a vicious counterattack that worked to demoralize and demobilize the black-led insurgency of the 1960s. Not unlike the period after Radical Reconstruction, there has been a feeling for several decades that nothing great can be accomplished for black people without deference to elite priorities. In the field of education, desegregation and redistribution of resources have been shelved by policy makers and what few resources there are, are devoted almost entirely to parsimonious market-oriented reforms. Washington would probably recognize the corresponding ideological landscape, including calls for black people to accept greater "personal responsibility" for their plights.[30]

Washington's critics often call him an "accommodationist," but even the most radical social actors make some accommodations to the status quo. The question is not whether to accommodate but what to accommodate and what to resist. Everyone must pick their battles. Few of his students would blame Booker T. Washington for taking white people's money to underwrite their work (everyone from Du Bois to the Black Panther Party has done the same), but some did criticize him for conceding the struggle for political rights in his public discourse, or for overworking (and undereducating) them. The terms of accommodation and protest are not fixed and absolute, but are relative and shift over time. Yesterday's audacious demand can be tomorrow's shameful accommodation. A challenge in one era can be a concession in the next. Washington opposed instruction in Latin and Greek, while parents and students demanded it. Teaching these languages in the postbellum South was seen as a challenge to the status quo because it implied that black people and white people were intellectual equals. In later years, by contrast, teaching these same languages would be perceived by Black Power activists to be an accommodation to Eurocentric curricula—an unacceptable concession to the white power structure.

There is always some element of challenge and some element of accommodation in every social action, especially when it comes to the attempt to develop and preserve an institution. No institution can be at war with the status quo in all ways all of the time and persist. For that reason, more conservative models of schooling are always more enduring, while liberatory models of schooling are more ephemeral. Tuskegee Institute's history is a story of leaders whose compromises made the institution possible: A local black tinsmith, Lewis Adams, negotiated the trading of black votes in 1881 in return for white people's support for the school that became Tuskegee Institute; Washington (publicly, at least) was willing to sacrifice the cause of civil rights to receive philanthropic support of his school; Moton and Patterson made compromises with the federal government and segregationists to secure a federally funded hospital and a pilot training program, respectively. But all compromises are not equal, and each new generation must confront the old agreements and renegotiate them. The social boundaries shifted over time and, in general, students moved with the times faster than did faculty and administrators. Washington promised a way up from slavery, but for some, it didn't go up far enough. During the First World War, the changes came fast and thick, but black college administrators were still bound to and by old arrangements. As mediators between the white power structure and the black students they served, black administrators sometimes developed conceptions of education that were different from those of powerful white people, but not always. The gap between students and administrators, between rising expectations and long-standing social accommodations on Tuskegee's campus set the stage for the student protests and strikes in the 1890s and 1900s as well as in the 1960s.

A school is a unique kind of institution. Schools produce people and ideas, and neither are easily reconciled to the social status quo. School leaders can try to contain and limit a curriculum, but literacy is a power that has no natural boundaries. Learning can lead to thoughts and questions beyond any given curriculum. At the heart of the educational conflict in the postbellum South was the question of whether or not schooling—however modest in scope—would in fact raise black people's social status or expectations or both. In this respect, white elites and black people of various classes more or less participated for opposite reasons in founding and supporting Tuskegee Institute.[31] The former wanted to use the school to keep black people in their place (to "make the people"), while the latter aimed to use it to change black people's status (to make themselves). Arguably, this same dynamic is true for the education of all subordinate classes of people, although in the case of Afro-Americans it takes on unique dimensions and twists because of racism and the legacy of slavery.

Without appreciating the record of internal dissent and protest at Tuskegee Institute, some historians tend to conflate Washington's interests and strategies with those of all black people. They make it seem as though Washington's approach was the only possible path, and the collective resistance of black people is ignored. Students were not the only ones with a history of collective action. The black mineworkers and sharecroppers who tried to organize unions after 1900 in Alabama represented an alternative outlook and strategy for advancement, and one that Washington and his successors sometimes actively opposed. Washington's emphasis on self-help and entrepreneurialism was primarily the strategy of the black middle class. After the Civil War, this small but fragile class grew more self-conscious and, at times, clashed with the black working class as well as with the ambitions of Tuskegee students. Some argue that Washington "wore the mask" as black people have had to do since slavery. However true, this interpretation misses the fact that black people did not all agree about how much of their views to disguise and how much to forthrightly declare. And while recognizing the need for a certain amount of obliqueness, black people did not necessarily agree about what did or should lie behind such a mask.

The histories of Alabama's labor movement and of the Tuskegee student movement suggest that there were multiple constituencies of local black people who disagreed with Washington's public presentation. Washington's program was controversial in his own place and time. When we imagine (as August Meier did) that the sum of opposition to Washingtonism came from elite northern black people such as Du Bois, we miss the ever-present and significant current of critique coming from southern black people, including Tuskegee Institute faculty members, students, and parents throughout the school's history.[32] Such critique, debate, and dissent are not at all unique to Tuskegee Institute. Rather, they are features of all human institutions. At Tuskegee Institute, however, that pattern takes on a special significance, given the school's unique place in black educational history.

The kind of critical history contained in the chapters of this book does not diminish the legacy of Tuskegee Institute or of other historically black colleges. It does, however, suggest that they are the products of more than just a founder's great vision. Another way to view this history is that Washington made the institution possible, but once they entered it, teachers, students, and parents had to struggle in order to realize its (and their) greater potential. Instead of the "great leader" version of Tuskegee Institute's past, this alternate history points to the role of parents, teachers, alumni, and administrators in defining and redefining the ways and means of the school. This push and pull between different actors within the campus community takes on greater significance given Tuskegee Institute's standing as a "capital" of black America in the first half of the twentieth century. The struggle over different strategies and expectations within the school, in some ways, is a microcosm of the conflict among black people as a whole, emerging from slavery, heroically trying to carve out and define a measure of freedom for themselves in extremely difficult circumstances.

We have benefited from new research into the ways that various strata in the field of black education contributed to historical social struggles, but the truth is that parents, teachers, students, and administrators didn't always pull in the same direction. At Tuskegee Institute, we see a campus community wherein various historical actors worked in concert in some moments, and were at odds at other times. This more complicated history can be harder to swallow, but it better equips us to recognize and grapple with our complicated present. The "we were all more unified back then" nostalgia is powerful, but it is disarming when it comes to figuring out what to do and how to move forward in our own time, when such unity can feel hard to come by. Like many institutions that continue to grapple with the challenge of their history and mandates for reform, Tuskegee Institute was a crucible in which many different groups invested hopes in sometimes opposing goals for social conservation or change.

Tuskegee Institute was founded in part to suppress black people's political aspirations, but became a place that nurtured them. Such aspirations for collective social change can be deferred, but they never die. In the right context, even elite schools—places where wealth and privilege are concentrated—can and have become centers of opposition. When collective aspirations for change burst through to the surface, they challenge old assumptions and ideas. Tuskegee students experienced this in the 1960s as their upbringing and education increasingly collided with their experience in a social struggle. These students were in a unique location both socially and geographically. They were students in an elite school in a surging economy. They were in a middle-class community surrounded by deep poverty. They were also black students in the Jim Crow South. Their movement was shaped by these locations; it is both recognizable as part of the larger trends in the region and the era, and also distinctive. On no other black college campus in the 1960s did students come to radical consciousness in the shadow of such a prominent political and educational figure as Tuskegee students did. While some students rejected Washington, it should not be surprising that others tried to embrace his legacy and effectively recruit him to their cause.

Black Education, Past and Future

The educational and political struggles of black people in the United States are far from over. In the long view of history, Afro-Americans have made astounding educational strides. Black students graduate high school at nearly the rate of white students, and attend and graduate from college in higher proportions than ever before. These achievements are even more remarkable in light of the fact that steep barriers persist: black students are more likely to be suspended from school, more likely to attend segregated and underfunded schools, and more likely to carry heavy debt burdens to fund their education.[33] At a time when students are told that education is their "ticket" to changing their lives as individuals, the price of that ticket has become astronomical. These conditions make schools, at all levels, sites of extreme pressure and contradiction, places that are likely to continue to be social battlegrounds for the foreseeable future.

As economic inequality reaches new extremes in this country, a profound financial gap has opened up between different classes of black people. There are still ways in which all black people, regardless of social class, are often lumped together in terms of social policy; encounters with the police in public places offer one glaring example. But the growing prominence, wealth, and power of black elites has not attenuated racism. The rise of "black faces in high places" has been entirely compatible with both heightened inequality and the growth of white supremacist organizations. Solutions that became part of the common sense among radicals in the 1960s—that college-educated, middle-class figures could lead the liberation struggle of the global Third World by forging a new, assertive national sovereignty—are not likely to reappear in exactly the same form as a new popular roadmap for social change. Black nationalism remains a powerful impulse, but contemporary black-led social movements and thinkers are finding creative ways to learn from the ancestors without merely imitating them.[34]

The radicalism of the Tuskegee student movement is not to be found in terms of its demands, which, even at its height, amounted mostly to modest reforms. Many of the militants—the engineering students, especially—insisted that they were not ideological. The Tuskegee student movement was radical because it elevated students to the position of decision making. The rhetorical questions posed by the president of Fisk University—just before the Fisk student movement drove him from office—still resonate a hundred years later: *Shall the factory be turned over to the workers and be run by the workingmen's council? Shall the colleges be turned over to the students and be run by undergraduate committees?* The Tuskegee student movement—fighting for democracy in the Black Belt and on campus—answered these questions in the affirmative.

The Tuskegee student uprising is part of a long pattern of black radical action in the center of empire and the citadels of knowledge production, expressing the tensions of both sides of the hyphenated "Afro" and "American." The contradictions of Tuskegee Institute's history are bound up with the contradictions of black history: the aspiration to reform the nation, and the imperative of forging the means of surviving it; the irrepressible need to fight for change, and the bitter necessity of reckoning with defeats. The Tuskegee student movement is a small part of the long Black freedom struggle, the battles of which have frequently taken place in (and for) schools. That experience of collective action, too, becomes a kind of school. In that school, students frequently become teachers and teachers become students. Its lessons belong to the future actors who step onto the stage of history and dare to speak.

ACKNOWLEDGMENTS

I took my first research trip to Tuskegee University in the spring of 2014 with my father, Robert Jones. Since that time, I have racked up some debts. First, I need to thank the former Tuskegee students, teachers, administrators, and community members who invited me into their homes and shared their memories with me. I hope this work brings greater awareness to their story.

I am grateful to Ashley Farmer, Ibram X. Kendi, and Clara Platter for bringing this work to the New York University Press Black Power series, and my friend and agent, Róisín Davis, for shepherding this first-time author through the process. The amazing copyediting and design team at New York University Press made this a better a book. Feedback from anonymous peer reviewers greatly improved the manuscript. Ashley Farmer was incredibly generous at every stage. As a graduate student, I was fortunate to have the guidance of an incredible community of scholars in this work, starting with my committee: Steve Brier, whose sharp intellectual eyes looked over my work more than anyone, thinking with me through each sentence; Ruth Wilson Gilmore, who modeled a method of generous and critical engagement with ideas; Ofelia Garcia, who stretched my thinking about what it means to "read the world"; and Barbara J. Fields, whose wit, wisdom, and precision sets a very high bar.

Many other colleagues gave time, energy, and advice to support my research, especially Wendy Luttrell, Anthony Picciano, Nicholas Michelli, Herman Bennett, Robyn Spencer, Duncan Faherty, Rebecca Mlynarczyk, and Jeanne Theoharis. Still more lent this work indispensable assistance in various phases, including Edwin Mayorga, Latoya Strong, Alisa Algava, Jodi Barnhart, Meghan Moore-Wilk, Carly Huesenbeck, Barbara Hubert, Kate Seltzer, Natalia Ortiz, Tahir Butt, Robert Robinson, Chloe Asselin, Sakina Laksimi, Francine Almash, Ricardo Gabriel, and Jennifer Stoops. Critical comments, questions, and feedback on parts of this research shaped this work and sharpened my writing, especially from Naomi Murakawa, Imani Perry, Joshua Guild, Martha Biondi, Jon Hale, James Anderson, Joy Williamson-Lott, Cally Waite, Eddie Cole, Deirdre Flowers, James Alford, and Clyde Robertson. Opportunities to make presentations of parts of this research and engage with colleagues in the History of Education Society, the American Educational Research Association, the Center for History and Education at Teachers College, and the NYU History of Educating Writing Group were essential. Robert Cohen was especially generous in taking the time to read and comment on several chapters. Christian Siener challenged me to rethink and reorganize the introduction.

Two groups of City University of New York fellows provided essential feedback to this work: at the Institute for Research in the African Diaspora in the Americas and the Caribbean (IRADAC) and the Center for Place, Culture, and Politics (CPCP). Both were sources of excellent discussion, dialogue, and critical thinking about this project. I could not have devoted the necessary time to research and writing without crucial financial support from CUNY's Magnet Program and summer research grants, and fellowships early in my process from the Lannan and Ford Foundations. A very special thanks to Brenda Coughlin, whose intervention made it possible for me to have time to begin this research.

So many amazing librarians and archivists guided me. The librarians at the Schomburg Center for Research in Black Culture in New York City, and at the CUNY Graduate Center lent incredible expertise and advice. I'd like to thank the archivists at Tuskegee University, especially Dana Chandler and Cheryl Ferguson. I also received expert assistance from librarians and archivists at Trenholm State Technical College and the Alabama State Archives in Montgomery. I felt like a real writer for the first time when I was granted a residency in the beautiful Shoichi Noma room of the New York Public Library.

In a later phase of writing, I received extremely useful feedback, thought-provoking comments, and very good food from a residency at the Schomburg Center. I am deeply appreciative of my colleagues from that very special year: Ansley Erickson, Anthony Rodriguez, Yuko Miki, Eric Herschthal, Tyesha Maddox, Ayesha Hardison, Imani Owens, Hisham Aidi, Naomi Lorrain, Margaret Odette, and Aisha Al-Adawiya. I learned so much from the brilliant Brent Hayes Edwards that year, and am deeply grateful for his guidance.

I had the good fortune to be able to join the staff of the Schomburg Center at the end of that residency. Reporting to work each day at the Schomburg Center was an incredible privilege, and the more I learned about the institution's history as a center of Black Studies and activism, the more I realized how fortunate I was. I was also grateful for another cohort of scholars-in-residence there who gave perceptive and useful feedback on parts of this work, including Neil Clarke, Jennifer De-Clue, Tobi Haslett, Laura Helton, Jarvis McInnis, Selena Doss, Tashima Thomas, Jaime Coan, Maya Harakawa, Ishmai'l Kushkush, and Cord Whitaker. Everyone at the Schomburg Center was a source of inspiration and joy, from our director Kevin Young, to Kevin Matthews, Michelle Commander, Novella Ford, Mary Yearwood, Joy Bivins, Maira Liriano, Shola Lynch, Tammi Lawson, Michael Mery, and Cheryl Beredo. Nicole Daniels, Lauren O'Brien, Zenzele Johnson, Kadiatou Tubman, M. Scott Johnson, and the whole Schomburg Junior Scholars team. I also learned a great deal from collaborating on special projects and programs with Zakiya Collier, Maryam Aziz, Jermaine Scott, Amaris Brown, Amoni Thompson, Aly Thomas, Jeanne Theoharis, Komozi Woodard, Erik Wallenberg, Ansley Erickson, Matthew Kautz, Karen Taylor, Khadijah Akeem, Jessica Murray, Subha Ahmed, Jesse Hagopian, Yolanda Sealey-Ruiz, Adam Sanchez, and with Nelson Luna and many other amazing youth leaders in Teens Take Charge.

Howard Zinn was a friend and a wonderful teacher, a model of scholar-activism, and he continues to inspire me. I was thrilled every time his name popped up in the archives of the southern movement.

His "bottom up" approach to writing social movement history guided this project, and I'm lucky to be able to work with so many like-minded colleagues who keep his vision alive through the Voices of a People's History of the United States project. I feel fortunate also to have been a student of the late Jean Anyon, if briefly. I remain eternally grateful and intend to pay her care forward. My comrades Anthony Arnove, Jesse Hagopian, Stanley Rosario Diaz, and Keeanga-Yamahtta Taylor have made themselves available for practical, political, and personal advice that has gotten me through these years—thank you.

I am grateful for the swift and generous support from brilliant photographers Chester Higgins Jr. and Jim Peppler, both of whom granted permission to reprint their gorgeous photographs in this book. I am also indebted to Alabama Department of Archives and History and the Tuskegee University Archives for their support in my use of reproductions from their collections here as well.

Each word on each of these pages was made possible by the wonderful people who took expert care of my children at various points in their lives: Maritza, Karen, Dolores, Linda, Liz, Liz, Joe, Della, Milana, Tasha, Regina, Anni, Shannille, Iliana, Alondra, Vera, Reeda, Avery, Cami, Sumaya, Alejandra, Jomayra, Lupe, and especially Irma. Thank you.

My mother and father have each gone above and beyond to support this work. They laid a foundation of intellectual curiosity that has come to fruition here. My mother, Barbara, was my first teacher. From her I learned the joy and power not only of literacy, but also of dreaming. My father has provided essential support, and a model of staying curious and of lifelong learning. My brother, Rick, his partner, Jacquie, and his sons, Ryan and Patrick, have cheered me on through thick and thin, and never fail to show up for me. I could not have a more amazing extended family by marriage. Thank you to Mohamad, Michael, Jennifer, Alex, and Caroline for your generosity, warmth, puns, and good counsel.

I have been conducting research for this book and writing it for most of my daughter's young life. In that time, she has grown into an intelligent and caring person, and an amazing writer herself. I am always impressed by my son, a true pre-K scholar, deeply invested in the project of making connections between books and the world. I can't wait for him and his sister to read this one. And to my wife, Susie: making this book has coincided with the second chapter of our time together. I'm so lucky to be on this journey with you.

If I have omitted any names, please forgive me. That error, and all the rest herein, are mine alone.

NOTES

INTRODUCTION

1 Bertrand Phillips, interview with the author, June 2016.

2 Tuskegee Institute had graduate programs in the 1960s, but formally became Tuskegee University in 1984. I therefore use the historically accurate "Institute" designation, except when writing about the school in the present.

3 Historical sources quoted in this book sometimes capitalize the letter *b* in the use of "Black" as a political designation and sometimes do not. Apart from quoting those sources or referring to widely used concepts such as Black Power, Black Studies, and Black University, I choose to use the lowercase *b* in most other instances, mainly as a stylistic preference.

4 "Black Power," C. L. R. James wrote, was a "political slogan and yet not a political slogan: rather a banner." See James, *C. L. R. James Reader*, 364.

5 James D. Anderson, *Education of Blacks in the South*.

6 James D. Anderson, *Education of Blacks in the South*, 50.

7 This movement is well described and documented: Washington, *Up from Slavery*; Woodson, *Mis-Education of the Negro*; Du Bois, *Black Reconstruction in America*; Gutman, *Power and Culture*; Siddle Walker, "Caswell County Training School"; Payne and Strickland, *Teach Freedom*; Heather A. Williams, *Self-Taught*; Fairclough, *Class of Their Own*; Butchart, *Schooling the Freed People*.

8 James D. Anderson, *Education of Blacks in the South*, 94.

9 Du Bois, *Souls of Black Folk*.

10 See, for example, Woodward, *Origins of the New South*; Spivey, *Schooling for the New Slavery*; Watkins, *White Architects of Black Education*; Kelly, "Sentinels for New South Industry"; and Michael R. West, *Education of Booker T. Washington*.

11 Harlan, *Making of a Black Leader*; and Harlan, *Wizard of Tuskegee*.

12 Jackson, *Booker T. Washington*; Verney, *Art of the Possible*; Norrell, *Up from History*.

13 Dagbovie, "Exploring a Century of Historical Scholarship," 257.

14 See, for example, Bradley, *Upending the Ivory Tower*; Kinchen, *Black Power in the Bluff City*; Biondi, *Black Revolution on Campus*; Rogers, *Black Campus Movement*; Turner, *Sitting In and Speaking Out*; Cohen, Snyder, and Carter, *Rebellion in Black and White*; and Meyers, *We Are Worth Fighting For*.

15 Hall, "Long Civil Rights Movement"; Rogers, *Black Campus Movement*.
16 See chapter 1.
17 See, for example, Flowers, "Launching of the Student Sit-In Movement."
18 Williamson, *Radicalizing the Ebony Tower*.
19 See Biondi, *Black Revolution on Campus*, 31–33, 159, 161, 163–64.
20 Favors, *Shelter in a Time of Storm*.
21 Cole, *Campus Color Line*.
22 Williamson-Lott, *Jim Crow Campus*.
23 Norrell, *Reaping the Whirlwind*. In 1958 the Anti-Defamation League of B'nai B'rith published a forty-six-page booklet on the (at the time, incomplete) Tuskegee voting rights struggle: Lewis Jones and Stanley Hugh Smith, *Tuskegee, Alabama: Voting Rights and Economic Pressure* (New York: Anti-Defamation League of B'nai B'rith, with the cooperation of the National Council of the Churches of Christ in the United States of America, 1958). In 1984 Jessie Guzman published a 226-page non-narrative catalog of the structure and activities of the main organization leading the voting rights struggle: Guzman, *Crusade for Civic Democracy*.
24 Norrell, *Reaping the Whirlwind*, x.
25 Norrell, *Reaping the Whirlwind*, 170.
26 Forman, *Sammy Younge, Jr.*
27 Marable, "Tuskegee Institute in the 1920's," 767, 768.
28 Marable, "Tuskegee and the Politics of Illusion," 21.
29 See dynamic and instructive discussions on the black middle class in Connolly, *World More Concrete*; and Taylor, *From #BlackLivesMatter to Black Liberation*.
30 Gaines, *Uplifting the Race*, xiii–xiv.
31 Zinn, *SNCC*; Carson, *In Struggle*; Hogan, *Many Minds, One Heart*.
32 Forman, *Making of Black Revolutionaries*; Carmichael and Thelwell, *Ready for Revolution*.
33 See, for example, Holsaert et al., *Hands on the Freedom Plow*; and Farmer, *Remaking Black Power*.
34 Patton, *My Race to Freedom*.
35 Jeffries, *Bloody Lowndes*. Donna Murch makes a point of highlighting the southern roots of Black Power in *Living for the City*. Robin D. G. Kelley also provides useful prehistory of radical political organizing in Alabama in *Hammer and Hoe*.
36 Ture and Hamilton, *Black Power*, chap. 6.
37 Ture and Hamilton, *Black Power*, 114.
38 For recent scholarship on Tuskegee's colonial legacy, see Beckert, "From Tuskegee to Togo"; and Zimmerman, *Alabama in Africa*.
39 Mary Dudziak writes about the ways Cold War anti-communism opened opportunities for democratic reform in the United States and at the same time, limited their scope, in *Cold War Civil Rights*.

40 See, for example, Bowles and Gintis, *Schooling in Capitalist America*; Anyon, *Radical Possibilities*; Freire and Macedo, *Literacy*; and Freire, *Pedagogy of the Oppressed*.

41 Perlstein, *Justice, Justice*; Marable, *Race, Reform, and Rebellion*; Rickford, *We Are an African People*.

42 I agree with Michael R. West that the term "conservative" doesn't accurately capture the politics of Booker T. Washington, for example. Jack Dougherty also grapples with what unites apparently disparate educational movements led by black people in *More Than One Struggle*.

43 I explore this pattern in "Washington and Canada" and in "The Struggle for Black Education," in Bale and Knopp, *Education and Capitalism*.

44 Joseph, *Black Power Movement*, chap. 10, "Black Studies, Student Activism, and the Black Power Movement."

45 See chapter 2 of this book; and Guzman, *New South and Higher Education*.

46 As I was completing this book, I discovered that my aunt Vivian knew Gwen Patton. They were cheerleaders together at Inkster High School. Confirming what many other people have told me, my aunt described her as "a little fire stick."

47 Michael Tullier, "US News Continues to Rank Tuskegee University as a Top HBCU Regionally, Nationally," Tuskegee University, September 13, 2017, www.tuskegee.edu.

48 Thompson, *Private Black Colleges*, 14.

49 Arthur H. Chamberlain, "Solving a Serious Problem," *Overland Monthly and Out West Magazine*, September 1930, 4.

50 Ronald Hill, interview with the author, June 2017.

51 At the time of writing, activists at Howard University occupied a campus building for a month to protest the poor quality of student housing. See Jonathan Franklin, "Howard University students reach an agreement with officials after a month of protest," National Public Radio, November 15, 2021, www.npr.org. For discussions of such contemporary debates and conflicts in black education and activism, see, for example, Ewing, *Ghosts in the Schoolyard*; Todd-Breland, *Political Education*; and James D. Anderson and Christopher M. Span, "History of Education in the News: The Legacy of Slavery, Racism, and Contemporary Black Activism on Campus," *History of Education Quarterly* 56, no. 4 (2016): 646–56.

CHAPTER 1. THE CONTRADICTIONS OF TUSKEGEE INSTITUTE, 1881–1960

1 Harlan, *Making of a Black Leader*, 282.

2 Harlan, *Wizard of Tuskegee*, 155.

3 Verney, *Art of the Possible*, 43.

4 Du Bois, *Black Reconstruction in America*, 185.

5 Norrell, *Reaping the Whirlwind*, 3.

6 Herbert George Gutman, "Schools for Freedom: The Post-Emancipation Origins of Afro-American Education," in Gutman, *Power and Culture*, 260–97; Heather A. Williams, *Self-Taught*; Steven Hahn, "To Build a New Jerusalem," in Payne and Strickland, *Teach Freedom*.

7 Bond, *Negro Education in Alabama*, 81.

8 James D. Anderson, *Education of Blacks in the South*, 36.

9 Du Bois, *Black Reconstruction*, 638.

10 "The last two decades of the nineteenth century," writes Meyer Weinberg, "were an educational catastrophe for black children and their parents." See *A Chance to Learn*, 47.

11 Litwack, *Trouble in Mind*, 87.

12 Beckert, *Empire of Cotton*.

13 Genovese, *Roll, Jordan, Roll*, 33.

14 Norrell, *Reaping the Whirlwind*, 6, 10.

15 Marable, *Race, Reform, and Rebellion*, 9.

16 Fields, "Nineteenth-Century American South."

17 Charles S. Johnson, *Shadow of the Plantation*, 19, 104, 109.

18 Weinberg, *A Chance to Learn*, 267.

19 Perlstein, "Westward Ho!"

20 James D. Anderson, *Education of Blacks in the South*, 94.

21 Fairclough, *Class of Their Own*, 121.

22 James D. Anderson, *Education of Blacks in the South*, 50.

23 James D. Anderson, *Education of Blacks in the South*, 106, 62.

24 Washington, *Up from Slavery*, 106.

25 Marable, *Black Leadership*, 27.

26 James D. Anderson, *Education of Blacks in the South*, 46, 89, 153.

27 Dennis, "Schooling along the Color Line," 153.

28 Bond, *Negro Education in Alabama*, 217; West argues that Washington's most significant legacy is in the realm of ideas, specifically the "race relations" theory. See Michael R. West, *Education of Booker T. Washington*.

29 James D. Anderson, *Education of Blacks in the South*, 75.

30 Moton, *Finding a Way Out*, 164.

31 Moton, *Finding a Way Out*, 112–15.

32 James D. Anderson, *Education of Blacks in the South*, 75, 78, 79.

33 Tuskegee Institute had stabilized at around one thousand students by the beginning of the twentieth century. Harlan, *Wizard of Tuskegee*, 144.

34 Washington, *Up from Slavery*, 77.

35 Harlan, *Making of a Black Leader*, 283.

36 Harlan, *Wizard of Tuskegee*, 276.

37 Harlan, *Wizard of Tuskegee*, 153–55; McMurry, "Black Intellectual in the New South," 335, 339–41.

38 McMurry, "Black Intellectual in the New South," 338.

39 Harlan, *Wizard of Tuskegee*, 146–47.

40 Spivey, *Schooling for the New Slavery*, 62.

41 Harlan, *Wizard of Tuskegee*, 147–48. Meanwhile, at Howard, in 1905 the president tried to introduce "industrial" education and was "ousted by a near-revolt of students and faculty" (177).

42 "Record of Warnings, Etc.," 1907, Tuskegee Institute Archives.

43 Harlan, *Wizard of Tuskegee*, 144–45.

44 Aptheker, "Negro College Student," 156.

45 Button, "Meaning of Tuskegee," 428.

46 Washington, *Up from Slavery*, 106–7.

47 Bond, *Negro Education in Alabama*, 122, 226–27, 236.

48 Bond, *Negro Education in Alabama*.

49 Kelly, *Race, Class, and Power*, 81, 89, 142, 99; Marable, *Black Leadership*, 33.

50 Bond, *Negro Education in Alabama*, 233.

51 Fairclough, *Class of Their Own*, 208, 250, 146, 272, 207.

52 Fairclough, *Class of Their Own*, 146, 419. See also Theoharis, *Rebellious Life of Mrs. Rosa Parks*.

53 Givens, *Fugitive Pedagogy*.

54 James D. Anderson, *Education of Blacks in the South*, 251–52.

55 Drewry, Doermann, and Anderson, *Stand and Prosper*, 72.

56 The 1914 and 1917 Smith-Lever and Smith-Hughes Acts established a county bureaucracy that deployed agents to make sure black schools receiving federal funds did not stray from vocationalism. See Wolters, *New Negro on Campus*, 13. I learned a great deal about black student protest movements in the 1920s from Wolters's book, which was published in 1975. I find his support for racist pseudoscience repugnant, and I don't profess to know when or how he became the sort of person who writes for white nationalist publications. In *The New Negro on Campus* he very much wrote from the standpoint of black college students, and I believe that the information and ideas quoted here hold up, and are corroborated by other authors, such as Du Bois, Aptheker, Marable, Rogers, and others. For more on Wolters's racism, see Nicole Hemmer, "The Renaissance of Intellectual Racism: How Institutions Gift a Veneer of Respectability to White Nationalists Who Promote Racist Pseudoscience," *US News & World Report*, April 18, 2017, www.usnews.com.

57 Aptheker, "Negro College Student," 152.

58 Wolters, *New Negro on Campus*, 17.

59 Wolters, *New Negro on Campus*, 44, 45, 48, 51, 64, 74, 76, 113, 118.

60 For example, compulsory chapel attendance at Tuskegee wasn't amended until 1967. See *Campus Digest*, March 11, 1967.

61 Aptheker, "Negro College Student," 164, 154.

62 Marable, "Tuskegee Institute in the 1920's," 764.

63 Graham and Meade, "Hampton Institute Strike," 673.

64 Hughes and Patterson, *Robert Russa Moton*, 87–89.

65 Quoted in Marable, "Tuskegee Institute in the 1920's," 766.

66 Wolters, *New Negro on Campus*, 142–44.

67 Larsen, *Quicksand*, 13.

68 Wolters, *New Negro on Campus*, 143, 145.

69 Jordan, "'Damnable Dilemma,'" 1572.

70 Moton, *Finding a Way Out*, 249.

71 Du Bois, "Moton of Hampton and Tuskegee," 348–49. See also "Haitian Masses Tell US Get Out," *Liberator*, March 8, 1930. The complicity of many black intellectuals (including Washington and, for a time, Du Bois) in the occupation of Haiti is well discussed in Byrd, *Black Republic*.

72 Wolters, *New Negro on Campus*, 151, 154, 152–53.

73 Wolters, *New Negro on Campus*, 171, 167, 172, 174, 175.

74 Fairclough, "Tuskegee's Robert R. Moton," 99.

75 Wolters, *New Negro on Campus*, 177–80, 183–84, 189, 190. On the residency programs, see Elizabeth D. Schafer, "Tildon, Toussaint Tourgee," *American National Biography Online*, February 2000, https://doi.org/10.1093/anb/9780198606697.article.1201128.

76 Wolters, *New Negro on Campus*, 191.

77 Moton, *What the Negro Thinks*.

78 See Patton, *My Race to Freedom*, 127.

79 Hughes and Patterson, *Robert Russa Moton*, 93.

80 Harlan, *Wizard of Tuskegee*, 235.

81 However, a medical assessment of both hospitals in 1931 found that neither had made a significant contribution to community health. See James H. Jones, *Bad Blood*, 64.

82 Reverby, *Examining Tuskegee*, 9.

83 Reverby, *Examining Tuskegee*, 1, 2, 28.

84 Reverby, *Examining Tuskegee*, 21, 54.

85 Fairchild and Bayer, "Uses and Abuses of Tuskegee," 919.

86 James H. Jones, *Bad Blood*, 1.

87 Fairchild and Bayer, "Uses and Abuses of Tuskegee," 919.

88 Robert M. White reviews some of the finer points in "Misrepresentations of the Tuskegee Study," 564.

89 "Presidential Apology," Centers for Disease Control and Prevention, last updated September 24, 2013, www.cdc.gov.

90 "Bioethics Minor Overview," Tuskegee University, accessed March 22, 2016, www.tuskegee.edu.

91 Bloom, *Class, Race, and the Civil Rights Movement*, 65, 60.

92 Marable, *Race, Reform, and Rebellion*, 13.

93 Fairclough, "Tuskegee's Robert R. Moton," 102.

94   Rogers, *Black Campus Movement*, 46.

95   Chamberlain, "Solving a Serious Problem," 4.

96   Rampersad, *Ralph Ellison*, 53, 56, 60, 58.

97   Ellison, *Invisible Man*, 101, 142.

98   Fairclough, "Tuskegee's Robert R. Moton," 96–97.

99   Ellison, *Invisible Man*, 36.

100   Favors, *Shelter in a Time of Storm*.

101   Rampersad, *Ralph Ellison*, 68.

102   Fairclough, "Tuskegee's Robert R. Moton," 103.

103   Kelley, *Hammer and Hoe*, 112, 51, 42.

104   Rogers, *Black Campus Movement*, 52; Kelley, *Hammer and Hoe*, 197.

105   Fairclough, "Tuskegee's Robert R. Moton," 102, 103.

106   Hughes, "We Demand Our Rights," 39, 42.

107   Kelley, *Hammer and Hoe*, 202.

108   Rogers, *Black Campus Movement*, 52; Fairclough, "Tuskegee's Robert R. Moton," 104.

109   Tucker, "Early Years of the United Negro College Fund," 418.

110   Gasman, "Origins of the United Negro College Fund," 86.

111   Patterson, *Chronicles of Faith*, 65, 43.

112   Rogers, *Black Campus Movement*, 58.

113   Patterson, *Chronicles of Faith*, 60.

114   Fairclough, "Tuskegee's Robert R. Moton," 103.

115   Patterson, *Chronicles of Faith*, 45, 46, 57–58, 43.

116   Patterson, *Chronicles of Faith*, 83, 65. Thirteen college presidents met at Tuskegee on April 9, 1943, to begin planning the effort. Their goal was to spend roughly $100,000 collectively in order to raise $1 to 2 million. They fell slightly short of that goal, reaching $765,000 by 1944. See Tucker, "Early Years of the United Negro College Fund," 417, 418, 421.

117   "Tuskegee Carries On," *New York Age*, July 26, 1941, 8.

118   Patterson, *Chronicles of Faith*, 31, 66.

119   Rampersad, *Ralph Ellison*, 74.

120   Patterson, *Chronicles of Faith*, 56.

121   "The land around Tuskegee is basically flat, and so we didn't need an airfield," Patterson remembered. "We could use a cow pasture—and we did!" Patterson, *Chronicles of Faith*, 74.

122   "Racial Quota System Is Bottleneck in Training Fliers, NAACP Tells Stimson," *Plain Dealer*, August 21, 1942, 2.

123   "Doings of the Race," *Cleveland Gazette*, July 26, 1941, 2; "$80,000 for Tuskegee Jim Crow Air Unit," *Plain Dealer*, June 27, 1941, 1.

124   Patterson, *Chronicles of Faith*, 79–81.

125   "Tuskegee Enrollment Increases," *Negro Star*, September 5, 1941, 1.

126   "Booker T. Washington 3rd Gets Defense Job," *New York Age*, August 2, 1941, 3.

127 "Tuskegee Airmen Facts," Tuskegee University, accessed April 6, 2016, www.tuskegee.edu.

128 Higginbotham, "Soldiers for Justice," 306–9, 275.

129 Norrell, *Reaping the Whirlwind*.

130 One recent acknowledgment of this effort was in an article about Fred Gray, the lawyer who successfully prosecuted the case: Elaina Plott, "For a Civil Rights Hero, 90, a New Battle Unfolds on His Childhood Street," *New York Times*, December 25, 2020, www.nytimes.com.

131 Hall, *Bibliography of the Tuskegee Gerrymander Protest*, i.

132 Quoted in Hamilton, *Minority Politics*, 1; Norrell paraphrases this quote on page 34 of *Reaping the Whirlwind*.

133 Norrell, *Reaping the Whirlwind*, 43.

134 Foster, "Inaugural Statement," in Guzman, *New South and Higher Education*, 124, 127, 128.

135 Hamilton, *Minority Politics*, 2.

136 Gomillion, "Tuskegee Voting Story," 22.

137 Norrell, *Reaping the Whirlwind*, 61–62.

138 Robert Jones, interview with the author, April 2014.

139 Jones, interview; Caroline Hilton, who arrived as a freshman in 1965, told a similar story. Caroline Hilton, interview with the author, August 2015.

140 Lucenia Dunn, interview with the author, July 2015.

141 Wendell Paris, interview with the author, July 2015.

142 Guy Trammell, interview with the author, July 2015.

143 Chester Higgins Jr., interview with the author, August 2015.

144 George Paris, interview with the author, July 2015.

145 Mosnier, "Kathleen Cleaver Interview," quoted in Forman, *Sammy Younge, Jr.*, 44–45.

146 Melvin Todd, interview with the author, June 2016.

147 Gwen Patton, interview with the author, July 2015.

148 Patton, interview.

149 Benson, "Interview with Gwendolyn M. Patton," 183–84.

150 Patton, interview.

151 Patton, interview.

152 Taper, "Gomillion versus Lightfoot," 37, 64.

153 Hamilton, *Minority Politics*, 1.

154 Ture and Hamilton, *Black Power*, 129.

155 Norrell, *Reaping the Whirlwind*, 85.

156 Taper, "Gomillion versus Lightfoot," 38.

157 Hamilton, *Minority Politics*, 2.

158 Hamilton, *Minority Politics*, 28.

159 Fritz, "Charles Gomillion," 14, 15.

160 Gomillion, "Tuskegee Voting Story," 23.

161 Fritz, "Charles Gomillion," 16.

162 Taper, "Gomillion versus Lightfoot," 39.

163 Elwood, "Interview with Charles G. Gomillion," 586, 596.

164 Hamilton, *Minority Politics*, 5.

165 Norrell, *Reaping the Whirlwind*, 109.

166 Hamilton, *Minority Politics*, 19, 26.

167 Rogers et al., *Alabama*, 540.

168 Taper, "Gomillion versus Lightfoot," 38.

169 Gomillion, "Tuskegee Voting Story," 25.

170 Quoted in Forman, *Sammy Younge, Jr.*, 44.

171 Hamilton, *Minority Politics*, 27.

172 Taper, "Gomillion versus Lightfoot," 57.

173 Taper, "Gomillion versus Lightfoot," 40, 42.

174 Fritz, "Charles Gomillion," 17.

175 Wilbur C. Rich, "From Muskogee to Morningside Heights: Political Scientist Charles V. Hamilton," *Columbia Magazine*, Spring 2004.

176 Norrell, *Reaping the Whirlwind*, 171–72.

177 Norrell, *Reaping the Whirlwind*, 118.

178 Marable, "Tuskegee and the Politics of Illusion," 17.

179 Norrell, *Reaping the Whirlwind*, 124.

180 Gomillion, "Tuskegee Voting Story," 25–26.

181 Norrell, *Reaping the Whirlwind*, 125–26.

182 Gomillion, "Tuskegee Voting Story," 26.

183 Elwood, "Interview with Charles G. Gomillion," 587.

CHAPTER 2. SCHOLAR-ACTIVISTS, 1960–1965

1 University of Alabama Center for Public Television, "Samuel 'Sammy' Younge Jr."; Wendell Paris, interview.

2 Sammy's father was director of Macon County's March of Dimes campaign. See "March of Dimes Gets Support of Schools," *Tuskegee News*, January 7, 1965, 1.

3 Norrell, *Reaping the Whirlwind*, 32.

4 Wendell Paris and George Paris, interviews.

5 Cooper, *Africa in the World*, 2.

6 Quoted in Norrell, *Reaping the Whirlwind*, 126.

7 Woodward, *Strange Career*, 167.

8 Sitkoff, *Struggle for Black Equality*, 83.

9 Weinberg, *Chance to Learn*, 281.

10 Sitkoff, *Struggle for Black Equality*, 70.

11 Marable, *Race, Reform, and Rebellion*, 67.

12 Weinberg, *A Chance to Learn*, 325. Thompson writes that by the summer of 1960, "over 70,000 students had taken an active part in disruptive civil rights demonstrations." Thompson, *Private Black Colleges*, 16.

13 Michael Wright, interview with the author, July 2015.

14 Patton, interview.

15 George Paris, interview.

16 "400 Students Parade in Support of Civil Rights," *Campus Digest*, March 1, 1960, 1.

17 Jones, interview.

18 Lee, "Case of Dixon v. Alabama."

19 Quoted in Carson, *In Struggle*, 23–34.

20 Sitkoff, *Struggle for Black Equality*, 81–82.

21 Patton, interview.

22 James D. McJunkins, "SNCC Leader Urges Freedom Crusade," *Campus Digest*, December 13, 1963, 1.

23 Phillips, interview.

24 Peter Scott II, "SNCC Representatives Seek Aid in 'Black Belt Project,'" *Campus Digest*, October 18, 1964, 1.

25 Richard Von Briscoe, "14 Students Aid Miss. Vote," *Campus Digest*, November 14, 1964, 1.

26 Marable, *Race, Reform, and Rebellion*, 67.

27 George C. Wallace, "Statement by George C. Wallace, Governor of Alabama, before the Senate Committee on Commerce, in Opposition to Senate Bill 1732," July 15, 1963, Papers of George C. Wallace, Box SG030859, Folder 43.

28 Joseph, *Waiting 'til the Midnight Hour*, 48.

29 Dr. L. H. Foster and O'Neal Smalls, "Communist Lecture Cancelled—Why?," *Campus Digest*, December 13, 1963, 1.

30 "House Joint Resolution 5," Papers of the Alabama Legislative Commission to Preserve the Peace, Reel SG21073, 4 (hereafter cited as ALCPP).

31 ALCPP, Reel SG21073, 6, 10, 13, 14.

32 Williamson-Lott, "Battle over Power, Control, and Academic Freedom," 880, 884.

33 Carter, *Politics of Rage*, 231.

34 George C. Wallace, "TV Statement by Gov," July 13, 1965, Papers of George C. Wallace, Box SG030859, Folder 43.

35 "1273 Maconites Self-Employed," *Tuskegee News*, August 19, 1965, 1.

36 "Net Income of Macon Countians Shows Rise," *Tuskegee News*, January 7, 1965, 1.

37 "Government Furnishes 25% of Local Income," *Tuskegee News*, September 30, 1965, 1.

38 "34.4% Increase in Business Recorded for Macon County," *Tuskegee News*, November 4, 1965, 1.

39 Rogers, "Black Campus Movement," 172–73; Weinberg, *A Chance to Learn*, 281.

40 "Record Enrollment Expected at Tuskegee," *Tuskegee News*, June 10, 1965, 1.

41 "Foster Outlines T.I. Philosophy," *Tuskegee News*, February 25, 1965, 1.

42 Todd, interview.

43 Wright, interview.

44 "Students March in Support of Selma Campaign," *Tuskegee News*, February 4, 1965, 1.

45 Patton, "Insurgent Memories."

46 "Students Stage Sympathy March," *Campus Digest*, February 13, 1965, 1.

47 Quoted in Benson, "Interview with Gwendolyn M. Patton," 184.

48 Patton, "Insurgent Memories."

49 Phillips, interview; Melvin Todd got to ask Malcolm a question, and recalls that he answered it in a "gracious manner." Todd, interview.

50 "Malcolm X Hits Press in Speech Here at College," *Tuskegee News*, February 11, 1965.

51 Malcolm X, *Malcolm X Speaks*.

52 Todd, interview.

53 "Deaths Mount in Alabama Campaign," *Student Voice*, March 26, 1965, 1–2.

54 "'New Inspiration' Gained by Negro Says Farmer in Speech at Institute," *Tuskegee News*, March 4, 1965, 1.

55 Peter Scott II, "A Dying Warning," *Campus Digest*, March 6, 1965, 3.

56 Patton, *My Race to Freedom*, 155.

57 "The Shame of Selma," *Tuskegee News*, March 11, 1965.

58 Patton, *My Race to Freedom*, chap. 13; Forman, *Sammy Younge, Jr.*, 80.

59 Wiley and Hartford, "Oral History/Interview: Ruby Nell Sales."

60 George Paris, interview.

61 Patton, "Insurgent Memories"; Forman, *Sammy Younge, Jr.*, 82; George Paris, interview.

62 Barbara Donaldson, "Minute by Minute," *Campus Digest*, March 20, 1965, 8; Forman, *Sammy Younge, Jr.*, 87.

63 Patton, "Insurgent Memories."

64 Patton, *My Race to Freedom*, 158; Forman, *Sammy Younge, Jr.*, 89.

65 Wiley and Hartford, "Oral History/Interview: Ruby Nell Sales."

66 Donaldson, "Minute by Minute"; Forman, *Sammy Younge, Jr.*, 92.

67 Wiley and Hartford, "Oral History/Interview: Ruby Nell Sales."

68 Atheal Pierce, "From an Exchange Student," *Campus Digest*, March 20, 1965, 9, quoted in Forman, *Sammy Younge, Jr.*, 107.

69 Quoted in Forman, *Sammy Younge, Jr.*, 109.

70 L. H. Foster, "Statement Prepared by L. H. Foster, President of Tuskegee Institute, for Conference with Governor George C. Wallace," March 16, 1965, Papers of George C. Wallace, Box SG21957, Folder 12.

71 George C. Wallace, "By George C. Wallace, Governor of Alabama," March 17, 1965, Papers of George C. Wallace, Box SG030859, Folder 43.

72 James McJunkins, "A Time to Act," *Campus Digest*, March 20, 1965, 2.

73 Forman, *Sammy Younge, Jr.*, 110.

74 "Prexy Views Civil Rights Trend," *Campus Digest*, April 10, 1965, 1.

75 Patton, interview.
76 ALCPP, Reel SG21073, 8, 13.
77 Forman, *Sammy Younge, Jr.*, 130.
78 Wiley and Hartford, "Oral History/Interview: Ruby Nell Sales." In loco parentis rules were in decline after the *Dixon v. Alabama State Board of Education* ruling that students had a right to due process proceedings in campus disciplinary cases. See Lee, "Case of Dixon v. Alabama."
79 Wiley and Hartford, "Oral History/Interview: Ruby Nell Sales."
80 Forman, *Sammy Younge, Jr.*, 130–31.
81 "Marxist Studies Director Will Lecture Here," *Tuskegee News*, March 11, 1965, 1.
82 "Statement to House Members of Information on Point of Privilege," ALCPP, Reel SG21072.
83 James D. Bales and George L. Knox Jr., "John Doe and . . . Communism," *Campus Digest*, May 8, 1965, 7.
84 Wiley and Hartford, "Oral History/Interview: Ruby Nell Sales."
85 "Patton Wins Presidency," *Campus Digest*, April 24, 1965; Patton, *My Race to Freedom*, 163.
86 Todd, interview.
87 Wiley and Hartford, "Oral History/Interview: Ruby Nell Sales."
88 Hilton, interview.
89 Marshall Cabiness Jr., "Students Picket A&P Protesting Job Policy," *Campus Digest*, May 24, 1965, 1.
90 James Rogers, "TIAL Group Aids Ala. Voting Drive," *Campus Digest*, May 24, 1965, 3.
91 "Major State Civil Rights Projects Seek Vote Registration, Education," *Southern Courier*, July 16, 1965, 1.
92 Peter Westover, "Tuskegee Summer Program Stirs Interest in Education," *Southern Courier*, September 4, 1965, 1.
93 Dunn, interview.
94 Cozetta Lamore, interview with the author, July 2016.
95 Todd, interview.
96 Dunn, interview.
97 Todd, interview.
98 Higgins, interview.
99 Edwina Hayes, "Tuskegee and Civil Rights," *Campus Digest*, September 18, 1965, 4.
100 "We Must Learn to Live Together as Brothers, King Tells Graduates," *Tuskegee News*, June 3, 1965, 1.
101 Forman, *Sammy Younge, Jr.*, 126, 129.
102 Wendell Paris, interview.
103 Forman, *Sammy Younge, Jr.*, 142–43; "Group Asks Open Pool on Segregated Basis," *Tuskegee News*, June 10, 1965, 1.
104 Quoted in Forman, *Sammy Younge, Jr.*, 153.

105 Ture and Hamilton, *Black Power*, 136.
106 Jeffries, *Bloody Lowndes*, 165.
107 Wendell Paris, interview.
108 "Eight Local Firms Drop Race Bars," *Tuskegee News*, June 3, 1965, 1.
109 "What We Believe and Where We Stand," *Tuskegee News*, April 20, 1965.
110 Norrell, *Reaping the Whirlwind*, 130–31. For example: "There Is a Solution," March 4, 1965, and "Wrong Choices," March 18, 1965.
111 Patton, "Insurgent Memories."
112 Forman, *Sammy Younge, Jr.*, 119.
113 Wendell Paris, interview.
114 Todd, interview.
115 George Ware, "The Middle Class Negro in Tuskegee," *Activist*, 1965, 17, 34.
116 Quoted in Altonia Baker, "Tuskegee," *Southern Courier*, August 6, 1965, 6.
117 Paris, "The Poor of Macon County," *Activist*, 1965, 24.
118 Forman, *Sammy Younge, Jr.*, 119.
119 Younge, "The Great Society," *Activist*, 1965, 22; Forman, *Sammy Younge, Jr.*, 155–56.
120 Younge, "Great Society," 22–23.
121 Martha Honey, "Sundays in Tuskegee: Trouble at the Church," *Southern Courier*, July 16, 1965, 1.
122 Autry, "Integration Attempt at the Presbyterian Church," *Activist*, 1965, 8, 28; Honey, "Sundays in Tuskegee."
123 "TIAL Publication Calls for More Activist Stance," *Tuskegee News*, July 8, 1965, 1.
124 Shields, "Editorial," *Activist*, 1965, 5.
125 Shields, "Editorial," 6–7.
126 Younge, "Great Society," 23.
127 "New Advisory Committee to Study City's Problems," *Tuskegee News*, July 15, 1965, 1.
128 Forman, *Sammy Younge, Jr.*, 157.
129 "Violence Breaks Out at Tuskegee Church during TIAL's Third Integration Attempt," *Southern Courier*, July 23, 1965, 1.
130 Forman, *Sammy Younge, Jr.*, 158.
131 Forman, *Sammy Younge, Jr.*, 158; "Violence Breaks Out at Tuskegee Church."
132 George Paris, interview.
133 Patton, "Insurgent Memories."
134 Forman, *Sammy Younge, Jr.*, 160–61.
135 Phillips, personal communication, July 2016.
136 Patton, "Insurgent Memories."
137 Forman, *Sammy Younge, Jr.*, 162–63.
138 Quoted in Forman, *Sammy Younge, Jr.*, 165, 166–67.
139 "Arrests Made Following Incident at Church Here," *Tuskegee News*, July 22, 1965, 1.
140 "An Appeal for Law and Order," *Tuskegee News*, July 22, 1965, 1.
141 Mrs. Wilhelmina R. Jones, letter to the editor, *Tuskegee News*, July 22, 1965.

142 "Fourth Integration Attempt Fails at Tuskegee Church," *Southern Courier*, July 30, 1965, 1.

143 National Advisory Commission on Civil Disorders, and Otto Kerner, *Report of the National Advisory Commission on Civil Disorders* (Washington, DC: US Government Printing Office, 1968), 20.

144 Valia Wallace, "TI Student Is Eye Witness," *Campus Digest*, October 9, 1965, 3.

145 "Foster Urges Tuskegee Staff to Be Ready for Much Change," *Tuskegee News*, September 16, 1965, 1.

146 President Foster, "No Cliches, Just Facts," *Campus Digest*, September 18, 1965, 5.

147 "Dr. Foster Cites Responsibility of Staff to Students," *Tuskegee News*, September 30, 1965, 1.

148 Peter Scott II, "Unexamined Life . . . ," *Campus Digest*, October 23, 1965, 4.

149 Jim McJunkins, "Students Voice Opinions on Compulsory Chapel Rule," *Campus Digest*, October 23, 1965, 5.

150 Hilton, interview.

151 David R. Underhill, "Tuskegee Students Vote against Taking Their Parade Downtown," *Southern Courier*, November 6, 1965, 6.

152 "Let Students Vote!," *Campus Digest*, November 20, 1965, 4.

153 Mary Ellen Gale, "Students Explain Gripes," *Southern Courier*, December 11, 1965, 2.

154 Leon White, "Weekend Protests Note Student Unrest Claims," *Campus Digest*, December 4, 1965, 1.

155 "No Berkeley, but a Tuskegee," *Campus Digest*, December 4, 1965, 3.

156 Quoted in Forman, *Sammy Younge, Jr.*, 183–84.

CHAPTER 3. A CENTER OF BLACK POWER, 1966–1967

1 Mary Ellen Gale, "Killing of Rights Worker Jolts Tuskegee Students," *Southern Courier*, January 8, 1966, 1, 5; "Sheriff Says New Evidence Discovered in Murder Case," *Tuskegee News*, January 6, 1966, 1; Wright, interview.

2 Phillips, interview.

3 George Paris, interview.

4 Wendell Paris, interview.

5 Recent studies have explored the southern roots of the Black Power movement, in particular, Jeffries, *Bloody Lowndes*; and Murch, *Living for the City*.

6 The colonial origins of "industrial education" and of Tuskegee Institute are discussed in chapter 1.

7 Patton, "Insurgent Memories."

8 "Tuskegee Student Slain," *Campus Digest*, January 8, 1966, 1.

9 Hilton, interview.

10 Lamore, interview.

11 "Tuskegee Student Slain."

12 Forman, *Sammy Younge, Jr.*, 201–2.

13 "Tuskegee Student Slain."

14 Gale, "Killing of Rights Worker."
15 Wright, interview.
16 Harry Belafonte, "A Message from Harry Belafonte," Papers of Gwendolyn Patton, Box 403055.
17 Wendell Paris, interview.
18 Wendell Paris, interview.
19 Forman, *Sammy Younge, Jr.*
20 Forman, *Sammy Younge, Jr.*, 23.
21 Mary Ellen Gale, "Tuskegee Students Continue Pressure on City Council," *Southern Courier*, January 15, 1966, 5.
22 Kaufman, "Murder in Tuskegee," 122.
23 George Geddis, Chuck Griner, Eddie Cotton, "Week-Long Protests Continue," *Campus Digest*, January 15, 1966, 1.
24 Todd, interview.
25 Kaufman, "Murder in Tuskegee," 122.
26 Geddis, Griner, and Cotton, "Week-Long Protests Continue," 1, 3; Luther Foster, untitled memo to Tuskegee Institute Community, Papers of Erik Krystall, Box 422.001, Folder 17.
27 Gale, "Tuskegee Students Continue Pressure."
28 Mary Ellen Gale, "Tuskegee March Erupts into Riot," *Southern Courier*, January 22, 1966, 1.
29 "1200 Students Join Protest," *Campus Digest*, January 17, 1966, 1.
30 Editorial, *Campus Digest*, January 17, 1966, 2.
31 J. H. M. Henderson, "Student Demonstrators Leadership Praised," *Campus Digest*, January 22, 1966, 4.
32 "A Dark Day—But Hope Lies Ahead," *Tuskegee News*, January 20, 1966, 4.
33 Beulah C. Johnson, letter to the editor, *Tuskegee News*, January 20, 1966, 2.
34 Mary Ellen Gale, "Tuskegee Council Passes Local Desegregation Law," *Southern Courier*, January 29, 1966, 1; "City Council Approves Accommodations Law," *Tuskegee News*, January 27, 1966, 1.
35 "Debate Ends in Free-for-All," *Campus Digest*, February 5, 1966, 1.
36 According to Patton, the Tuskegee student movement coined this phrase. Patton, interview.
37 Mary Ellen Gale, "Tuskegee Institute Asks, Civil Rights or Classes?," *Southern Courier*, February 5, 1966, 5.
38 Forman, *Sammy Younge, Jr.*, 215–16.
39 James E. Jackson, "Gus Hall, James Jackson Speak at Tuskegee," *Worker*, February 20, 1966, 1, Papers of Erik Krystall, Box 422.001, Folder 20; Mrs. Arthur C. Fortner to George C. Wallace, February 12, 1966, Mrs. Jimmie Jean Price to George C. Wallace, February 15, 1966, and Wallace to Fortner and Wallace to Price, February 18, 1966, Papers of George C. Wallace, Box SG21957, Folder 12.

40 Mary Ellen Gale, "Tuskegee Institute Disputes Local School over Teacher," *Southern Courier*, February 26, 1966, 1.

41 Board of Trustees of Tuskegee Institute, "Minutes of the Board of Trustees," *Tuskegee Institute*, April 2, 1966, 6, 8–9.

42 Mary Ellen Gale, "Pool Integrated Quietly: No Splash," *Southern Courier*, July 16, 1966, 1.

43 Marable, *Race, Reform, and Rebellion*, 21–26; Fairclough, *Better Day Coming*, 213.

44 Fairclough, "Martin Luther King, Jr. and the War in Vietnam," 24–25.

45 Marable, *Malcolm X*, 272.

46 Marable, *Race, Reform, and Rebellion*, 97–98.

47 Carson, *In Struggle*.

48 See Vietnam Veterans Memorial Fund, accessed online January 31, 2017, www.vmf.org; George Paris, interview.

49 George Paris, interview.

50 Forman, *Making of Black Revolutionaries*, 445.

51 Student Nonviolent Coordinating Committee, "Statement on Vietnam," January 6, 1966, www.crmvet.org.

52 Robert Analavage and James Smith, "Viet Nam Stand Stirs Storm," *Southern Courier*, January 15, 1966, 1; Wendell Paris, interview.

53 David Colker and Laura J. Nelson, "Julian Bond, Former NAACP Board Chairman, Dies at 75," *Los Angeles Times*, August 16, 2015, www.latimes.com.

54 Mary Ellen Gale, "Tuskegee Hears Two CR Views," *Southern Courier*, February 4, 1967, 5.

55 The phrase "Black Power" was not invented by Carmichael. Others used it long before him. See, for example, Richard Wright, *Black Power: A Record of Reactions in a Land of Pathos* (New York: Perennial, 1954).

56 Rogers, "Black Campus Movement," 173.

57 Biondi, *Black Revolution on Campus*, 26.

58 Joseph, *Black Power Movement*, 3.

59 On women's activism and the state, see Sanders, *Chance for Change*; on education and schooling, see Rickford, *We Are an African People*; and on health care activism, see Jenna M. Loyd, *Health Rights Are Civil Rights* (Minneapolis: University of Minnesota Press, 2014).

60 Wendell Paris, interview.

61 Gene Roberts, "2 Rights Groups Promote All-Negro Slates for Local Elections in the South," *New York Times*, January 23, 1966, 73.

62 "Unwise SNCC Advice," *Tuskegee News*, June 2, 1966, 2.

63 Michael F. Wright, letter to the editor, *Campus Digest*, April 30, 1966, 4; Todd, interview.

64 Michael Wright, "Black Power and the Press," July 1966, Papers of Michael Wright, Box 099.001.

65 Patton, interview.
66 Stokely Carmichael, "What We Want," *New York Review of Books*, September 22, 1966.
67 Ernest Stephens, "Black Power and Black Backlash," *Campus Digest*, September 17, 1966.
68 Edwin Strickland, "Confidential Report to Governor George C. Wallace," September 13, 1966, ALCPP, Reel SG21074, Folder 18.
69 "'Impediments' Hit in Foster Speech," *Tuskegee News*, September 29, 1966, 2.
70 Higgins, Hilton, Wright, George Paris, Wendell Paris, interviews; Arthur Pfister, interview with the author, July 2016.
71 Wendell Paris, interview.
72 Dr. G. W. Cooper, "Assimilationists and Revolutionists," *Campus Digest*, October 8, 1966, 5.
73 Speeches at Tuskegee by King, Forman, and Malcolm X are discussed in chapter 2.
74 Higgins, interview.
75 "Stokely Carmichael Confronts Tuskegee," *Southern Courier*, October 22, 1966, 3.
76 "Speakers Probe Problems," *Campus Digest*, October 15, 1966, 1. The article misspelled his last name as "Parish."
77 Rogers, *Black Campus Movement*, 78.
78 "Speakers Probe Problems," 1, 4. Advocating for the TICEP program, Dean Phillips at times gave speeches right after Carmichael at many of the same Black Belt churches (not an easy act to follow!). Years later, Phillips and Carmichael bumped into each other at an event at Howard University. Phillips remembers that Carmichael told him, "Well, Dean, I'll tell you, you know things have changed a little bit, but they still haven't changed too much since you and I used to be on that circuit talking at the churches." Phillips, interview.
79 See chapter 1.
80 For Washington's attitude toward colonialism, see chapter 1. Writing later in his life, from Ghana, about the role of the French, English, and German governments in Africa, Du Bois admitted that he "did not question the interpretation which pictured this as the advance of civilization and the benevolent tutelage of barbarians." Du Bois, *Dusk of Dawn*, 21.
81 Cruse, "Revolutionary Nationalism," 13.
82 Carmichael, "What We Want."
83 Higgins, interview.
84 Holsaert et al., *Hands on the Freedom Plow*, 580.
85 Todd, interview.
86 Michael Wright, "Economics and Racism," Papers of Michael Wright, Box 099.001.
87 Marable, *Race, Reform, and Rebellion*, 108.
88 Turner, *Sitting In and Speaking Out*, 189.

89 See, for example, C. L. R. James's 1966 analysis, "The Rise and Fall of Nkrumah," in James, *C. L. R. James Reader*, 354–61.

90 See, for example, Du Bois, *Black Reconstruction*.

91 In 1967 George Wallace received a list of Black Power organizations, prefaced by an assertion that "these groups always oppose the capitalist system." Papers of George C. Wallace, Box SG19973, Folder 18. For a more sympathetic reaction to Carmichael and the slogan, see C. L. R. James, "Black Power" (1967), in James, *C. L. R. James Reader*, 365; also, historian Jeffrey Turner argues that the black student movement was essentially reformist because it aimed to alter, not destroy, higher education. *Sitting In and Speaking Out*, 7. For further discussion, see chapter 4.

92 Wendell Paris, interview.

93 Trammell, interview; Forman, *Sammy Younge, Jr.*, 208.

94 Dunn, interview; see chapter 2.

95 Todd, interview.

96 US Census Bureau, "Characteristics of the Population, for Census County Divisions, 1960," Alabama Population Table 25, accessed January 16, 2017, www.census.gov.

97 Amerson, *Great Courage*, 69.

98 According to Amerson, his only law enforcement credential was the completion of two courses on civil and criminal investigations while in the Army. "Scott Davis, Lucius Amerson, Candidates for Sheriff Post," *Tuskegee News*, March 3, 1966, 1.

99 Wendell Paris, Patton, and Wright, interviews.

100 Norrell, *Reaping the Whirlwind*, 189.

101 Mary Ellen Gale, "Macon Sheriff Nominee Takes Victory in Stride," *Southern Courier*, June 4, 1966, 1; Mary Ellen Gale, "Amerson Elected Macon Sheriff Despite Sadler Write-In Effort," *Southern Courier*, November 12, 1966, 1.

102 Wendell Paris, interview.

103 Gene Roberts, "A Kind of Black Power in Macon County, Ala.," *New York Times Magazine*, February 26, 1967.

104 Michael E. Ruane, "Sheriff Made History Simply by Doing His Job," *Washington Post*, August 14, 2008; Amerson, *Great Courage*, 94–95.

105 *Tick . . . Tick . . . Tick. . .* , Metro-Goldwyn-Mayer, 1970; Amerson, *Great Courage*, 130–31.

106 Sokol, *There Goes My Everything*, 263.

107 Ture and Hamilton, *Black Power*.

108 On Hamilton's career at Tuskegee, see chapter 1.

109 Ture and Hamilton, *Black Power*, 144.

110 See, for example, Murch, *Living for the City*; and Spencer, *Revolution Has Come*.

111 John Klein, "Civil Rights Leaders Disagree on Using Votes in Black Belt," *Southern Courier*, January 22, 1966, 1.

112 The Democratic Party did not abandon the slogan "white supremacy" until December 1966. See Roy Reed, "Democrats Scrap Alabama Slogan in Bid to Negroes," *New York Times*, January 23, 1966, 1.

113 Mary Ellen Gale, "A Night of Speeches at Tuskegee," *Southern Courier*, February 12, 1966, 2.

114 Ture and Hamilton, *Black Power*, 144.

115 Ture and Hamilton, *Black Power*, 145.

116 Mary Ellen Gale, "Mayor's Order Starts Dispute," *Southern Courier*, December 3, 1966, 5.

117 Mary Ellen Gale, "More Troubles for Amerson," *Southern Courier*, February 25, 1967, 2.

118 Amerson, *Great Courage*, chap. 15; Mary Ellen Gale, "Constables Run Loose in Macon," *Southern Courier*, January 28, 1967, 5.

119 James O. Hadnott, "Amerson Says Party Helped Him Win," *Southern Courier*, March 18, 1967, 2.

120 Forman, *Sammy Younge, Jr.*, 227.

121 Amerson, *Great Courage*, chap. 17; Mary Ellen Gale, "High Bond in Macon," *Southern Courier*, August 19, 1967, 1, 5; "Alabama's First Negro Sheriff Arrests White Chief of Police," *Madera Tribune*, March 20, 1968, 2.

122 Wendell Paris, interview.

123 Mary Ellen Gale, "Church Doors Are Locked in Tuskegee Again . . . ," *Southern Courier*, July 30, 1966, 1; "You'll Have to Leave," *Southern Courier*, August 6, 1966, 2.

124 Mary Ellen Gale, "Extent of School Integration Is Anybody's Guess in Tuskegee," *Southern Courier*, September 10, 1966.

125 Jeffries, *Bloody Lowndes*, 201–4; Gwendolyn Patton, "Lowndes County Election Fraud," *Liberator*, December 1966, 8–9; Ture and Hamilton, *Black Power*, 118–20.

126 Higgins, interview.

127 Amerson, *Great Courage*, 116.

128 "Segrest Gets Venue Shift," *Tuskegee News*, November 10, 1966, 1.

129 "A Mockery of Justice," *Southern Courier*, December 17, 1966, 2.

130 Mary Ellen Gale, "Anatomy of a Murder Trial," *Southern Courier*, December 24, 1966, 4.

131 "Not Guilty Verdict Told," *Tuskegee News*, December 15, 1966, 1.

132 Tom Richardson, letter to the editor, *Tuskegee News*, December 15, 1966, 2.

133 Quoted in Forman, *Sammy Younge, Jr.*, 249.

134 Forman, *Sammy Younge, Jr.*, 250.

135 "Slayer Goes Free; Students Riot," *Campus Digest*, December 19, 1966, 1.

136 Forman, *Sammy Younge, Jr.*, 254.

137 "Town Rocked by Students," *Campus Digest*, December 19, 1966, 3.

138 Forman, *Sammy Younge, Jr.*, 257.

139 "Foster Puts Clamp on Demonstrations," *Tuskegee News*, December 15, 1966, 1; "A Wise Statement," *Tuskegee News*, December 15, 1966, 2.

140 A Tuskegee Merchant, letter to the editor, *Tuskegee News*, December 22, 1966, 6.

141 "City Council against Student March Here," *Tuskegee News*, January 5, 1967, 1.

142 Mary Ellen Gale, "After a Year, Tuskegee Remembers," *Southern Courier*, January 7, 1967, 5.

143 Patton, interview.

144 Wendell Paris, interview.

145 "Compulsory Chapel Ends—Next Year," *Campus Digest*, March 25, 1967.

146 See Robert Cohen, "Prophetic Minority versus Recalcitrant Minority," in Cohen, Snyder, and Carter, *Rebellion in Black and White*, 12.

147 Rogers, "Black Campus Movement," 173.

148 Eddie Cotton, "Student Conference Views Statewide Campus Problems," *Campus Digest*, April 23, 1966, 2; Program, Student Human Relations Conference, Papers of Erik Krystall, Box 422.001, Folder 14.

149 Valia Wallace, "Patton Resigns SGA," *Campus Digest*, October 1, 1966, 2. It was later revealed that the NSA was funded by the Central Intelligence Agency. See Louis Menand, "A Friend of the Devil," *New Yorker*, March 23, 2015.

150 The origins of the Tuskegee Institute Community Education Program (TICEP) and its effect on student participants are described in chapter 2.

151 Wright, interview.

152 Lamore, interview.

153 Michael Wright, "An Open Letter to Black Youth," July 1966, Papers of Michael Wright, Box 099.001.

154 Ernest Stephens, "Our Role as Black Student," *Campus Digest*, October 1, 1966, 4.

155 Quoted in Board of Trustees of Tuskegee Institute, "Minutes of the Board of Trustees," *Tuskegee Institute*, October 28, 1966, 20.

156 S. E. Anderson, "Black Students," 41.

157 Quoted in Roger Rapaport, "Tuskegee Students Apathetic on Goals, Favor Personal Goals," *Campus Digest*, November 5, 1966, 1.

158 Gwen Patton, "Schools 'Better Wake Up,'" *Southern Courier*, November 19, 1966, 2.

159 Mary Ellen Gale, "Students Attack Negro Colleges," *Southern Courier*, February 18, 1967, 5.

160 "Jones Visits Campus," *Campus Digest*, February 28, 1967, 1.

161 Elizabeth Keen, letter to the editor, *Tuskegee News*, March 9, 1967, 2.

162 Mary Ellen Gale, "SNCC an Issue in SGA Election," *Southern Courier*, April 22, 1967, 2.

163 Barbara Flowers, "Two Weeks of Protest at Alabama State," *Southern Courier*, April 29, 1967, 3.

164 Marvin McMillan, "Up from Apathy," *Campus Digest*, April 15, 1967.

165 Tony Mohr, "Southern Stereotypes," *Campus Digest*, May 1, 1967, 1.

166 Tom Robischon, "An Open Letter to Marvin McMillan," *Campus Digest*, May 6, 1967, 2.

167 Trammell, interview; Rogers, "Black Campus Movement," 173.

168 Quoted in Turner, *Sitting In and Speaking Out*, 181.

169 Stephens, "Black University," 131.

170 Stephens, "Black University," 131–32, 134, 135–36.

171 Stephens, "Black University," 136–37.

172 Charles V. Hamilton, "The Place of the Black College in the Human Rights Struggle," *Negro Digest*, September 1967, 4–10. Hamilton's article was based on a speech of the same title (unpublished). See Biondi, "Controversial Blackness," 227.

173 Hamilton, "Place of the Black College," 5–7.

174 Michael Wright, "Gentlemen" (1967), Papers of Michael Wright, Box 099.001.

175 James Norton Jr., "Black Is Beautiful," *Campus Digest*, November 11, 1967, 6.

176 Thomas W. Schmidt, letter to the editor, *Campus Digest*, November 18, 1967.

177 The global perspective of the 1960s and 1970s black radical movements is described by many historians. See, for example, Biondi, *Black Revolution on Campus*; Rickford, *We Are an African People*; and Bloom and Martin, *Black against Empire*.

178 See chapter 1.

179 See "Muhammad Ali Speaks Out against the War in Vietnam," in Zinn and Arnove, *Voices of a People's History of the United States*, 431.

180 Mary Ellen Gale, "Anti-War Demonstrators Accompany ROTC Parade," *Southern Courier*, March 18, 1967, 2.

181 See Martin Luther King Jr., "Beyond Vietnam," in Zinn and Arnove, *Voices of a People's History of the United States*, 423–27.

182 "Greatest Purveyor . . . ," *Campus Digest*, April 15, 1967, 3. In June a group of seventy-seven faculty and staff members signed a resolution to support the Johnson administration's conduct of the war. See "Tuskegee Group Endorses US Viet Nam Role," *Southern Courier*, June 17, 1967, 2.

183 "Should the US Remain in Viet Nam," *Campus Digest*, May 8, 1965, 7.

184 Gwendolyn Patton, "Views of Vietnam War," *Southern Courier*, January 28, 1967, 2; Gwendolyn Patton, "Black People and War," *Liberator*, February 1967.

185 Student Mobilization Committee, "Working Committee Meeting—Minutes," June 6, 1967, www.marxists.org.

186 "Carmichael Discusses Black Power in Havana Press Conference," *World Outlook*, August 25, 1967, 731, www.marxists.org.

187 "Exile Says: Americans Go Home," *Campus Digest*, April 15, 1967, 1.

188 "Exploring Afro-Americanism," *Campus Digest*, April 15, 1967, 2.

189 Mary Ellen Gale, "We're Not Americans, Brother," *Southern Courier*, December 2, 1967, 1; Alenda A. Hicks, "James Forman Addresses South African Forum," *Campus Digest*, December 2, 1967, 1.

190 Forman, *Sammy Younge, Jr.*; Patton and Wright, interviews.

191 Trammell, interview.

192 Mary Ellen Gale, "Court Orders Desegregation of All State Schools," *Southern Courier*, March 25, 1967, 1.

193 Mary Ellen Gale, "US Order 'Impossible,' Educators Say at Hearing," *Southern Courier*, April 8, 1967, 1.

194 Mary Ellen Gale, "Reed Protests Tuskegee Cut-Off," *Southern Courier*, May 13, 1967, 6.

195 Carter, *Politics of Rage*, 235.

196 "Wallace's Revenge," *Southern Courier*, May 20, 1967, 2.

197 "Cynical Education Budgeting," *Tuskegee News*, June 22, 1966, 2.

198 Mary Ellen Gale, "Educators Plead for More Money," *Southern Courier*, May 27, 1967, 1.

199 "Tuskegee Inst. Makes Bid to Regain Funds," *Tuskegee News*, May 25, 1967, 1.

200 "Race Relations Grant of $300,000 Given TI," *Tuskegee News*, May 25, 1967, 1.

201 "Senate Passes Measure Restoring Funds to TI," *Tuskegee News*, August 10, 1967, 1.

202 Mary Ellen Gale, "Can Gov. Keep Tuskegee Money? Radney Says Yes, Cooper Says No," *Southern Courier*, September 16, 1967, 1; Mary Ellen Gale, "Tuskegee Gets Funds after All," *Southern Courier*, October 28, 1967, 1.

203 "Negro Rights Aide Slain in Alabama," *New York Times*, January 5, 1966.

CHAPTER 4. A BLACK UNIVERSITY? 1968

1 Soldiers also came to campus in 1940 to stop a Tuskegee student strike. See chapter 1.

2 Higgins, *Student Unrest*, 4–9.

3 Higgins, *Student Unrest*, 5–8.

4 Higgins, *Student Unrest*, 8–9.

5 Hughes and Patterson, *Robert Russa Moton*, 117.

6 Charles Johnson Jr., *African Americans and ROTC*.

7 See chapter 1.

8 Hill, interview.

9 George Geddis, interview with the author, June 2017.

10 Warren Hamilton, interview with the author, July 2017.

11 Bass and Nelson, *Orangeburg Massacre*, 16, 15–46, 46–47.

12 Bass and Nelson, *Orangeburg Massacre*, 61–65, 73.

13 Bass and Nelson, *Orangeburg Massacre*, 89.

14 Bass and Nelson, *Orangeburg Massacre*, 87–88.

15 Bass and Nelson, *Orangeburg Massacre*, 92.

16 Lawrence B. de Graaf, "Howard: The Evolution of a Black Student Revolt," in *Protest! Student Activism in America* (New York: Morrow, 1970), 332.

17 Caroline Hilton, "SGA Group Goes to S.C.," *Campus Digest*, February 17, 1968, 3, 5.

18 Todd, interview.

19 Todd, interview.

20 Mary Ellen Gale, "Tuskegee Students Tell of Deaths in Carolina," *Southern Courier*, February 24, 1968, 1.

21 Melvin Todd, "Massacre at Orangeburg," *Campus Digest*, February 17, 1968, 1–2.

22 Forman, *Sammy Younge, Jr.*, 264.

23 Todd, interview.

24 Mary Ellen Gale, "Muslims Tell Students: Blacks In, Whites Out," *Southern Courier*, February 17, 1968, 1.

25 Mary Ellen Gale, "Flying Eggs, Words Greet US Speakers at Tuskegee," *Southern Courier*, March 9, 1968, 1.

26 Higgins, *Student Unrest*, 12.

27 Forman, *Sammy Younge, Jr.*, 264.

28 Higgins, *Student Unrest*, 13–14.

29 Higgins, *Student Unrest*, 14–15.

30 Higgins, *Student Unrest*, 153–54.

31 Carmichael spent a lot of time in the region and got to know many Tuskegee activists well. The impact of his previous speaking engagements on campus is discussed in chapter 3.

32 Higgins, *Student Unrest*, 154, 15–16.

33 Higgins, *Student Unrest*, 155.

34 Higgins, *Student Unrest*, 22–23; "Chronology of Protest," *Campus Digest*, March 23, 1968, 1.

35 Higgins, *Student Unrest*, 21–22.

36 "Foster Holds Faculty Meet," *Campus Digest*, March 23, 1968, 1.

37 Higgins, *Student Unrest*, 21.

38 Higgins, *Student Unrest*, introduction. It may in fact be the most comprehensive documentary record compiled for any student movement in the United States.

39 Higgins, *Student Unrest*, 24–25.

40 Higgins, *Student Unrest*, 37.

41 Dock Anderson, "Engineers Take Over Building," *Campus Digest*, March 30, 1968, 1.

42 *Campus Digest*, various issues, 1966–1968.

43 Higgins, *Student Unrest*, 156.

44 Higgins, *Student Unrest*, 37–39.

45 Electronics Senior Class, "What about Us?," *Campus Digest*, March 23, 1968, 2.

46 Bert Phillips was a very popular figure among students on campus. His resignation was a big deal because he was widely perceived as defending students and student activists in 1965–1967. See chapter 2.

47 Deborah McGregor, "Dean Phillips Resigns," *Campus Digest*, March 23, 1968, 1.

48 Higgins, *Student Unrest*, 157; "Students' Demands Met after Boycott," *Campus Digest*, March 30, 1968, 1.

49 Higgins, *Student Unrest*, 44.

50 Torrens, "Tuskegee Years," 11.

51 Mary Ellen Gale, "Revolution at Tuskegee," *Southern Courier*, March 30, 1968, 1, 6.

52 Higgins, *Student Unrest*, 40–42.

53 Higgins, *Student Unrest*, 157.

54 Higgins, *Student Unrest*, 49.

55 Higgins, *Student Unrest*, 158; "Engineers Take Over," 2.

56 James Norton Jr., "Courage or Comforts," *Campus Digest*, March 30, 1968, 4.

57 Higgins, *Student Unrest*, 55–56, 61, 58.

58 Geddis, interview.

59 Wright, interview.

60 Wright, "Affidavit," Papers of Michael F. Wright, Box 099.001.

61 Student "Mandate" document (untitled), Papers of Erik Krystall, Box 422.001, Folder 24.

62 Wright, interview; Geddis, interview.

63 Except for two pages proposing a new Department of Oral Communications, signed by a young white instructor, Sue Pendell. She went on to an academic career in the field of communications studies, but has no memory of how this proposal ended up in the student "Mandate" document. She taught in Tuskegee's English department for two semesters, 1967–1968, and her contract was not renewed. Sue Pendell, interview with the author, October 2017.

64 Student "Mandate" document.

65 Student "Mandate" document, 1–2.

66 Student "Mandate" document, 3–18.

67 Student "Mandate" document, 4.

68 Student "Mandate" document, 15. Emphasis in the original.

69 Dock Anthony Anderson III, "Engineers Reject Foster's Request," *Campus Digest*, April 6, 1968, 1, 3.

70 Geddis, interview; Wright, interview.

71 Trustees, "Minutes," April 6, 1968, 13.

72 On Bouldin, see Thornton, *Dividing Lines*, 235. On Gaston, see Jenkins and Hines, *Black Titan*.

73 "Lucius Clay Dies; Led Berlin Airlift," *New York Times*, April 17, 1978.

74 Wolfgang Saxon, "Melvin Glasser, 79, Supervisor of Field Trials of Salk Vaccine," *New York Times*, March 17, 1995.

75 "Richard Waddell, Art Dealer, 50, Dies," *New York Times*, February 8, 1974; "In Memoriam: William Gill Gridley, Jr., Trustee of Battell Stoeckel Estate in Norfolk," Norfolk Chamber Music Festival website; "Obituary: Alexander Aldrich," *Saratogian*, July 23, 2017.

76 "Tuskegee Students Lock Up Trustees 13 Hours," *St. Petersburg Times*, April 8, 1968, A1, A8.

77 Wright, interview.

78 Geddis, interview.

79 Hill, interview.

80 Wright, interview.

81 Geddis, interview.

82 Honey, *Going down Jericho Road*, 444.

83 Earl Caldwell, "Guard Called Out," *New York Times*, April 5, 1968.

84 Ben A. Franklin, "Army Troops in Capital as Negroes Riot; Guards Sent into Chicago, Detroit, Boston," *New York Times*, April 6, 1968.

85 Quoted in Franklin, "Army Troops in Capital."

86 Geddis, interview.

87 Lamore, interview.

88 "Students Polled on 11 Questions," *Campus Digest*, April 6, 1968, 2; "Vote Shows: Students Support Tuition Grants, Fee for Athletics," *Campus Digest*, April 6, 1968, 7.

89 Wright, "Affidavit."

90 Geddis, interview.

91 Higgins, *Student Unrest*, 160.

92 In attendance were Frances Bolton, Lucius Clay, Arthur Cook, A. G. Gaston, Melvin Glasser, E. B. Goode, William Gridley, Robert Mulreaney, Basil O'Connor, Montague Oliver, and Frederick Patterson. Trustees, "Minutes," April 5, 1968, 4.

93 Trustees, "Minutes," April 6, 1968, 5.

94 Trustees, "Minutes," April 6, 1968, 15–16.

95 Mary Ellen Gale, "Trouble at Tuskegee," *Southern Courier*, April 13, 1968, 6.

96 Trustees, "Minutes," April 6, 1968, 3–5, 8–9.

97 Geddis, interview.

98 Hill, interview.

99 Trustees, "Minutes," April 6, 1968, 9.

100 Olaf O. McJunkins Jr., "Students Push for Demands," *Campus Digest*, May 4, 1968, 2.

101 Lena Agnew, interview with the author, November 2016.

102 Agnew, interview.

103 Alenda A. Hicks, "On Trial," *Campus Digest*, May 4, 1968, 2.

104 Quoted in Mary Ellen Gale, "Tuskegee 'Court' Hears Senior Class President," *Southern Courier*, May 4, 1968, 2.

105 Geddis, interview.

106 Higgins, interview.

107 In his memoir he writes, "I called the governor and requested that the National Guard and state troopers be sent to Tuskegee in case we had to forcefully restore order." See Amerson, *Great Courage*, 113. However, in Gwen Patton's memoir, she recounts a conversation with him years later and claims that he explicitly denied doing that, out of fear that it could "turn into a bloodbath." See Patton, *My Race to Freedom*, 343.

108 Higgins, *Student Unrest*, 160.

109 "Foster Closes Tuskegee Institute; Sheriff Calls In Guard, Troopers," *Tuskegee News*, April 11, 1968, 1.

110 Wright, "Affidavit."

111 Wright, interview.

112 Wright, interview.

113 Wright, interview.

114 "Foster Closes Tuskegee Institute."

115 Higgins, *Student Unrest*, 161.

116 Agnew, interview.

117 Wright, "Affidavit."

118 Hilton, interview.

119 Phillips, interview.

120 "Foster Closes Tuskegee Institute."

121 Pendell, interview.

122 "Institute May Open Latter Part of Month," *Tuskegee News*, April 11, 1968, 1.

123 Hilton, interview.

124 Higgins, *Student Unrest*, 92–93.

125 Higgins, *Student Unrest*, 94–95.

126 Forman, *Sammy Younge, Jr.*, 278. As the Tuskegee student movement was brought to an abrupt halt, student activism continued to explode around the country. On the day after Tuskegee Institute reopened, April 23, students occupied five buildings at Columbia University. Police stormed the buildings seven days later.

127 Quoted in Mary Ellen Gale, "US Judge Tells Tuskegee to Re-Admit All Students," *Southern Courier*, April 27, 1968, 1.

128 Higgins, *Student Unrest*, 123–24.

129 Hill, interview.

130 Geddis, interview.

131 "In Good Faith!," *Campus Digest*, May 18, 1968, 2.

132 Phillips, interview.

133 Wright, interview.

134 Geddis, interview.

135 Hamilton, interview.

136 Hilton, interview.

137 Geddis, interview.

138 Zamma, "'Forgive Them'—Says Zamma," *Campus Digest*, May 4, 1968, 1.

139 Edwin Strickland to Gov. Albert Brewer, September 15, 1968, Files of ALCPP.

140 Ali, *Street Fighting Years*, chap. 8.

141 Quoted in Mary Ellen Gale, "Tuskegee Speaker Calls for a 'Quiet Rebellion,'" *Southern Courier*, June 15, 1968, 4.

142 Tuskegee's fall enrollment ticked upward to its highest level to date: 3,184 students. See Pernella Peavy, "Institute Increases Enrollment," *Campus Digest*, October 26, 1968, 1.

143 James Norton Jr., "Editorial: Welcome Freshmen, An Observation," *Campus Digest*, September 21, 1968, 2.

144 Those Who Know, "Dear Freshmen," *Campus Digest*, September 21, 1968, 2.

145 Anonymous, letter to the editor, *Campus Digest*, September 28, 1968, 2.

146 Caroline Hilton, "A Foreword: Instilling Trust," *Campus Digest*, October 5, 1968, 2.

147 Dementreous Clifton, "Judge Johnson Grants Tuskegee Institute Permanent Injunction," *Campus Digest*, October 19, 1968, 1.

148 James M. Fallows, "Keever Elected in Tuskegee," *Southern Courier*, August 17, 1968, 1.

149 Geddis, interview.

150 Caroline Hilton, "Election May Decide Future for Tuskegee," *Southern Courier*, October 19, 1968, 4.

151 Torrens, "Tuskegee Years," 14, 23.

152 Caroline Hilton, "Afro-American Responsibility Begins in a Black Oriented University," *Campus Digest*, October 19, 1968, 4.

153 Beatrice Berry, "Role of Black University Discussed by Labrie," *Campus Digest*, October 19, 1968, 3.

154 Caroline Hilton, "A New Breed Approacheth," *Campus Digest*, October 26, 1968, 4.

155 Arthur Pfister, "Ain't That Sad?," *Campus Digest*, November 9, 1968, 5.

156 "Students Form New Organization S.O.B.U.-T.I.," *Campus Digest*, November 16, 1968, 2. See also Jelani Favors, "North Carolina A&T Black Power Activists and the Student Organization for Black Unity," in Cohen, Snyder, and Carter, *Rebellion in Black and White*.

157 Turner, *Sitting In and Speaking Out*, 168–69.

158 Julia Ann Fuller, "Views On: The Dismissal of White Instructors," *Campus Digest*, November 2, 1968, 5.

159 Dick Wasserstrom, interview with the author, June 26, 2017; Maggie Magee, interview with the author, June 29, 2017; Torrens, "Tuskegee Years," 28.

160 Caroline Hilton, "A Return To What?," and "Will You Come Home?," *Campus Digest*, November 16, 1968, 6.

161 E. B. Henderson, letter to the editor, *Tuskegee News*, March 28, 1968, 2.

162 Neal Jackson, "Isom States Reasons for Refusing to Attend Black Concept Meeting," *Campus Digest*, October 26, 1968, 1.

163 Hamilton, interview.

164 See Kelley, *Freedom Dreams*, ix, on the problem of evaluating movements merely by whether or not they "succeed."

165 "Special Joint Committee Report," *Campus Digest*, November 2, 1968, 6.

166 Biondi, *Black Revolution on Campus*, 146, chap. 2.

167 Rogers, *Black Campus Movement*, 123, 138.

168 Hill, interview.

169 Geddis, interview.

170 See Michael Wright's assessment in Forman, *Sammy Younge, Jr.*, 274.

171 Hilton and Lamore, interviews.

172 Annual Report of the President, *Bulletin of Tuskegee Institute*, December 1968, 2.

CHAPTER 5. CONCLUSION

1 US Census Bureau, "Community Facts," website for Tuskegee city, Alabama, accessed March 8, 2018, factfinder.census.gov.

2 Anna Claire Vollers, "Alabama Is 6th Poorest State in Nation; Poverty Rate at 40 Percent in Some Counties," Al.com, accessed March 4, 2018, www.al.com.

3 Manning Marable analyzed this pattern in "Tuskegee and the Politics of Illusion," 18.

4 Norrell, *Reaping the Whirlwind*, 201–2; Marable, "Tuskegee and the Politics of Illusion," 18.

5 Cedric Johnson, *Revolutionaries to Race Leaders*; Taylor, *From #BlackLivesMatter to Black Liberation*.

6 Connolly, *World More Concrete*, 285.

7 Norrell, *Reaping the Whirlwind*, 217.

8 Chester Higgins and Betsy Kissam, *Sacred Nile* (Harrison, NY: BCH Fulfillment & Distribution, 2021).

9 Wright, interview.

10 Wendell Paris, George Paris, Higgins, Wright, Dunn, Pfister, interviews.

11 See Patton, *My Race to Freedom*.

12 Farmer, *Remaking Black Power*, 166.

13 Trenholm State Community College, "Biography," Gwen Patton Collection.

14 Charles V. Hamilton, "Afterword, 1992," in Ture and Hamilton, *Black Power*, 209.

15 Hamilton, "Afterword," 210.

16 Cooper, *Africa in the World*.

17 Joseph, *Black Power Movement*, 252; James Preston, "Tuskegee: A Study of the Emergence of a Black Studies Program," Tuskegee Institute, July 30, 1970, Tuskegee Institute Archives, 3; Au, Brown, and Calderón, *Reclaiming the Multicultural Roots of US Curriculum*, chap. 5.

18 Joseph, *Black Power Movement*, 273; Murch, *Living for the City*.

19 Preston, "Tuskegee," 14–15, 18, 20, 22.

20 Rojas, *From Black Power to Black Studies*.

21 Joseph, *Black Power Movement*, 251.

22 Ferguson, *Reorder of Things*.

23 "Lucius Clay Dies; Led Berlin Airlift."

24 Quoted in Gale, "Tuskegee Speaker Calls for a 'Quiet Rebellion.'"

25 Trip Gabriel and Dana Goldstein, "Disputing Racism's Reach, Republicans Rattle American Schools," *New York Times*, June 1, 2021.

26 N. B. D. Connolly, "The Enduring, Gilded Periphery: Colonialism and Grand Cayman in Capital's Atlantic World," *Journal of the Gilded Age and Progressive Era* 19, no. 2 (2020): 206–16.

27 I compare the ideas and career of Booker T. Washington to those of famed charter school CEO Geoffrey Canada in "Washington and Canada."

28 For some professions, such as teaching, unions have provided an indispensable vehicle for challenging racism. See, for example, Brian Jones, "Keys to the Schoolhouse: Black Teachers, Education Reform and the Growing Teacher Rebellion," in Mayorga, Aggarwal, and Picower, *What's Race Got to Do with It?* For reflections on the role of scholars and students in higher education, see Steven

Osuna, "Class Suicide: The Black Radical Tradition, Radical Scholarship, and the Neoliberal Turn," in Johnson and Lubin, *Futures of Black Radicalism*, 21–38; and Roderick A. Ferguson, *We Demand: The University and Student Protests* (Oakland: University of California Press, 2017).

29 Imani Perry, *Vexy Thing: On Gender and Liberation* (Durham: Duke University Press, 2018), 94.

30 Jason J. Riley, "50 Years of Blaming Everything on Racism," *Wall Street Journal*, March 7, 2018.

31 James D. Anderson, *Education of Blacks in the South*.

32 Meier, "Negro Class Structure," 264.

33 Jesse Hagopian and Denisha Jones, eds., *Black Lives Matter at School: An Uprising for Educational Justice* (Chicago: Haymarket, 2020).

34 See, for example, Love, *We Want to Do More Than Survive*; and Kaba, *We Do This 'til We Free Us*.

BIBLIOGRAPHY

MANUSCRIPT COLLECTIONS

Alabama Legislative Commission to Preserve the Peace. Papers. Alabama Department of Archives and History, Montgomery.

Army National Guard. Administrative Files. Alabama Department of Archives and History, Montgomery.

Higgins, Chester, Jr. Papers. Tuskegee University Archives, Tuskegee, AL.

Krystall, Erik. Papers. Tuskegee University Archives, Tuskegee, AL.

Patton, Gwendolyn. Papers. H. Councill Trenholm State Community College, Special Collections, Montgomery, AL.

Student Unrest Collection. Tuskegee University Archives, Tuskegee, AL.

Wallace, George C. Papers. Alabama Department of Archives and History, Montgomery.

Wallace, Lurleen. Papers. Alabama Department of Archives and History, Montgomery.

Wright, Michael. Papers. Tuskegee University Archives, Tuskegee, AL.

Younge, Sammy, Jr. Papers. Tuskegee University Archives, Tuskegee, AL.

NEWSPAPERS AND MAGAZINES

Campus Digest
Liberator
Los Angeles Times
Madera Tribune
Nation
Negro Star
New York Age
New Yorker
New York Review of Books
New York Times
Plain Dealer
Saratogian
Southern Courier
St. Petersburg Times
Tuskegee News
US News & World Report
Wall Street Journal

Washington Post
World Outlook

INTERVIEWS BY AUTHOR
Lena Agnew: Cleveland, OH, November 11, 2016.
Kathleen Cleaver: New York, NY, June 8, 2017.
Lucenia Dunn: Montgomery, AL, July 19, 2015.
George Geddis: phone, June 15, 2017.
Warren Hamilton: phone, July 28, 2017.
Chester Higgins Jr.: New York, NY, August 11, 2015.
Ronald Hill: phone, June 14, 2017.
Caroline Hilton: New York, NY, August 4, 2015.
Robert Jones: Twinsburg, OH, February 22, 2015.
Cozetta Lamore: phone, July 6, 2016.
Maggie Magee: phone, June 29, 2017.
George Paris: Tuskegee, AL, July 9, 2015.
Wendell Paris: phone, July 14, 2015.
Gwen Patton: Montgomery, AL, July 11, 2015.
Sue Pendell: phone, October 3, 2017.
Arthur Pfister: New York, NY, July 7, 2016.
Bertrand Phillips: phone, June 22, 2016.
Melvin Todd: phone, June 20, 2016.
Guy Trammel: Tuskegee, AL, July 20, 2015.
Richard Wasserstrom: phone, June 26, 2017.
Michael Wright: phone, July 15, 2015.

PUBLISHED AND ARCHIVED INTERVIEWS
Benson, Richard D., II. "Interview with Gwendolyn M. Patton." *Journal of Civil and Human Rights* 1, no. 2 (2015): 182–89.
Elwood, William A. "An Interview with Charles G. Gomillion." *Callaloo*, no. 40 (1989): 577–99.
Feeley, Diane. "No Outside Saviors! ATC Interviews Gwen Patton." *Against the Current* 136 (October 2008), www.solidarity-us.org.
Mosnier, Joseph. "Kathleen Cleaver Interview." *Civil Rights History Project* (blog), September 16, 2011. loc.gov.
Wiley, Jean, and Bruce Hartford. "Oral History/Interview: Ruby Nell Sales." *Veterans of the Civil Rights Movement* (blog), September 2005. www.crmvet.org.

BOOKS
Ali, Tariq. *Street Fighting Years: An Autobiography of the Sixties*. New York: Verso, 2005.
Allen, Robert L. *Black Awakening in Capitalist America: An Analytic History*. New York: Doubleday, 1970.

Amerson, Lucius. *Great Courage: The First Black Sheriff Elected in the South since Reconstruction*. Fort Washington: What's Your Story Publishing, 2004.

Anderson, James D. *The Education of Blacks in the South, 1860–1935*. Chapel Hill: University of North Carolina Press, 1988.

Anyon, Jean. *Radical Possibilities: Public Policy, Urban Education, and a New Social Movement*. New York: Routledge, 2014.

Au, Wayne, Anthony L. Brown, and Dolores Calderón. *Reclaiming the Multicultural Roots of US Curriculum: Communities of Color and Official Knowledge in Education*. New York: Teachers College Press, 2016.

Bale, Jeff, and Sarah Knopp, eds. *Education and Capitalism: Struggles for Learning and Liberation*. Chicago: Haymarket, 2012.

Bass, Jack, and Jack Nelson. *The Orangeburg Massacre*. 2nd ed. Macon: Mercer University Press, 1984.

Beckert, Sven. *Empire of Cotton: A New History of Global Capitalism*. London: Penguin UK, 2014.

Biondi, Martha. *The Black Revolution on Campus*. Berkeley: University of California Press, 2012.

Bloom, Jack M. *Class, Race, and the Civil Rights Movement*. Bloomington: Indiana University Press, 1987.

Bloom, Joshua, and Waldo E. Martin. *Black against Empire: The History and Politics of the Black Panther Party*. Berkeley: University of California Press, 2013.

Bond, Horace Mann. *Negro Education in Alabama: A Study in Cotton and Steel*. 1939; New York: Atheneum, 1969.

Bowles, Samuel, and Herbert Gintis. *Schooling in Capitalist America: Educational Reform and the Contradictions of Economic Life*. 1976; Chicago: Haymarket, 2014.

Bradley, Stefan M. *Upending the Ivory Tower: Civil Rights, Black Power, and the Ivy League*. New York: New York University Press, 2018.

Butchart, Ronald E. *Schooling the Freed People: Teaching, Learning, and the Struggle for Black Freedom, 1861–1876*. Chapel Hill: University of North Carolina Press, 2010.

Byrd, Brandon. *The Black Republic: African Americans and the Fate of Haiti*. Philadelphia: University of Pennsylvania Press, 2020.

Carmichael, Stokely, and Michael Thelwell. *Ready for Revolution: The Life and Struggles of Stokely Carmichael (Kwame Ture)*. New York: Simon and Schuster, 2003.

Carson, Clayborne. *In Struggle: SNCC and the Black Awakening of the 1960s*. Cambridge: Harvard University Press, 1981.

Carter, Dan T. *The Politics of Rage: George Wallace, the Origins of the New Conservatism, and the Transformation of American Politics*. Baton Rouge: Louisiana State University Press, 2000.

Cohen, Robert, David J. Snyder, and Dan T. Carter, eds. *Rebellion in Black and White: Southern Student Activism in the 1960s*. Baltimore: Johns Hopkins University Press, 2013.

Cole, Eddie. *The Campus Color Line: College Presidents and the Struggle for Black Freedom*. Princeton: Princeton University Press, 2020.

Connolly, Nathan D. B. *A World More Concrete: Real Estate and the Remaking of Jim Crow South Florida*. Chicago: University of Chicago Press, 2014.

Cooper, Frederick. *Africa in the World*. Cambridge: Harvard University Press, 2014.

Cruse, Harold. *The Crisis of the Negro Intellectual: A Historical Analysis of the Failure of Black Leadership*. New York: New York Review of Books, 1967.

Delmont, Matthew F. *Why Busing Failed: Race, Media, and the National Resistance to School Desegregation*. Berkeley: University of California Press, 2016.

Dougherty, Jack. *More Than One Struggle: The Evolution of Black School Reform in Milwaukee*. Greensboro: University of North Carolina Press, 2004.

Drewry, Henry N., Humphrey Doermann, and Susan H. Anderson. *Stand and Prosper: Private Black Colleges and Their Students*. Princeton: Princeton University Press, 2001.

Du Bois, W. E. B. *Black Reconstruction in America: Toward a History of the Part Which Black Folk Played in the Attempt to Reconstruct Democracy in America, 1860–1880*. 1936; New York: Atheneum, 1969.

———. *Dusk of Dawn: An Essay toward an Autobiography of a Race Concept*. Piscataway: Transaction, 1968.

———. *The Souls of Black Folk*. 1903; New York: Bantam, 1989.

Dudziak, Mary L. *Cold War Civil Rights: Race and the Image of American Democracy*. Princeton: Princeton University Press, 2011.

Ellison, Ralph. *Invisible Man*. 1952; New York: Vintage, 2010.

Ewing, Eve L. *Ghosts in the Schoolyard: Racism and School Closings on Chicago's South Side*. Chicago: University of Chicago Press, 2018.

Fabricant, Michael, and Stephen Brier. *Austerity Blues: Fighting for the Soul of Public Higher Education*. Baltimore: Johns Hopkins University Press, 2016.

Fairclough, Adam. *Better Day Coming: Blacks and Equality, 1890–2000*. New York: Penguin, 2002.

———. *A Class of Their Own: Black Teachers in the Segregated South*. Cambridge: Harvard University Press, 2009.

Fanon, Frantz. *The Wretched of the Earth*. Translated by Constance Farrington. New York: Grove, 1963.

Farmer, Ashley D. *Remaking Black Power: How Black Women Transformed an Era*. Chapel Hill: University of North Carolina Press, 2017.

Favors, Jelani. *Shelter in a Time of Storm: How Black Colleges Fostered Generations of Leadership and Activism*. Chapel Hill: University of North Carolina Press, 2019.

Ferguson, Roderick A. *The Reorder of Things: The University and Its Pedagogies of Minority Difference*. Minneapolis: University of Minnesota Press, 2012.

Fields, Barbara J., and Karen Fields. *Racecraft: The Soul of Inequality in American Life*. New York: Verso, 2012.

Fitch, Robert, and Mary Oppenheimer. *Ghana: End of an Illusion*. New York: Monthly Review Press, 1966.

Foner, Eric, ed. *America's Black Past: A Reader in Afro American History*. New York: Harper Collins, 1970.

———. *Reconstruction: America's Unfinished Revolution, 1863–1877*. 1988; New York: Harper Collins, 2011.

Forman, James. *The Making of Black Revolutionaries*. 1972; Seattle: Open Hand, 1985.

———. *Sammy Younge, Jr.: The First Black College Student to Die in the Black Liberation Movement*. New York: Grove, 1968.

Frazier, Franklin. *Black Bourgeoisie: The Rise of a New Middle Class*. New York: Free Press, 1957.

Freire, Paulo. *Pedagogy of the Oppressed*. 1968; London: Bloomsbury, 2000.

Freire, Paulo, and Donaldo Macedo. *Literacy: Reading the Word and the World*. New York: Routledge, 2005.

Gaines, Kevin K. *Uplifting the Race: Black Leadership, Politics, and Culture in the Twentieth Century*. Chapel Hill: University of North Carolina Press, 1996.

Genovese, Eugene D. *Roll, Jordan, Roll: The World the Slaves Made*. New York: Vintage, 1976.

Givens, Jarvis R. *Fugitive Pedagogy: Carter G. Woodson and the Art of Black Teaching*. Cambridge: Harvard University Press, 2021.

Gutman, Herbert George. *Power and Culture: Essays on the American Working Class*. Edited by Ira Berlin. New York: Pantheon, 1987.

Guzman, Jessie Parkhurst. *Crusade for Civic Democracy: The Story of the Tuskegee Civic Association, 1941–1970*. New York: Vantage, 1984.

———. *The New South and Higher Education: What Are the Implications for Higher Education of the Changing Socio-Economic Conditions of the South? A Symposium and Ceremonies Held in Connection with the Inauguration of Luther Hilton Foster, Fourth President of Tuskegee Inst.* Tuskegee: Tuskegee Institute, 1954.

Hale, Jon N. *The Freedom Schools: Student Activists in the Mississippi Civil Rights Movement*. New York: Columbia University Press, 2016.

Hall, Woodrow W. *A Bibliography of the Tuskegee Gerrymander Protest: Pamphlets, Magazine and Newspaper Articles Chronologically Arranged*. Tuskegee: Department of Records and Research, Tuskegee Institute, 1960.

Hamilton, Charles V. *Minority Politics in Black Belt Alabama*. New York: McGraw-Hill, 1960.

Harlan, Louis R. *The Making of a Black Leader, 1856–1901*. Vol. 1 of *Booker T. Washington*. New York: Oxford University Press, 1972.

———. *The Wizard of Tuskegee, 1901–1915*. Vol. 2 of *Booker T. Washington*. New York: Oxford University Press, 1986.

Haynes, Stephen R. *The Last Segregated Hour: The Memphis Kneel-Ins and the Campaign for Southern Church Desegregation*. New York: Oxford University Press, 2012.

Higgins, Chester, Jr. *Student Unrest, Tuskegee Institute: A Chronology*. Tuskegee: Tuskegee Institute, 1968.

Hogan, Wesley C. *Many Minds, One Heart: SNCC's Dream for a New America*. Chapel Hill: University of North Carolina Press, 2007.

Holsaert, Faith S., et al., eds. *Hands on the Freedom Plow: Personal Accounts by Women in SNCC*. Champaign: University of Illinois Press, 2010.

Honey, Michael K. *Going down Jericho Road: The Memphis Strike, Martin Luther King's Last Campaign*. New York: Norton, 2011.

Hughes, William Hardin, and Frederick Douglass Patterson. *Robert Russa Moton of Hampton and Tuskegee*. Chapel Hill: University of North Carolina Press, 1956.

Jackson, David H. *Booker T. Washington and the Struggle against White Supremacy*. New York: Palgrave Macmillan, 2008.

James, C. L. R. *The C. L. R. James Reader*. Edited by Anna Grimshaw. Hoboken: Blackwell, 1992.

Jeffries, Hasan Kwame. *Bloody Lowndes: Civil Rights and Black Power in Alabama's Black Belt*. New York: New York University Press, 2010.

Jenkins, Carol, and Elizabeth Gardner Hines. *Black Titan: A. G. Gaston and the Making of a Black American Millionaire*. New York: One World/Ballantine, 2003.

Johnson, Cedric. *Revolutionaries to Race Leaders: Black Power and the Making of African American Politics*. Minneapolis: University of Minnesota Press, 2007.

Johnson, Charles S. *Shadow of the Plantation*. Piscataway: Transaction, 1996.

Johnson, Charles, Jr. *African Americans and ROTC: Military, Naval and Aeroscience Programs at Historically Black Colleges, 1916–1973*. Jefferson: McFarland, 2002.

Johnson, Gaye Theresa, and Alex Lubin, eds. *Futures of Black Radicalism*. New York: Verso, 2017.

Jones, James H. *Bad Blood: The Tuskegee Syphilis Experiment*. New ed. New York: Simon and Schuster, 1993.

Joseph, Peniel E. *The Black Power Movement: Rethinking the Civil Rights-Black Power Era*. New York: Taylor and Francis, 2006.

———. *Waiting 'til the Midnight Hour: A Narrative History of Black Power in America*. New York: Macmillan, 2007.

Kaba, Mariame. *We Do This 'til We Free Us: Abolitionist Organizing and Transforming Justice*. Chicago: Haymarket, 2021.

Kean, Melissa. *Desegregating Private Higher Education in the South: Duke, Emory, Rice, Tulane, and Vanderbilt*. Baton Rouge: Louisiana State University Press, 2008.

Kelley, Robin D. G. *Freedom Dreams: The Black Radical Imagination*. Boston: Beacon, 2002.

———. *Hammer and Hoe: Alabama Communists during the Great Depression*. Chapel Hill: University of North Carolina Press, 1990.

Kelly, Brian. *Race, Class, and Power in the Alabama Coalfields, 1908–21*. Champaign: University of Illinois Press, 2001.

Kendi, Ibram X. *Stamped from the Beginning: The Definitive History of Racist Ideas in America*. New York: Nation Books, 2016.

Kinchen, Shirletta. *Black Power in the Bluff City: African American Youth and Student Activism in Memphis, 1965–1975*. Knoxville: University of Tennessee Press, 2016.

King, Martin Luther. *The Radical King*. Edited by Cornel West. Boston: Beacon, 2016.

Larsen, Nella. *Quicksand; and Passing*. Mansfield Centre: Martino, 2011.

Litwack, Leon F. *Trouble in Mind: Black Southerners in the Age of Jim Crow*. New York: Knopf, 1998.

Love, Bettina L. *We Want to Do More Than Survive: Abolitionist Teaching and the Pursuit of Educational Freedom*. Boston: Beacon, 2019.

Malcolm X. *Malcolm X Speaks: Selected Speeches and Statements*. Edited by George Breitman. New York: Grove, 1965.

Marable, Manning. *Black Leadership*. New York: Columbia University Press, 1998.

———. *How Capitalism Underdeveloped Black America: Problems in Race, Political Economy, and Society*. London: Pluto, 2000.

———. *Malcolm X: A Life of Reinvention*. New York: Penguin, 2011.

———. *Race, Reform, and Rebellion: The Second Reconstruction and Beyond in Black America, 1945–2006*. Jackson: University Press of Mississippi, 2007.

Mayorga, Edwin, Ujju Aggarwal, and Bree Picower, eds. *What's Race Got to Do with It: How Current School Reform Policy Maintains Racial and Economic Inequality*. 2nd ed. New York: Peter Lang, 2020.

Melamed, Jodi. *Represent and Destroy: Rationalizing Violence in the New Racial Capitalism*. Minneapolis: University of Minnesota Press, 2011.

Meyers, Joshua M. *We Are Worth Fighting For: A History of the Howard University Student Protest of 1989*. New York: New York University Press, 2019.

Moton, Robert Russa. *Finding a Way Out: An Autobiography*. New York: Doubleday, Page, 1920.

———. *What the Negro Thinks*. New York: Doubleday, 1929.

Murch, Donna Jean. *Living for the City: Migration, Education, and the Rise of the Black Panther Party in Oakland, California*. Chapel Hill: University of North Carolina Press, 2010.

Nkrumah, Kwame. *Class Struggle in Africa*. Bedford: Panaf, 1980.

Norrell, Robert Jefferson. *Reaping the Whirlwind: The Civil Rights Movement in Tuskegee*. New York: Knopf, 1998.

———. *Up from History: The Life of Booker T. Washington*. Cambridge: Harvard University Press, 2009.

Olson, Lynne. *Freedom's Daughters: The Unsung Heroines of the Civil Rights Movement from 1830 to 1970*. New York: Simon and Schuster, 2001.

Patterson, Frederick D. *Chronicles of Faith: The Autobiography of Frederick D. Patterson*. Tuscaloosa: University of Alabama Press, 2002.

Patton, Gwendolyn. *My Race to Freedom: A Life in the Civil Rights Movement*. Montgomery: New South Books, 2020.

Payne, Charles M., and Carol Sills Strickland, eds. *Teach Freedom: Education for Liberation in the African-American Tradition*. New York: Teachers College Press, 2008.

Perlstein, Daniel Hiram. *Justice, Justice: School Politics and the Eclipse of Liberalism*. New York: Peter Lang, 2004.

Rampersad, Arnold. *Ralph Ellison: A Biography*. New York: Vintage, 2007.

Reverby, Susan M. *Examining Tuskegee: The Infamous Syphilis Study and Its Legacy*. Chapel Hill: University of North Carolina Press, 2009.

Rickford, Russell. *We Are an African People: Independent Education, Black Power, and the Radical Imagination*. New York: Oxford University Press, 2016.

Rogers, Ibram H. *The Black Campus Movement: Black Students and the Racial Reconstitution of Higher Education, 1965–1972*. New York: Palgrave Macmillan, 2012.

Rogers, William Warren, Robert D. Ward, Wayne Flynt, and Leah Rawls Atkins. *Alabama: The History of a Deep South State*. Tuscaloosa: University of Alabama Press, 2010.

Rojas, Fabio. *From Black Power to Black Studies: How a Radical Social Movement Became an Academic Discipline*. Baltimore: Johns Hopkins University Press, 2007.

Sanders, Crystal R. *A Chance for Change: Head Start and Mississippi's Black Freedom Struggle*. Chapel Hill: University of North Carolina Press, 2016.

Schulman, Bruce J. *From Cotton Belt to Sunbelt: Federal Policy, Economic Development, and the Transformation of the South, 1938–1980*. Durham: Duke University Press, 1994.

Schwartz, Edward. *Student Power: A Collection of Readings*. Washington, DC: US National Student Association, 1969.

Scranton, William W. *The Report of the President's Commission on Campus Unrest*. Washington, DC: US Government Printing Office, 1970.

Sellers, Cleveland, and Robert L. Terrell. *The River of No Return: The Autobiography of a Black Militant and the Life and Death of SNCC*. Jackson: University Press of Mississippi, 1973.

Shaw, Nate, and Theodore Rosengarten. *All God's Dangers: The Life of Nate Shaw*. Chicago: University of Chicago Press, 2000.

Singh, Nikhil Pal. *Black Is a Country: Race and the Unfinished Struggle for Democracy*. Cambridge: Harvard University Press, 2005.

Sitkoff, Harvard. *The Struggle for Black Equality, 1954–1992*. New York: Macmillan, 1993.

Sokol, Jason. *There Goes My Everything: White Southerners in the Age of Civil Rights, 1945–1975*. New York: Vintage, 2008.

Spencer, Robyn C. *The Revolution Has Come: Black Power, Gender, and the Black Panther Party in Oakland*. Durham: Duke University Press, 2016.

Spivey, Donald. *Schooling for the New Slavery: Black Industrial Education, 1868–1915*. Westport: Greenwood, 1978.

Taylor, Keeanga-Yamahtta. *From #BlackLivesMatter to Black Liberation*. Chicago: Haymarket, 2016.

Theoharis, Jeanne. *The Rebellious Life of Mrs. Rosa Parks*. Boston: Beacon, 2013.

Thompson, Daniel Calbert. *Private Black Colleges at the Crossroads*. Westport: Greenwood, 1973.

Thornton, J. Mills. *Dividing Lines: Municipal Politics and the Struggle for Civil Rights in Montgomery, Birmingham, and Selma*. Tuscaloosa: University of Alabama Press, 2002.

Todd-Breland, Elizabeth. *A Political Education: Black Politics and Education Reform in Chicago since the 1960s*. Chapel Hill: University of North Carolina Press, 2018.

Ture, Kwame, and Charles Hamilton. *Black Power: Politics of Liberation in America*. New York: Vintage, 1967.

Turner, Jeffrey A. *Sitting In and Speaking Out: Student Movements in the American South, 1960–1970*. Athens: University of Georgia Press, 2010.

Verney, Kevern J. *The Art of the Possible: Booker T. Washington and Black Leadership in the United States, 1881–1925*. New York: Routledge, 2013.

Washington, Booker T. *Up from Slavery*. 1901; New York: Penguin, 1986.

Watkins, William Henry. *Black Protest Thought and Education*. New York: Peter Lang, 2005.

———. *The White Architects of Black Education: Ideology and Power in America, 1865–1954*. New York: Teachers College Press, 2001.

Weinberg, Meyer. *A Chance to Learn: The History of Race and Education in the United States*. Long Beach: California State University Press, 1995.

West, Michael Rudolph. *The Education of Booker T. Washington: American Democracy and the Idea of Race Relations*. New York: Columbia University Press, 2006.

White, Derrick E. *The Challenge of Blackness: The Institute of the Black World and Political Activism in the 1970s*. Gainesville: University Press of Florida, 2011.

Williams, Heather Andrea. *Self-Taught: African American Education in Slavery and Freedom*. Chapel Hill: University of North Carolina Press, 2009.

Williamson, Joy Ann. *Radicalizing the Ebony Tower: Black Colleges and the Black Freedom Struggle in Mississippi*. New York: Teachers College Press, 2008.

Williamson-Lott, Joy. *Jim Crow Campus: Higher Education and the Struggle for a New Southern Social Order*. New York: Teachers College Press, 2018.

Wolters, Raymond. *The New Negro on Campus: Black College Rebellions of the 1920s*. Princeton: Princeton University Press, 1975.

Woodard, Komozi. *A Nation within a Nation: Amiri Baraka (LeRoi Jones) and Black Power Politics*. Chapel Hill: University of North Carolina Press, 1999.

Woods, Jeff R. *Black Struggle, Red Scare: Segregation and Anti-Communism in the South, 1948–1968*. Baton Rouge: Louisiana State University Press, 2004.

Woodson, Carter G. *The Mis-Education of the Negro*. 1933; San Diego: Book Tree, 2006.

Woodward, C. Vann. *Origins of the New South, 1877–1913*. Baton Rouge: Louisiana State University Press, 1971.

———. *The Strange Career of Jim Crow*. New York: Oxford University Press, 2001.

Zimmerman, Andrew. *Alabama in Africa: Booker T. Washington, the German Empire, and the Globalization of the New South.* Princeton: Princeton University Press, 2010.

Zinn, Howard. *SNCC: The New Abolitionists.* Cambridge: South End, 1964.

Zinn, Howard, and Anthony Arnove. *Voices of a People's History of the United States.* New York: Seven Stories, 2014.

JOURNAL ARTICLES

Ahmad, Muhammad. "On the Black Student Movement—1960–70." *Black Scholar* 9, nos. 8–9 (May 1, 1978): 2–11.

Anderson, James D. "Eleventh Annual Brown Lecture in Education Research: A Long Shadow: The American Pursuit of Political Justice and Education Equality." *Educational Researcher* 44, no. 6 (2015): 319–35.

Anderson, James D., and Christopher M. Span. "History of Education in the News: The Legacy of Slavery, Racism, and Contemporary Black Activism on Campus." *History of Education Quarterly* 56, no. 4 (2016): 646–56.

Anderson, S. E. "Black Students: Racial Consciousness and the Class Struggle, 1960–1976." *Black Scholar* 8, no. 4 (1977): 35–43.

———. "Revolutionary Black Nationalism Is Pan-African." *Black Scholar* 2, no. 7 (1971): 16–22.

Anyon, Jean. "Social Class and School Knowledge." *Curriculum Inquiry* 11, no. 1 (1981): 3–42.

Aptheker, Herbert. "The Negro College Student in the 1920s—Years of Preparation and Protest: An Introduction." *Science & Society* 33, no. 2 (April 1969): 150–67.

Bauerlein, Mark. "Booker T. Washington and W. E. B. Du Bois: The Origins of a Bitter Intellectual Battle." *Journal of Blacks in Higher Education*, no. 46 (2004–2005): 106–14.

———. "Washington, Du Bois, and the Black Future." *Wilson Quarterly* 28, no. 4 (2004): 74–86.

Beckert, Sven. "From Tuskegee to Togo: The Problem of Freedom in the Empire of Cotton." *Journal of American History* 92, no. 2 (2005): 498–526.

Berman, Edward H. "Tuskegee-in-Africa." *Journal of Negro Education* 41, no. 2 (1972): 99–112.

Biondi, Martha. "Controversial Blackness: The Historical Development and Future Trajectory of African American Studies." *Daedalus* 140, no. 2 (2011): 226–37.

Butchart, Ronald E. "'Outthinking and Outflanking the Owners of the World': A Historiography of the African American Struggle for Education." *History of Education Quarterly* 28, no. 3 (October 1988): 333–66.

Button, W. J. "The Meaning of Tuskegee." *Journal of Education*, 1916, 428–29.

Chennault, Ronald E. "Pragmatism and Progressivism in the Educational Thought and Practices of Booker T. Washington." *Philosophical Studies in Education* 44 (2013): 121–31.

Cleaver, Eldridge. "Education and Revolution." *Black Scholar* 1, no. 1 (November 1969): 44–52.

Cobb, Charlie. "Revolution: From Stokely Carmichael to Kwame Ture." *Black Scholar* 27, nos. 3–4 (1997): 32–38.

Cruse, Harold W. "Revolutionary Nationalism and the Afro-American." *Studies on the Left* 2, no. 3 (1962): 12–25.

Dagbovie, Pero Gaglo. "Exploring a Century of Historical Scholarship on Booker T. Washington." *Journal of African American History* 92, no. 2 (April 2007): 239–64.

Dennis, Michael. "Schooling along the Color Line: Progressives and the Education of Blacks in the New South." *Journal of Negro Education* 67, no. 2 (April 1998): 142–56.

Du Bois, W. E. B. "Behold the Land." *Freedomways* 4 (1964): 8–15.

——. "Moton of Hampton and Tuskegee." *Phylon* 1, no. 4 (1940): 302–51.

Ellison, Ralph. "An American Dilemma: A Review." *Shadow and Act*, 1973, 303–17.

Erickson, Ansley T. "The Rhetoric of Choice: Segregation, Desegregation, and Charter Schools." *Dissent* 58, no. 4 (2011): 41–46.

Fairchild, Amy L., and Ronald Bayer. "Uses and Abuses of Tuskegee." *Science* 284, no. 5416 (1999): 919–21.

Fairclough, Adam. "Martin Luther King, Jr. and the War in Vietnam." *Phylon* 45, no. 1 (1984): 19–39.

——. "Tuskegee's Robert R. Moton and the Travails of the Early Black College President." *Journal of Blacks in Higher Education*, no. 31 (April 2001): 94–105.

Fields, Barbara J. "Dysplacement and Southern History." *Journal of Southern History* 82, no. 1 (February 2016): 7–26.

——. "The Nineteenth-Century American South: History and Theory." *Plantation Society* 2, no. 1 (1983): 7–27.

——. "Slavery, Race and Ideology in the United States of America." *New Left Review*, no. 181 (1990): 95–118.

Flowers, Deidre B. "The Launching of the Student Sit-In Movement: The Role of Black Women at Bennett College." *Journal of African American History* 90, nos. 1–2 (2005): 52–63.

Foster, Luther H. "Annual Report of the President: 1960–1961." *Bulletin of Tuskegee Institute* 54, no. 3 (October 1961): 1–21.

Frady, Marshall. "God and Man in the South." *Atlantic Monthly* 219 (1967): 37–42.

Fritz, Jan M. "Charles Gomillion, Educator-Community Activist." *Clinical Sociology Review* 6, no. 1 (1988): 13–21.

Gasman, Marybeth. "The Origins of the United Negro College Fund as the Cornerstone of Private Black Colleges." *Journal of Blacks in Higher Education*, no. 56 (2007): 86–89.

——. "Scylla and Charybdis: Navigating the Waters of Academic Freedom at Fisk University during Charles S. Johnson's Administration (1946–1956)." *American Educational Research Journal* 36, no. 4 (1999): 739–58.

Gilmore, Ruth Wilson. "Public Enemies and Private Intellectuals: Apartheid USA." *Race & Class* 35, no. 1 (1993): 69–78.

Givens, Jarvis Ray. "A Grammar for Black Education beyond Borders: Exploring Technologies of Schooling in the African Diaspora." *Race Ethnicity and Education* 19, no. 6 (2016): 1288–1302.

Gomillion, C. G. "The Negro Voter in Alabama." *Journal of Negro Education* 26, no. 3 (1957): 281–86.

———. "Questions Which Might Be Asked in Planning a Program of Social Action." *Clinical Sociology Review* 6, no. 1 (1988): 33–34.

———. "Reply." *Clinical Sociology Review* 6, no. 1 (1988): 29–32.

———. "The Role of the Sociologist in Community Action in the Rural South." *Clinical Sociology Review* 6, no. 1 (1988): 35–41.

———. "The Tuskegee Voting Story." *Clinical Sociology Review* 6, no. 1 (1988): 22–26.

Graham, Edward K., and Margaret Mead. "The Hampton Institute Strike of 1927: A Case Study in Student Protest." *American Scholar* 38, no. 4 (October 1969): 668–83.

Guridy, Frank A. "From Solidarity to Cross-Fertilization: Afro-Cuban/African American Interaction during the 1930s and 1940s." *Radical History Review* 87, no. 1 (2003): 19–48.

Hall, Jacquelyn Dowd. "The Long Civil Rights Movement and the Political Uses of the Past." *Journal of American History* 91, no. 4 (2005): 1233–63.

Hamilton, Charles V. "Education in the Black Community: An Examination of the Realities." *Freedomways* 8 (1968): 319–24.

Harding, Vincent. "Black Students and the Impossible Revolution." *Journal of Black Studies* 1, no. 1 (September 1970): 75–100.

Hare, Nathan. "The Challenge of a Black Scholar." *Black Scholar* 1, no. 2 (December 1969): 58–63.

Harlan, Louis R. "Booker T. Washington and the White Man's Burden." *American Historical Review* 71, no. 2 (1966): 441–67.

———. "The Secret Life of Booker T. Washington." *Journal of Southern History* 37, no. 3 (1971): 393–416.

Harris, Donald J. "The Black Ghetto as Colony: A Theoretical Critique and Alternative Formulation." *Review of Black Political Economy* 2, no. 4 (1972): 3–33.

Harrison, E. C. "Student Unrest on the Black College Campus." *Journal of Negro Education* 41, no. 2 (1972): 113–20.

Higginbotham, F. Michael. "Soldiers for Justice: The Role of the Tuskegee Airmen in the Desegregation of the American Armed Forces." *William & Mary Bill of Rights Journal* 8, no. 2 (2000): 273–321.

Hughes, C. Alvin. "We Demand Our Rights: The Southern Negro Youth Congress, 1937–1949." *Phylon* 48, no. 1 (1987): 38–50.

Jeffries, Hasan Kwame. "What's Old Is New Again: Recentering Black Power and Decentering Civil Rights." *Journal of Civil and Human Rights* 1, no. 2 (2015): 245–48.

Johnson, Roosevelt. "Black Administrators and Higher Education." *Black Scholar* 1, no. 1 (November 1969): 66–76.

Jones, Allen W. "The Role of Tuskegee Institute in the Education of Black Farmers." *Journal of Negro History* 60, no. 2 (April 1975): 252–67.

Jones, Brian. "Washington and Canada: Free Market Idealism in the Context of Social Defeat." *Journal of Negro Education* 87, no. 1 (2018): 33–45.

Jordan, William. "'The Damnable Dilemma': African-American Accommodation and Protest during World War I." *Journal of American History* 81, no. 4 (March 1995): 1562–83.

Joseph, Peniel E. "Dashikis and Democracy: Black Studies, Student Activism, and the Black Power Movement." *Journal of African American History* 88, no. 2 (April 2003): 182–203.

Kaufman, Arnold. "Murder in Tuskegee: Day of Wrath in the Model Town," *Nation*, January 31, 1966, 118–25.

Kelley, Robin D. G. "'But a Local Phase of a World Problem': Black History's Global Vision, 1883–1950." *Journal of American History* 86, no. 3 (1999): 1045–77.

———. "'We Are Not What We Seem': Rethinking Black Working-Class Opposition in the Jim Crow South." *Journal of American History* 80, no. 1 (1993): 75–112.

Kelly, Brian. "'Gradualism and Militancy in the Struggle for Racial Equality,' Review of Fairclough, Adam, *Better Day Coming: Blacks and Equality, 1890–2000*." *H-Net Reviews* H-South (January 2004). www.h-net.org.

———. "No Easy Way Through: Race Leadership and Black Workers at the Nadir." *Labor* 7, no. 3 (September 2010): 79–93.

———. "Sentinels for New South Industry: Booker T. Washington, Industrial Accommodation and Black Workers in the Jim Crow South." *Labor History* 44, no. 3 (2003): 337–57.

Kliebard, Herbert M. "'That Evil Genius of the Negro Race': Thomas Jesse Jones and Educational Reform." *Journal of Curriculum and Supervision* 10, no. 1 (1994): 5–20.

Lee, Philip. "The Case of *Dixon v. Alabama*: From Civil Rights to Students' Rights and Back Again." *Teachers College Record* 116 (2014): 1–18.

Lynd, Staughton, and Roberta Yancy. "The Unfamiliar Campus—Southern Negro Students: The College and the Movement." *Dissent* 11, no. 1 (1964): 39–45.

Malczewski, Joan. "Weak State, Stronger Schools: Northern Philanthropy and Organizational Change in the Jim Crow South." *Journal of Southern History* 75, no. 4 (2009): 963–1000.

Marable, Manning. "Booker T. Washington and African Nationalism." *Phylon* 35, no. 4 (December 1974): 398–406.

———. "Tuskegee and the Politics of Illusion in the New South." *Black Scholar* 8, no. 7 (May 1977): 13–24.

———. "Tuskegee Institute in the 1920's." *Negro History Bulletin* 40, no. 6 (November 1977): 764–68.

McKissick, Floyd B. "The Way to a Black Ideology." *Black Scholar* 1, no. 2 (December 1969): 14–17.

McMurry, Linda O. "A Black Intellectual in the New South: Monroe Nathan Work, 1866–1945." *Phylon* 41, no. 4 (1980): 333–44.

Meier, August. "Negro Class Structure and Ideology in the Age of Booker T. Washington." *Phylon* 23, no. 3 (September 1962): 258–66.

Murtadha, Khaula, and Daud Malik Watts. "Linking the Struggle for Education and Social Justice: Historical Perspectives of African American Leadership in Schools." *Educational Administration Quarterly* 41, no. 4 (October 2005): 591–608.

Norrell, Robert J. "Booker T. Washington: Understanding the Wizard of Tuskegee." *Journal of Blacks in Higher Education*, no. 42 (December 2003): 96–109.

Patterson, Frederick D. "Foundation Policies in Regard to Negro Institutions of Higher Learning." *Journal of Educational Sociology* 32, no. 6 (1959): 290–96.

Patton, Gwendolyn. "Insurgent Memories." *Southern Exposure*, Spring 1981.

———. "Open Letter to Marxists." *Black Scholar* 6, no. 7 (1975): 50–52.

Perlstein, Daniel. "Westward Ho! Progressive Education and American Colonialism in Hawai'i and the Philippines." Presentation, History of Education Society conference, 2016.

Polletta, Francesca. "'It Was Like a Fever . . .': Narrative and Identity in Social Protest." *Social Problems* 45, no. 2 (May 1998): 137–59.

Rogers, Ibram H. "The Black Campus Movement: The Case for a New Historiography." *The Sixties* 4, no. 2 (2011): 171–86.

Rosenthal, Joel. "Southern Black Student Activism: Assimilation vs. Nationalism." *Journal of Negro Education* 44, no. 2 (April 1975): 113–29.

Sehat, David. "The Civilizing Mission of Booker T. Washington." *Journal of Southern History* 73, no. 2 (May 2007): 323–62.

Seidman, Sarah. "Tricontinental Routes of Solidarity: Stokely Carmichael in Cuba." *Journal of Transnational American Studies* 4, no. 2 (2012). escholarship.org.

Sherman, Richard B. "The 'Teachings at Hampton Institute': Social Equality, Racial Integrity, and the Virginia Public Assemblage Act of 1926." *Virginia Magazine of History and Biography* 95, no. 3 (July 1987): 275–300.

Siddle Walker, Emilie. "Caswell County Training School, 1933–1969: Relationships between Community and School." *Harvard Educational Review* 63, no. 2 (1993): 161–83.

Simmons, LaKisha Michelle. "The Poetry of Vesta Stephens: In Search of Black Girls' Gardens." *Tulsa Studies in Women's Literature* 36, no. 2 (Fall 2017): 449–61.

Smallwood, Stephanie E. "The Politics of the Archive and History's Accountability to the Enslaved." *History of the Present* 6, no. 2 (2016): 117–32.

Stephens, Ernest. "The Black University in America Today." *Freedomways* 7 (1967): 131–37.

Taper, Bernard. "Gomillion versus Lightfoot." *New Yorker*, June 10, 1961, 37–93.

Taylor, Orlando L. "New Directions for American Education: A Black Perspective." *Speech Teacher* 19, no. 2 (March 1970): 111–16.

"Thoughts of a White Citizen Council Member." *Clinical Sociology Review*, 1988, 27–28.

Torrens, James S. "Tuskegee Years: What Father Arrupe Got Me Into." *Studies in the Spirituality of Jesuits* 37, no. 3 (2005): 1–39.

Tucker, Shuana K. "The Early Years of the United Negro College Fund, 1943–1960." *Journal of African American History* 87 (2002): 416–32.

Watkins, William. "Black Curriculum Orientations: A Preliminary Inquiry." *Harvard Educational Review* 63, no. 3 (September 1993): 321–39.

West, Michael O. "The Tuskegee Model of Development in Africa: Another Dimension of the African/African-American Connection." *Diplomatic History* 16, no. 3 (1992): 371–87.

White, Robert M. "Misrepresentations of the Tuskegee Study of Untreated Syphilis." *Journal of the National Medical Association* 97, no. 4 (2005): 564–81.

Williams, Vernon J. "Monroe N. Work's Contribution to Booker T. Washington's Nationalist Legacy." *Western Journal of Black Studies* 21, no. 2 (1997): 85–91.

Williamson, Joy Ann. "'This Has Been Quite a Year for Heads Falling': Institutional Autonomy in the Civil Rights Era." *History of Education Quarterly* 44, no. 4 (2004): 554–76.

Williamson-Lott, Joy Ann. "The Battle over Power, Control, and Academic Freedom at Southern Institutions of Higher Education, 1955–1965." *Journal of Southern History* 79, no. 4 (2013): 879–920.

INDEX

Page numbers in *italic* refer to illustrations.

Worthy, William, 72

Wright, Michael, 19, 68, 75, 115, 126, 130, 141; anti-war protest, 131; on Black Power, 109–10; crisis of 1968, 154, 155, 157, 160, 162; de-escalation of student march, 143; Dorothy Hall occupation, 157, 160; expulsion, 163; on King assassination, 155; "Mandate," 150–51; Orangeburg, S.C., visit, 139; in *Sammy Younge, Jr.* (Forman), 12; in twenty-first century, 175; Younge death and, 101

X, Malcolm. *See* Malcolm X

Young, Whitney, 106

Younge, Sammy, Jr., 11–12, 65–66, 76, 78, 80, 88, 91–93; Carmichael relations, 96–97, 119; death, 98–100, 103, 105, 107, 109, 117, 122–25, 131, 135; Forman on, 88, 90; naval service, 107, *107*; swimming pool desegregation, 87; Todd on, 89; trial of Marvin Segrest, 122–24

ABOUT THE AUTHOR

BRIAN JONES is the Director of the Center for Educators and Schools at the New York Public Library. He was formerly the Associate Director of Education at the Schomburg Center for Research in Black Culture, where he was also a scholar in residence. He received a PhD in urban education from the City University of New York Graduate Center and writes about black education history and politics.